KT-367-411

List of Text Figures

List of Tables

Preface

This publication is an attempt to bring the Report of the Working Group on Inequalities in Health (known as the Black Report, because its Chairman was Sir Douglas Black, formerly Chief Scientist at the Department of Health and now President of the Royal College of Physicians) to a wider audience. The report was submitted to the Secretary of State in April 1980, but instead of being properly printed and published by the DHSS or HM Stationery Office, it was arranged for only 260 duplicated copies of the typescript to be publicly made available in the week of the August Bank Holiday in that year. Major organizations within the NHS, including health authorities, did not receive copies. However, this led to an unforeseen reaction. Attention was called in the medical press and elsewhere to the off-hand method of bringing the work of a group appointed by the government to the attention of the public. The contents of the report, once it could be bought or borrowed in grudging numbers, were also recognized to be important and came to be debated vigorously at meetings throughout Britain. A House of Commons debate on the report was arranged for the autumn of 1981. Inequalities in health are of concern to the whole nation and represent one of the biggest possible challenges to the conduct of government policy.

This book is a slightly slimmed-down version of the report and has been read and approved in general terms by the original Working Group of four members. Some statistical and technical details, and elaborations of the text, have been cut, but a large body of information remains in this version, which is nearly two thirds of the length of the detailed report. Most of the book remains in identical form to the report which was submitted to the Secretary of State, but, where there have been cuts, linking passages have been written and, in some cases, the discussion of certain issues has been summarized for the sake of brevity and communication to a wide readership. In a few instances statistics have been updated, but in general the question of what events have occurred since the report was written has been left to a new introduction, which follows this preface. The members of the Working Group would wish to point out that changes in the administration of the health services, the deepening problem of mass unemployment and changes in the government's social policies represent major matters which would need to be dealt with at some length if the same exercise were to be attempted today. We have sought, therefore, in the introduction to fulfil three objectives: (i) to explain how major developments of social and economic structure and policy during 1980 and 1981 might affect the arguments of the report; (ii) to describe and discuss the reactions to the publication of the report after August 1980; and (iii) to refer to specialized information and research on inequalities in health and provision of health services, which has been published in the last two years and which affects the continuing discussion of this national issue.

*

The authors would like to thank the Controller of Her Majesty's Stationery Office for permission to reproduce sections of the original report. The Department of Health and Social Security has asked us to make it clear that this permission in no way implies their authorization or approval of the book.

Introduction to the Pelican Edition

Peter Townsend and Nick Davidson

The future of health policies has become an immediate and often controversial issue in rich and poor countries alike. On the one hand, rich industrial countries like the United States, Canada, Western Germany, France, Sweden and the United Kingdom have been spending an ever-increasing percentage of their national income on health services (Abel-Smith, 1967; Simanis, 1973; Abel-Smith, 1979) and at the same time have been unable to demonstrate satisfactorily to themselves that much higher spending is clearly related to much better health – as judged by conventionally accepted indicators. In consequence, the relationship between spending on health services and health is being examined more and more closely (for example, Lalonde, 1975; Centre for Health Studies, Yale University, 1977). On the other hand, the poor countries, supported by the World Health Organization, have become wary of slavishly adopting health care systems like those of the rich countries, and are beginning to emphasize the need for both a broader approach to the achievement of the positive health of their populations and a less hierarchical and status-ridden organization of treatment for illness (for example, Djukanovic and Mach, 1975; Abel-Smith, 1976; IDS, 1978). 'Development' in both kinds of country is increasingly recognized as being a process which involves social and not just economic values, and one which, so far as the goal of good health is concerned, entails better universal education, good conditions of work, good amenities in the environment and in the home, well-integrated social services, and relatively high minimum living standards as well as reasonable standards of medicine and nursing.

This debate about the best strategy for achieving health, which is taking place at different ends of the spectrum of economic development, is increasingly concerned with the relations between the rich and the poor – within countries, as well as between countries.

In the Third World people have been raising the issues of the so-called diseases of industrialization or of western culture, the hazards of shanty towns on the outskirts of the cities, and the poorly supervised activities of multi-national corporations, by which large sections of the population are exposed to new kinds of health risk. In the rich countries comparable themes have been taken up – such as the hazards of chemical plants and the nuclear power industry, lead emissions on the roads, the constriction of the activities of children and families in high blocks of flats as well as the risks of living high up in such blocks, and the problems of regulating food additives. The world is becoming more sensitive to undesirable as well as desirable consequences for health of economic growth and industrial, urban and technological change.

The Black Report illustrates for Britain this accelerating concern. It provides an example, which is rare anywhere in the world, of an attempt authorized by a government to explain trends in inequalities in health and to relate these to the policies intended to promote health. Because it concentrates on Britain, the report also provides a commentary on the achievements of more than thirty years of a National Health Service in reducing these inequalities, and, by the same token, a standard by which to judge the current attempts of the government to develop a new mixture of private and public services. A version of the Black Report which is two thirds as long as the original follows this introduction, and speaks for itself. We shall try in the next pages only to show what has happened since the report was published in terms of how it has been received as well as what new events and evidence may be regarded as affecting its conclusions.

The appointment of the working group

We begin with some necessary background to the preparation of the report. In its publications the Department of Health and Social Security has frequently expressed concern with Britain's failure to match the improvement in health observed in some other countries and has acknowledged the relationship of this to persistent internal inequalities of health (for example, *Prevention and Health: Everybody's Business*, 1976, especially Chapters 1 and 4). In a speech on 27 March 1977, David Ennals, the Secretary of State for Social Services, stated:

... the crude differences in mortality rates between the various social classes are worrying. To take the extreme example, in 1971 the death rate for adult men in social class V (unskilled workers) was nearly twice that of adult men in social class I (professional workers) ... when you look at death rates for specific diseases the gap is even wider ... the first step towards remedial action is to put together what is already known about the problem ... it is a major challenge for the next ten or more years to try to narrow the gap in health standards between different social classes.

There were those like Sir John Brotherston, the Chief Medical Officer of Scotland, who in 1976 voiced the concern of many working in the health services and who had called the nation's attention to the social gulf in health which still existed and were calling for action. Many of those inside as well as outside the National Health Service were also aware that such inequalities might account for the failure of mortality rates in Britain to improve as far or as fast as in some other rich societies. Thus, among the countries of the world having the lowest infant mortality Britain ranked eighth in 1960 but had slipped to fifteenth by 1978. In the latter year, the infant mortality rates for Hong Kong and Singapore were slightly lower than the rate for Britain (World Bank, 1981).

The broad findings

Following its appointment in 1977 the Working Group sought to assemble national and international evidence and draw some of the implications for policy from the evidence about inequalities in health. The group found that the poorer health experience of the lower occupational groups applied at all stages of life. If the mortality rates of occupational class I (professional workers and members of their families) had applied to classes IV and V (partly skilled and unskilled manual workers and members of their families) during 1970–72 (the dates of the latest review of mortality experience) 74,000 lives of people aged under seventy-five would not have been lost. This estimate includes nearly 10,000 children and 32,000 men aged fifteen to sixty-four. The Group's main finding is therefore that despite more than thirty years of a National Health Service expressly committed to offering equal care for all, there remains a marked class gradient in standards of health. Indeed, that gradient seems to be more marked than in some comparable countries (though it must be said that the data for the United Kingdom almost invariably are fuller) and in certain respects has been becoming more marked. During the twenty years up to the early 1970s covered by the report the mortality rates for both men and women aged thirty-five and over in occupational classes I and II had steadily diminished while those in IV and V changed very little or had even deteriorated.

The report records

present social inequalities in health in a country with substantial resources like Britain are unacceptable and deserve to be so declared by every section of public opinion ... we have no doubt that greater equality of health must remain one of our foremost national objectives and that in the last two decades of the twentieth century a new attack upon the forces of inequality has regrettably become necessary.

What has gone wrong? The Working Group argues that much of the problem lies outside the scope of the National Health Service. Social and economic factors like income, work (or lack of it), environment, education,

housing, transport and what are today called 'life-styles' all affect health
and all favour the better-off. Yet they have largely remained outside the
ambit of national health policy. The Group also finds that those belonging
to the manual classes make smaller use of the health care system in a number
of different respects, yet need it more. Its thirty-seven recommendations
include giving effect to improvements in information, research and organization so that better plans might be drawn up, redressing the balance of
the health care system so that more emphasis is given to prevention, primary
care and community health, and, most important of all, radically improving
the material conditions of life of poorer groups, especially children and
people with disabilities, by increasing or introducing certain cash benefits,
like child benefit, maternity grant and infant care allowance, and a comprehensive disablement allowance, and developing new schemes for day
nurseries, ante-natal clinics, sheltered housing, home improvements, improved conditions at work and community services. So there are two policy
thrusts:

(i) Calling for a total and not merely a service-oriented approach to the
problems of health;

(ii) Calling for a radical overhaul of the balance of activity and proportionate distribution of resources within the health and associated services.

The government's reaction

Mr Patrick Jenkin, then Secretary of State for Social Services, received the
report early in April 1980. His department made a small number of copies
publicly available later that year – during August Bank Holiday week. The
Lancet referred to his reception as 'frosty', and pointed out that publicity
for the report was 'in the lowest possible key' and that Ministers and officials
gave the impression of being 'keen to reduce the report's impact to a
minimum' (6 September 1980, pp. 513 and 545). The *British Medical Journal*
wrote angrily of the failure to take measured account of the work of experts
and urged that the report 'should be examined more closely than Patrick
Jenkin's foreword suggests that it has been' (6 September 1980, p. 690, and
20 September 1980, p. 763). It said that, like the Short Report of 1980, it
had been discarded with 'shallow indifference' (20 December, p. 1663).

The Secretary of State's dismissal was brief. After stating in two short
paragraphs the scope of the Working Group's task he went on:

I must make it clear that additional expenditure on the scale which could result
from the report's recommendations – the amount involved could be upwards of £2
billion a year – is quite unrealistic in present or any foreseeable economic circum-

stances, quite apart from any judgement that may be formed of the effectiveness of such expenditure in dealing with the problems identified. I cannot, therefore, endorse the Group's recommendations.

Both the specialist and general press began to display keen interest in the manner of the appearance of the report and its substance. There was vigorous correspondence within the pages of the medical journals. Interested trade unions, and the TUC itself, published summaries for their members (COHSE, 1980; TUC, 1981), and quite exceptional efforts were made by bodies connected with the health and welfare services to bring the evidence and arguments in the report to a wide audience (for example, Gray, 1981; Black, 1981a; Deitch, 1981; Watkins and Elton, 1981; Townsend, 1981; and Radical Community Medicine, 1980). In July 1981, following a special conference devoted to the report, the association of community health councils for England and Wales adopted a resolution which deplored 'the negative response of Her Majesty's Government ... We call upon the Secretary of State for Health and Social Services to present a report to Parliament and to allow a debate on the important issues raised. We call upon the Minister to press for the necessary resources to provide the services and to analyse and give guidance to health authorities on the many recommendations which have little or no revenue consequences.' Partly at the prompting of bodies like the Socialist Health Association the Labour Party took an active interest in the report and a resolution passed in October at the annual conference called on the next Labour government to give priority to the implementation of its recommendations and, since many measures in the report could be introduced by local authorities, Labour representatives on councils and health authorities should 'do all in their power to ensure the implementation of these recommendations'. The General Secretary wrote to all Labour Groups accordingly (*Labour Weekly*, 4 December 1981).

By the spring of 1981 the Secretary of State found it necessary to elaborate on his first reaction and in a speech in Cardiff he drew attention to what he considered to be the report's three principal shortcomings. First, he claimed it did not adequately explain the causes of inequalities in health, and 'its enormously expensive' programme of recommendations could not therefore be accepted.

Secondly, Mr Jenkin argued that new evidence disproved the thesis that the working-class suffered poorer access to the health services.

My department has looked at a whole lot more evidence. We have compared the total use of the health services and we have found that people with lower incomes, more of whom are likely to be elderly, tend to receive proportionately more services than the average for the population as a whole. Moreover, there is support for this finding from an independent source – a recent analysis by two researchers at Bath University who have used quite different data based on the General Household Survey. The widely held view, therefore, that the poor do not have a proper crack of the whip when it comes to using the National Health Service is simply not supported by the facts. This is a very encouraging finding. (Cardiff, 13 March 1981)

Thirdly, Mr Jenkin argued in his Cardiff speech, and elsewhere (Deitch, 1981, p. 159), that there was no evidence that more money would make any difference (so missing the main point of the report).

We have been spending money in ever-increasing amounts on the NHS for thirty years and it has not actually had much effect on increasing people's health. (Deitch, 1981, p. 159)

The first and third of these objections were reiterated by Sir George Young, the Under-Secretary of State for Health and Social Security, on 31 July, in a short adjournment debate in the House of Commons, when replying to Mr William Hamilton, MP for Fife Central, who had drawn attention to the report. He repeated the costs given in the report (for November 1979); child benefit increases £970 m., infant care allowance £870 m., expansion of day provision for children £150 m., free school meals £200 m., universal allowance for disablement £24 m., special programme for deprived areas £30 m. 'The total is £2,244 m.' he claimed, and added, 'My department has provided an up-to-date estimate based on November 1980 prices of the net cost, which is £3,683 m., to which one has to add an increase in the maternity grant, which would amount to £55 m., and age-related child benefits of £1,110 m. That produces a total of £4,848 m.' He did however go on to say that the government agreed with some of the recommendations, particularly those on prevention. But, disappointingly, he did not seem to have recognized the gulf between the Working Group's concept of prevention and that of the government.

I see the progress being made by encouraging health education, personal responsibility for health, and encouraging voluntary organizations to help in the personal social services and helping to complement the NHS. That is the right way forward, given the difficult economic circumstances in which we find ourselves, rather than committing ourselves to the rather expensive solutions outlined by the Black Report, which we are not absolutely convinced would deliver the goods. (*British Medical Journal*, 22 August 1981)

The causes of inequalities in health

All three objections raised by government Ministers – explanation, access and money – have been strongly contested by the members of the Working Group, who have not only reaffirmed the original findings, but called attention to new evidence that has become available since the publication of the report (Black, 1981a and 1981b; Morris, 1980a, 1980b and 1980c; Townsend, 1981). We shall discuss the three in turn. First we shall consider trends in inequalities in health. Both in August 1980 and in March 1981 the Secretary of State accepted that there remained marked inequalities in health and also that 'some of the evidence ... suggests that the inequalities may actually have widened' (Cardiff, 13 March 1981). New texts have reviewed some of the latest evidence (Forster, 1979; Doyal, 1980; Morris, 1979 and 1980; Hollingsworth and Rogers, 1981; OPCS, 1981). In the late 1970s the class differences in infant mortality diminished, but there tend to be fluctuations in such rates from year to year and it will be a few years before this welcome trend can be confirmed (personal communication, OPCS, 1981). So far as we are aware, no other substantial evidence of any qualifications that may be attached to the conclusions about class have emerged. On the contrary, later evidence would seem to confirm the greater part of the analysis in the report.

There has been further work on area variations in infant mortality (Bradshaw, Edwards, Staden and Weale, 1981); low birth-weight, poor nutrition and resistance to disease (Chandra, 1980; Wynn and Wynn, 1981); variations in the need of the elderly for care (Vetter, Jones and Victor, 1981) and ill-health among unemployed school-leavers (Banks et al., 1980) and adults generally (Colledge, 1981; Fagin, 1981; Popay, 1981; and GP's Report, 1981). The work of Brenner is at the centre of a current controversy about the link between unemployment and ill-health or early mortality (Brenner, 1979; Ramsden and Smee, 1981; Stern, 1981; and Gravelle, Hutchinson and Stern, 1981). But, while calling attention to the importance of Brenner's research, the Working Group had already expressed reservations about his interpretation of cause and effect and in particular the prominence given to the concept of 'stress' rather than that of material deprivation. But there is no doubt that he has contributed most to the task of reopening a major line of investigation. Some of Brenner's subsequent critics have gone out of their way to point out that they do not deny that unemployment has 'no adverse effects on mortality or ill-health' – only that his approach suffers from certain weaknesses (for example, Gravelle, Hutchinson and Stern, 1981, p. 1). Some also associate themselves with 'sceptics who emphasize the role played by underlying social and economic inequalities rather than unemployment *per se*' (Stern, 1981, pp. 57–8).

Recent studies could be said to be filling in our knowledge of the long-term, pervasive effects of class membership on health and development throughout life. Thus, we know that there is a link between low birth-weight and congenital abnormality and we now have a sharper understanding of the relationships between low birth-weight and occupational class. A recent study has shown that even when allowance is made for whether it is the first or a subsequent child the poorest occupational class gave birth to three times as many babies under 2,500 grammes as the richest (Dowding, 1981; see also Wynn and Wynn, 1975, 1978 and 1981). Further evidence is also being collected about the difference according to social class in height and weight after making allowance for age (OPCS Monitor, 1981).

At the end of 1981 a report of a national survey carried out in 1979 showed pronounced inequalities in health between both the unskilled and partly skilled manual classes and the professional classes, and the indicators of inequalities in acute sickness were more pronounced than in any of the preceding years of the 1970s. As in previous surveys, general practitioner consultation rates were found not to match the apparently greater need for health care of the poorer occupational classes. For every female in the professional class there were 3.1 in the unskilled manual class who reported limiting long-standing illness, and 1.8 who reported restricted activity because of acute sickness. For males the corresponding ratios were 2.3 and 1.6 respectively. The ratios for persons in the partly skilled classes were nearly as high. Class gradients were pronounced at all ages except among the very youngest and oldest persons (OPCS, 1981, pp. 119–21). Females in the partly skilled class had an average of thirty-two days, and females in the unskilled manual class thirty-five days a year of restricted activity because of acute sickness, compared with thirteen in the professional classes. For males the corresponding figures were twenty-nine and twenty-five, compared with twelve. The relative differences on a variety of indicators are shown in Table A.

Such evidence, together with the known growth of unemployment since 1979 and, over the last two decades, the known increase in the numbers in the population on low incomes (see especially p. 116), amounts to a gloomy prognosis for inequalities in health. Trends in smoking also provide an indicator of such inequalities. According to the OPCS, smoking among men and women in professional occupations has declined by over a third since 1972, whereas that among unskilled manual classes has declined by only eleven per cent for men and two per cent for women (see Table B and OPCS Monitor, 1981).

Table A: *Indicators of ill-health: rates for partly skilled and unskilled persons expressed as a percentage of persons in the professional class (professional class rates = 100 in all cases) (1979)*

Indicator	Partly skilled		Unskilled	
	Females	*Males*	*Females*	*Males*
Acute sickness (restricted activity during previous 14 days)	178	144	178	156
Acute sickness (days per person per year of restricted activity)	248	215	273	250
Long-standing illness	183	158	217	179
Limiting long-standing illness	244	190	311	230
GP consultations: persons consulting	167	120	167	130
: number of consultations	167	130	160	120

Source: OPCS, *General Household Survey, 1979*, HMSO, 1981, pp. 117–23.

Only one of the further studies by the DHSS, promised by the Secretary of State, has so far (at the time of writing, January 1982) been published. This deals with health inequalities and not the utilization of health services. Using information from the 1976 General Household Survey on self-reported morbidity, a multivariate analysis was undertaken to identify the major influences upon the presence or absence of long-standing illness among adults. The study confirms that while the variables of age, sex and marital status are of course important, after other factors are held constant the upper non-manual groups are favoured.

The results are consistent with the conclusion of the Black Report which states that the 'rates of long-standing illness (as defined by the General Household Survey) rise with falling socio-economic status'. (Burchell, 1981, pp. 38–9)

Members of the Working Group are wary of claiming too much for their analysis of the *causes* of inequalities in health. Too little work of a wide-ranging kind on different age groups, and on the interrelationships between mortality or, even more, morbidity, and social and economic as well as biological and clinical factors has been carried out. But the Working Group were convinced that it is difficult to begin to explain the pattern of inequali-

Table B: *Prevalence of cigarette smoking among persons aged 16 and over* by sex and socio-economic group, Great Britain, 1972 to 1980*

Socio-economic group	% smoking cigarettes				
	1972	1974	1976	1978	1980
Males					
Professional	33	29	25	25	21
Employers and managers	44	46	38	37	35
Intermediate and junior non-manual	45	45	40	38	35
Skilled manual and own account non-professional	57	56	51	49	48
Semi-skilled manual and personal services	57	56	53	53	49
Unskilled manual	64	61	58	60	57
Total	52	51	46	45	42
Females					
Professional	33	25	28	23	21
Employers and managers	38	38	35	33	33
Intermediate and junior non-manual	38	38	36	33	34
Skilled manual and own account non-professional	47	46	42	42	43
Semi-skilled manual and personal service	42	43	41	41	39
Unskilled manual	42	43	38	41	41
Total	42	41	38	37	37

* *Aged 15 and over in 1972.*

Source: OPCS, Monitor, *General Household Survey, 1981.*

ties except by invoking material deprivation as a key concept. In looking at the causes of death for different age groups where differences between the classes are at their greatest, it is particularly difficult to deny the relevance of socio-economic variables. While it is as yet often impossible to pinpoint exactly how poverty and the class structure *cause* ill-health and death, there is little doubt about the kind of strategy which deserves to be pursued. While the Group appreciate that such a strategy involves major institutional changes in society (set out in the early pages of Chapter 9), they give priority to the interests of young children and people with disabilities, and secondly to *some* of those measures supporting a general strategy which are most likely to command public confidence at the present time. It is fair to say that the Group brings out more clearly than ever before the sharp inequalities in health which exist, and that in some respects and for some age groups these inequalities may have widened in recent years. The Group also begin the task of setting out the differences in working, home, environmental and social conditions which are correlated with level of income or equivalent resources, and hence with level of health or expectation of life. They are aware that the structure of inequality has many dimensions and needs to be examined much more systematically in relation to the distribution of health. They are also conscious of the biological and cultural as well as material influences on human behaviour, but they consider that it is possible to take the right general direction in policy without necessarily yet being aware which are precisely the best and cheapest measures to secure the objectives most quickly.

Cigarette smoking might be quoted as an illustration of their approach.

It is no good treating cigarette smoking as an aberrant or irresponsible behavioural response while society as a whole permits, even depends on the wide-scale production and promotion of tobacco goods. Human health is part of the organization of material existence. It is both produced and endangered by the work which men and women do in order to earn their livelihood. The manufacture and consumption of tobacco products and its effects on health provide a very clear example of the limitations of conventional health policy as a means to reduce health inequality. The prematurely lost lives of working class men and women will not be saved in the acute hospital or in the G P's surgery. (See chapters 6 and 8.)

It was not enough therefore to persuade or encourage individuals to give up smoking. There were powerful economic interests served by the production of tobacco products which were seeking to maximize consumption. A theory of health must of course include appropriate references to the organization of human society and production.

Unequal access to the NHS

The Secretary of State also drew on selected studies to cast doubts on the voluminous evidence marshalled by the Working Group showing that on the whole the richer occupational classes make more use of the National Health Service than do poorer occupational groups. In Chapter 4 the Working Group spell out the evidence in detail. They point out that inequalities appear to be greatest and most worrying in the case of the preventive services, but that in the case of GP attendance the evidence is not so clear-cut. This is partly because of differences in the measures used, but also because of year-to-year fluctuations in the sample information collected in the General Household Survey. The study quoted by the Secretary of State (Collins and Klein, 1980) is based on material from the General Household Survey *for only one year*. Because of the wide fluctuations reported by class in utilization of services the Working Group, with full support from DHSS statisticians, had deliberately analysed such material for a succession of years. Secondly, the paper by Collins and Klein was based on the *numbers* of users of primary care, and not on the *frequency* of use. Thirdly, the data considered were not related to *severity* of need as measured by days of illness or seriousness of condition. Fourthly, even the restricted data discussed in the paper were not re-examined in relation to the much higher percentage of partly skilled and unskilled manual workers who were in the categories of *'chronic sick'*. And, finally, no data are given on *children*, among whom there is the greatest inequality of access (Morris, 1979, 1980). Other commentators, who have themselves contributed to the evidence about unequal access, have consequently criticized this evidence of Collins and Klein. Thus, one analyst who concluded that 'the higher socio-economic groups received 40 per cent more NHS expenditure per person reporting illness than the lower groups' (LeGrand, 1978) now suggested that the GP consultation rates among the poorer manual groups were inflated artificially because of their relatively greater need for sickness absence certificates (LeGrand, *British Medical Journal*, 11 July 1981). In Chapter 4 the Working Group review the evidence in relation to separate criteria of need and point out that in general the poorer classes consult GPs less frequently than do the richer classes. The evidence from the latest General Household Survey to be published suggests that poorer occupational groups continue to consult GPs less than do their counterparts in richer groups when indicators of their greater needs are taken into the reckoning (OPCS, 1981 and Table A, p. 21).

The availability of resources and their distribution

Lack of resources is the third, and superficially the most conclusive, of the three arguments of government Ministers against the Black Report. Are there resources available to commit to new positive health strategies? First, other countries which are at a comparable stage of economic development are spending more of their GNP on health services. The figures quoted as the cost of the Black Report's recommendations represent an addition of only $4\frac{1}{2}$ per cent of total public expenditure on the social services (social security, health and personal social services, education and housing), or less than 3 per cent of total public expenditure. Secondly, the Working Group made clear that the recommendations deserve to be phased, with priorities, and that the full cost need not be met all at once. The Working Group take a modest view. As many as twenty-three of their thirty-seven recommendations would not be expensive to implement and the remaining recommendations could be implemented by stages. They take the view that the inception and development of an effective co-ordinated health strategy is all-important and that such a strategy will begin to bear fruit even if it cannot be backed for some time with massive resources. Thirdly, while it was no part of the Working Group's terms of reference to go into detail about methods of financing the proposed changes, illustrations were given of three possible strategies for reducing the total cost. Thus, the huge cost of the married man's tax allowance could be redistributed more effectively in the form of cash benefits for children and infants. The falling birth rate implied that without lowering standards resources and facilities might be found for nursery provision for the under-5s and for health education. And the prosecution of a more successful community care policy would have long-term implications for the reduction of the costs of residential care.

Fourthly, there were all kinds of indirect benefits from developing a more efficient social policy in the interests of a healthy workforce and population. There were implications for production by reducing mortality and morbidity among adults of economically active age but also the long-term contribution to morale and vitality from a reduction in pain, discomfort and stress and the enhancement of a sense of security.

What is at stake is the priority accorded to health by a nation, and the extent to which a programme for health is analysed and accepted as an integral part of the development of a healthy economy. The fundamental point in a still wealthy country like Britain is that the money for health is only not there if it is being spent on something else – like defence, roads or the marketing of consumer goods. Underlying the Working Group's judgement of the measures which might be possible in the current political and economic climate there runs a powerful argument: that a positive health strategy depends on political and economic priorities. The choice of those priorities is partly a question of arguing that health deserves to have a higher place in the claims that can be made on a nation's resources, partly that this in turn will necessarily involve spreading wealth around more equally than has been customary in Britain, and partly that expenditure on health has a lot to do with national production and hence with wealth *and* with welfare. Substantial expenditure on a programme for health represents a necessary part of wise national investment in a thriving economy.

What the nation can afford to spend on health

This point about investment in health deserves to be explained more clearly, because successive governments seem disinclined to accept it as a necessary assumption of planning. Much public discussion about social objectives is distorted by the rigid division invariably made between the public and private sector and the assumption that the former is financed by the latter. Part of the conventional wisdom is that expenditure on the welfare state, including health, is 'unproductive', and that the amounts available for welfare depend on the prosperity of the private sector – which tends to be equated with the prosperity of the national economy as a whole. On these assumptions governments have no choice but to reduce welfare spending during periods of recession. Both these assumptions can be questioned.

The welfare state was born at a time when public expenditure was seen as an aid or adjunct to economic growth and the pioneers of the welfare state, in making a case for spending some public money on welfare, did so without any doubt that welfare expenditure was conditional on that growth taking place; a desirable spin-off. It was not seen, except in the most incidental sense, as contributing in its own right to that growth. Welfare expenditure came to be regarded as something different from economic growth and efficiency; at best neutral, at worst a potential 'burden' on growth.

Since then governments of all political persuasions have repeated the same message, over and over again. Yet it is a distortion of reality. To understand this we need to understand what is usually meant by economic growth. To simplify, economic growth is a measure of the increase in the value of the sum total of goods and services that are sold by either a company or a national economy. And that is all. Consider an example. Every extra unit produced and sold from a factory is a contribution to the growth of that factory and, in as much as that factory is part of the national economy, to the growth of the national economy. But suppose that in increasing the number of units sold safety standards are reduced, thereby increasing the number of industrial injuries and also raising the levels of stress among the workforce and reducing work satisfaction. This 'hidden cost', known as an externality in mainstream economics, is not deducted or in any way connected with the increased 'wealth' generated by that factory. Yet the community as a whole will have to meet the cost of treating and caring for the casualties, which must imply some decrease in overall well-being. The apparent wealth generated by an industrial unit and the actual wealth taking into account such 'externalities' are therefore two very different measures. To get a real sense of the increased wealth and prosperity of the community we have to take the formal figure for economic growth and then deduct the externalities. It is not, of course, a calculation that is evident or, indeed, one which can easily be done. It is hard enough to quantify the costs of injury, still less treatment given free in the home and the lowered levels of positive health which represent a by-product. Yet, as Richard Titmuss has argued, social costs 'if allowed to lie where they fall, may result in larger costs in the shape of physical or psychological handicaps, destitution, deprived children, ill-educated workers unable or unwilling to acquire new skills and a general slackening in the sense of social involvement'. When either economic growth or economic loss is considered in range or depth, it cannot be distinguished from social growth or social loss.

Economic and social development are intertwined in ways which still require analysis. Whether we consider the urban riots in the summer of 1981 or the millions of people who are unemployed, social costs can be very real costs, even if not easily measurable in pounds and pence. To quote Richard Titmuss again: 'We need to find ways of seeing economic growth and social growth as interdependent in the sense that lagging behind in one has, necessarily, negative consequences on the other.' To see welfare merely as a potential by-product from economic growth, and as having no contribution to make to that growth, is at best shortsighted and at worst profoundly misguided. What requires at least as much consideration is the possibility that by according priority to the pursuit of social objectives there may be beneficial by-products for the economy.

The problem is in quantifying the money costs and gains of social policy. Cost-benefit analysis and output budgeting cannot be taken very far. It is hard, and perhaps at the moment impossible, to demonstrate and quantify social costs; to turn intangibles into tangibles. The technical wizardry of accountants, actuaries, statisticians and econometricians is hard to apply to even a fraction of the daunting problems, particularly health problems, of an entire population. It is difficult to put a cost on injury, unhappiness or dissatisfaction and to measure matters pertinent to 'positive' health like exuberance and ebullience. There is a sense in which the amount a nation can afford to spend on the pursuit of health is what it chooses to spend. Qualitative judgements as well as quantitative measures of health have to be combined. Certainly there is an impressive case to be made – whether by comparison with other equally rich societies, the demonstrated need in our own society, or the health benefits which accrue from lessening inequality

– for a more generous national commitment of resources to lessening inequality.

But the way that commitment of resources is made matters acutely. Investment to reduce the worst features of deprivation and markedly raise the lowest levels of income will have ramifying effects in promoting good health. The commitment of additional resources to the National Health Service, together with a change in the percentage distribution of allocated expenditure and in the power structure of the service itself, could also have a marked effect in reducing inequalities in health.

It is perfectly true that the money devoted to the NHS has risen annually since 1948 and is now over twice as much as it was then at equivalent prices. But it is not only that Britain is devoting less of its national resources to health care than industrial countries like Sweden, the United States, West Germany, Italy and Ireland: Britain is spending significantly less absolutely than other countries. Thus in 1977 Britain spent £123 per head of population on health care, compared with £280 in France and £450 in Sweden (OHE, 1979). So the argument that a state-run service involves runaway costs simply does not hold water.

While the low spending on the NHS is partly a consequence of its efficiency, at least relative to the systems of some other countries, there is also a long history of inadequate funding of some sectors of health care. For long periods different categories of long-stay patients in hospital and living at home have found it hard to get the services they need. And for many years health centres were slow to develop. In 1956 the Guillebaud Committee exposed the scaremongering about the alleged runaway costs of the NHS and in 1974 the House of Commons Public Expenditure Committee declared that 'it is the opinion of this committee that no Government has ever provided sufficient money to allow the health service to function and react to growing needs effectively'.

Against this background it is hard to believe that funding for the health service as a whole, as opposed to some parts of it, has ever been more than just adequate. Extra money for mentally and physically handicapped people, for the mentally ill and for large numbers of the elderly would make an enormous difference to the quality of their lives. Many long-stay hospitals need to be transformed in their amenities and conditions. NHS waiting lists for many routine but important operations are too long. Large numbers of hospitals and clinics have outlived their useful life. The conditions and wages of some low-paid staff need to be greatly improved. This being so, where has the argument that more money would not make any difference come from? Is it not transparently clear that additional resources would be helpful, even if they are concentrated in certain sectors?

The Working Group make a powerful case for greater spending on prevention and community health. But this is more of a political and medical
minefield than is often appreciated. The question is whether there is room
for a direct shift of resources from curative to preventive medicine when
there is little or no growth in the economy and little opportunity to increase
the overall resources for the health service. The Black Working Group split
on the issue, and as the Chairman, Sir Douglas Black, has explained,

we were all agreed that education and preventive measures, specifically directed
towards the socially deprived, were necessary. But the sociological members of the
group (Townsend and Smith) considered that the consequent expenditure should be
obtained by diversion from the acute services. On the other hand the medical members
– and that means both of us (Black and Morris) – felt that the acute services played
a vital part in the prevention of chronic disability and could not be further cut back
without serious effects on emergency care, on the training of doctors for both hospital
work and for family practice and on the length of waiting lists. We spent a long
time, without real success, trying to resolve this matter. (Black, 1981b)

Sir Douglas went on,

I regard this conflict, for such it was, as evidence of a widespread belief that
curative and preventive services are somehow in opposition, whereas in fact they are
both necessary, and indeed they may complement each other. It is argued, for example,
that a switch of resources from 'care and cure' to 'prevention' would achieve the
same benefits more economically. Not so; the benefits are not the same, but different.

And he concludes,

There is a related tendency to over-estimate the savings which may arise from a
reduction in acute hospital beds. To the extent that this is made possible by their
more intensive use, the undoubted savings in 'hotel costs' is considerably offset by
the increased cost of investigation and treatment as more patients pass through the
system.

It is a complicated argument. Certainly there are those who call for a
dramatic reduction in treatment services on the grounds that they are nothing
more than a wasteful holding operation and that the money could be better
spent elsewhere. Yet those working in any health service must aspire to
offer the best possible treatment they can. Heart transplants, often cited as
an example of expensive and wasteful medicine, may not be a solution to
heart disease, but equally heart disease that has not been prevented will
continue to exist even in the best-regulated society, and if the operation is
beneficial it must be considered for those who would benefit from it. The
problem is in balancing benefits, both potential as well as current. (Morris,
1980c.)

Successive governments have produced plans suggesting there could be a direct trade-off between preventive and community services and curative services and that absolute or relative cuts in the latter could directly finance improvements in the former. But the plans have not really taken into full account the administrative structures within which the health services are operated, together with the power distribution of different interests not only in the decision-making parts of the hierarchical structure of the National Health Service but in the relevant professions, unions and other representative organizations of the service. The implicit contradiction between plans and structures could be illustrated in different ways. Table C shows the numbers of doctors working in hospitals and in the community in England in 1949 and in 1980. In the formative years of the health service two thirds of the nation's doctors worked in general practice; today two thirds work in hospital. And Table C also shows that the absolute increase in numbers of nurses working in hospital has dwarfed the additional numbers working in the community, such that nearly ten times as many now work in hospital as in the community. To the sheer numbers has to be added the status and seniority of the leading personnel who are involved in the crucial arguments about resources in both hospitals and community. Senior consultants exercise a powerful influence at every level of the structure of the service, so much so that the present government has conceded the case for greater numbers of consultants at the same time as it is trying to hold down the costs of the service. Despite the priority expressed in principle for services outside the hospital, priority in practice has been steadily accorded to the hospital. These are the facts which underlie the debates about the allocation of resources.

A similar kind of analysis is required to explain the confusion of the

Table C: *Medical and nursing staff in England*

Health Service Personnel*	1949	1980	Percentage increase since 1949
Doctors: Hospital	11,735	31,421	168
General Practice	18,000	22,674	26
Nurses: Hospital	137,636	297,684†	116
Community	9,529	32,162†	238

* Whole-time equivalent.
† 1979.

debate about the Resource Allocation Working Party's proposals to channel money to the under-financed regions of the north from the relatively favoured areas of the south, in which a disproportionately large number of the teaching hospitals are to be found. The traditional sources of power in the health service have been resisting this equalization plan, as the Working Group pointed out and as some of the latest specialized research on the relationship between need and the resources committed to different areas within one of the metropolitan regions shows (Best, 1981; Cooper, 1981). This study shows that the districts in which teaching hospitals are placed secure a greater share of the available resources.

The growth of private medicine

It is in demonstrating the benefits of the principles of equalization that the Black Report will be read by a wide audience. In its stance and analysis the report stands four square behind the basic principles of the NHS. Until the late 1970s there was an uneasy political consensus about these principles. Despite the fractious exchanges with the negotiating body for the medical profession before 1948, the NHS proved to be the most popular development in the establishment of the post-war welfare state and had not been seriously altered by the governments in the 1950s and 1960s of Churchill, Eden, Home, and Macmillan as well as those of Attlee and Wilson. From time to time sections of the medical profession and advisers to the Conservative Party called for fundamental changes.

But a major transformation in the basis of operation of the National Health Service now threatens to take place and on all sides passions have been aroused. Different factors have all brought the development of the NHS back into the centre of the political stage: the world-wide escalating costs of clinical medicine and especially of drugs; the attempt by successive governments to cut public expenditure; the burgeoning power on the one hand of health service unions and on the other of hospital consultants; public resistance to high personal taxation; and, since 1979, the resurgence of private medicine. The conflicts reflect perhaps the long-standing and even deepening inequality of British society.

As yet the scale of private practice remains small. About 2 per cent of all acute hospital beds and 6 per cent of all hospital beds are in private hospitals and nursing homes. In 1976 total expenditure on private health care was about £200 m. or under 3 per cent of total NHS expenditure in that year of £6,300 m. Unlike in the United States, only a small percentage of elderly people in long-stay residential accommodation are to be found in private nursing or residential homes. The Royal Commission on the

National Health Service examined the relationship between the service and private practice and concluded 'the private sector is too small to make a significant impact on the NHS, except locally and temporarily' (Report of the Royal Commission, p. 294). Almost as categorically the Commission advised against the kind of changes in the finance of the service which might pave the way for more private medicine. 'We are not convinced,' they concluded, 'that the claimed advantages of insurance finance or substantial increases in charge revenue would outweigh their undoubted disadvantages in terms of equity and administrative costs. The same disadvantages arise from the existing NHS charges' (p. 353).

In the late 1970s and early 1980s inequalities in service became sharper with the increase in private hospital care. In 1975 the then Secretary of State set out to try to limit private medicine. A consultative document (DHSS, 1975) announced imminent legislation to separate private practice from the NHS, and introduced a licensing system to control and restrict the private sector to a size of only 9,000 beds. But the Health Services Act of 1976 designated only 1,000 of the 4,900 NHS pay beds for transfer to the NHS for general use, and, in setting up a Health Services Board to review the remaining pay beds, followed a leisurely timetable with a great deal of emphasis on 'reasonable alternative facilities' being available in the private sector. It has since been argued that the 1976 Act opened the way to an expansion of the private medical sector to the detriment of the NHS. It did not set a final date for the removal of all pay beds from the NHS and did not provide an effective means of controlling and limiting the growth of private hospitals outside the NHS. The Health Services Board exercised little control over private hospital developments and though it produced a programme in May 1977 for the operation of common waiting lists, the Secretary of State had no obligation to implement that programme. No action was taken by the time of the election of 1979. In the late 1970s registration for private medical insurance increased swiftly and new private hospitals were planned. BUPA has opened or is opening new hospitals in Manchester, Bushey, Harpenden, Cardiff and Wirrall. The Nuffield Nursing Homes Trust owns 1,000 of the 4,500 beds in the private sector and works closely with the Provident Associations. It built four hospitals in 1978. Two major profit-making companies, Humana, which owns the Wellington Hospital in London, and American Medical (Europe), which is a subsidiary of American Medical International, are also opening new hospitals. 'Hot-shot hospital companies', as they have been called by the *Financial Times* (4 April 1981), have grown fast in the United States and are taking advantage of the new market in Britain.

The present government, which came to power two months before the publication of the Royal Commission's Report, was committed to cutting back public expenditure in order to benefit the private sector. The Secretary of State for Social Services had argued for more of the cost of the service to be transferred from taxes to insurance 'either by extending the existing health contribution or by offering people a choice of insuring with the state or with the private sector' (*Lancet*, 28 July 1979). Similar themes were reiterated by government ministers late in 1981. Steps were taken to increase existing or introduce new charges. Thus between April 1979 and April 1982 the prescription charge was increased from 20p to £1.30 (although more than half of the volume of prescriptions are for people, including children and old people, who are exempt from charges). In 1980 the Health Service Bill was passed to stop the enforced withdrawal of pay beds from NHS hospitals, change the control over private practice and abolish the Health Service Board, which had been created by the Labour government to supervise private hospitals. Full-time consultants were permitted to gain additional earnings of 10 per cent of their gross earnings from private practice. The Conservative Minister of State for Health said that he would like at least 25 per cent of treatment to be carried out in the private sector.

Perhaps without realizing it the government is trying to go in two directions at once. It is following a policy of restraining the growth of total NHS expenditure, but simultaneously increasing the number of hospital consultants and conceding the consultants' case for more pay for less time, and expanding private medicine, with its necessary preoccupation with hospitalization of the acute sick. This policy implies a bigger imbalance between the resources committed to the hospitals and to the other sectors of the health care system, with a likely real *fall* in the resources obtained by the latter.

But there are signs of a strong reaction, both among health care staff and among the public, to the scale of cuts in public services made necessary by government policies on the one hand, and the encouragement that has been given to private medicine on the other. Issues of priorities in health care policy have been forced into the forefront of public and professional consciousness. The advocates of primary care and community health cannot but gain if the argument is sharpened.

Behind the present government's approach to medicine and health care is a tenacious set of market values; a belief in the virtue of individualism – that people should have the 'freedom' to buy the best medical care they can afford and that those who are able and willing to pay more should get more. Against this, those of all political colours who have for three decades favoured a very strong NHS have emphasized the importance of collective responsibility and equal access to medical attention regardless of individual financial, social or cultural constraints. These are two different visions of society. It is this difference which, more than anything else, seems to underlie the government's rejection of 'inequalities in health'. But fundamentally these two views have to be thought through and worked out in relationship to the achievement of health and the organization and future development of health services. In affirming belief in the basic principles of the NHS many people in Britain must accept the challenge to develop a better theory about health and translate such theory into an effective programme for health.

List of Abbreviations and Definitions

GHS: General Household Survey. Carried out annually by the Office of Population and Census Surveys. Based on a sample of 15,000 households in the UK, it provides data on a range of topics including health, education, employment, housing and migration. It has been running annually since 1970.

HIPE: Hospital Inpatient Enquiry. An annual survey carried out jointly by the Department of Health and Social Security, the OPCS and the Welsh Office and designed to find out how fully hospitals are used and what for.

MRC: Medical Research Council.

Neonatal mortality: Deaths during the first four weeks of life.

OPCS: Office of Population and Census Surveys. A government department which is in charge of the national census and many other recurrent and occasional surveys and collections of statistics.

Perinatal mortality: Still-births and deaths in the first week of life.

Post-neonatal mortality: Deaths after the first month but before the end of the first year of life.

Registrar General: Overlord at the OPCS. The current Registrar General is Mr Roger Thatcher, a statistician and career civil servant.

Registrar General's Decennial Supplements: The OPCS gathers mortality and morbidity data annually. Every ten years it supplements these annual data with extra information from the ten year census and publishes it as decennial supplements, one on occupational mortality and the other on area mortality.

SMR: Standardized Mortality Ratio. A method of comparing death rates between different sections of the population, holding other variables constant. That is comparing one area with another holding age, sex and occupation constant. Thus Merseyside has a higher SMR than East Anglia, even allowing for the different population structures of the two areas.

WHO: World Health Organization.

The Black Report

Foreword by Patrick Jenkin

The Working Group on Inequalities in Health was set up in 1977, on the initiative of my predecessor as Secretary of State, under the Chairmanship of Sir Douglas Black, to review information about differences in health status between the social classes; to consider possible causes and the implications for policy; and to suggest further research.

The Group was given a formidable task, and Sir Douglas and his colleagues deserve thanks for seeing the work through, and for the thoroughness with which they have surveyed the considerable literature on the subject. As they make clear, the influences at work in explaining the relative health experience of different parts of our society are many and interrelated; and, while it is disappointing that the Group were unable to make greater progress in disentangling the various causes of inequalities in health, the difficulties they experienced are perhaps no surprise given current measurement techniques.

It will come as a disappointment to many that over long periods since the inception of the NHS there is generally little sign of health inequalities in Britain actually diminishing and, in some cases, they may be increasing. It will be seen that the Group has reached the view that the causes of health inequalities are so deep-rooted that only a major and wide-ranging programme of public expenditure is capable of altering the pattern. I must make it clear that additional expenditure on the scale which could result from the report's recommendations – the amount involved could be upwards of £2 billion a year – is quite unrealistic in present or any foreseeable economic circumstances, quite apart from any judgement that may be formed of the effectiveness of such expenditure in dealing with the problems identified. I cannot, therefore, endorse the Group's recommendations. I am making the report available for discussion, but without any commitment by the government to its proposals.

PATRICK JENKIN
Secretary of State for
Social Services

August 1980

Foreword

In April 1977, at the request of Mr David Ennals, the then Secretary of State for Health and Social Security, the DHSS Chief Scientist appointed a working group with the following broad objectives:

(i) To assemble available information about the differences in health status among the social classes and about factors which might contribute to these, including relevant data from other industrial countries;

(ii) To analyse this material in order to identify possible causal relationships, to examine the hypotheses that have been formulated and the testing of them, and to assess the implications for policy; and

(iii) to suggest what further research should be initiated.

The membership of the Working Group was:

Sir Douglas Black (Chairman), Chief Scientist at the DHSS (to April 1978) and now President of the Royal College of Physicians;

Professor J. N. Morris, Professor of Community Health in the University of London at the London School of Hygiene and Tropical Medicine;

Dr Cyril Smith, Secretary of the Social Science Research Council;

Professor Peter Townsend, Professor of Sociology at the University of Essex, now Professor of Social Policy, University of Bristol.

Dr Stuart Blume was Scientific Secretary to the Group, and the Administrative Secretary was Mr A. J. Forsdick. Dr Nicky Hart was seconded by the University of Essex to act as Research Fellow to the Group.

The final report was published in August 1980.

Chapter 1

Concepts of Health and Inequality

Throughout history different meanings have been given to the idea of 'health'. One is freedom from clinically ascertainable disease, which has been central to the development of medicine. In ancient Greece the followers of Asclepius believed that the chief role of the physician was to 'treat disease, to restore health by correcting any imperfections caused by the accidents of birth or life' (Dubos, 1960, p. 109). Beginning with primitive surgical intervention and herbal treatment, a tradition was established which was to prove extraordinarily powerful, accelerating in the eighteenth century with the rise of science and again in the twentieth century as a consequence of the massive resources provided for research and innovation in medical technologies. The Cartesian philosophy of the body conceived as a machine and the body controlled as a machine provided an impetus for scientific experiment and a stream of practical outcomes which for an increasing proportion of the population seemed to validate a mechanistic perspective.

There can be no doubt about the success with which such an 'engineering' approach in medicine has been applied. Medical education became concerned with the structure and functions of the body and with disease processes, and medical science became represented predominantly by the acute hospital with its concentration of technological resources (Abel-Smith, 1964). The relatively restricted and familiar use of the word 'health' is therefore associated with the belief systems and the practice of a medicine from which its origins can be traced. Health, which derives from a word meaning whole, is the object of the healing process. To heal is literally to make whole or to restore health. The structure of medicine and of the health services helps to sustain this meaning. Some (for example, McKeown, 1976) have argued however that this development in medicine has distorted our understanding of the problems of human health and well-being and that there are alternative or complementary approaches which it is increasingly important to clarify and properly finance.

Much wider meanings have been given to the word 'health', which hold major implications for the organization of society and the pattern upon which personal life may be modelled. To the followers of the ideas symbolized in ancient Greece by the goddess Hygeia, rational social organization and rational individual behaviour were all-important to the promotion of human health. It was an attribute to which men were entitled if they governed their lives wisely and is echoed in today's 'life-style' approaches to good health. According to them, 'the most important function of medicine is to discover and teach the natural laws which will ensure a man a healthy mind in a healthy body' (Dubos, 1960, p. 109). Implicit also are ideas of the good life: not just freedom from pain, discomfort, stress and boredom, which themselves extend beyond the competence of clinicians to diagnose or treat, but positive expression of vigour, well-being and engagement with one's environment or community. In some respects this more comprehensive approach reached its apogee in the definition of health adopted at the foundation of the World Health Organization at the end of the Second World War as a 'state of complete physical, mental and social well-being and not merely the absence of disease or infirmity'. Adherents of this more comprehensive approach, which is usually called 'social', have worked both within and outside medicine. In most countries there are movements for physical fitness and good diet. Immunization is a standard public health practice. And through direct and indirect 'health education' and counselling, higher standards of health are encouraged. In the case of children this wider conception of health directs concern not only to the presence or absence of disease, but to growth and development, physical, cognitive and emotional. (There is, anyway, abundant evidence for the interaction of disease and development in infants. Low-birth-weight babies show a higher mortality and also incidence of neurological and physical disorder (Birch and Gussow, 1970, p. 52) and, later in life, there is evidence for the aetiological significance of even mild under-nutrition in inhibiting growth (Marshall, 1977, p. 118).) It becomes relevant to look at evidence relating to acuity of hearing and vision in children, and at heights, weights and age at the onset of puberty, even though none of these things is in any sense an aspect of 'disease'. Given the significance of this kind of thinking, we consider that the different meanings of 'health' and hence of national objectives in maintaining and promoting health are often not given as much attention as they might be, a point we shall return to. Plainly for our purposes the 'social model' of health is more relevant than the 'medical' and we have therefore in the main followed it.

The two models are not, of course, either exclusive or exhaustive. (Discussions based essentially on the 'medical model' are given by Black (1979) and by Dollery (1978).) Conceptions of health and illness vary among different groups within a single society and between societies, as well as in any single society over time (Morris, 1975). It is in part for this reason that

'illness behaviour' – the response to symptoms and the tendency or reluctance to define any symptom as a health problem and to seek medical care
– varies between cultural and social groups (Mechanic, 1968). Conceptions
are moreover in constant process of adaptation or revision. Changes occur
by virtue of scientific discovery and innovation, and developments in
professional judgements of needs and the status of different diseases and
treatments. They also occur in response to the pressure of established
interests, and the extent of public anxiety about illness or safety, as well as
the current level of demand for health, environmental and social services.
Thus one result of research on the elderly and disabled, and the heightening
of public interest and concern about their problems, has been that pain,
discomfort, debility and different forms of incapacity have come to play a
more prominent part in social and medical conceptions. If we consider
mental illness or mental handicap, or the history of 'fringe' medicine, to
take very diverse examples, we can see how conceptions of health and illness
have changed. And just as conceptions themselves may gradually change,
elements within them are accorded different weight or priority. We make
this point for two reasons. The first is that our understanding of 'health'
will always be evolving, and we must be prepared to absorb new knowledge
about changes in health and social conditions. The second is to make better
judgements about the strengths and weaknesses of the present health care
services.

Within for instance any general approach to the meaning of 'health',
views are reached about the seriousness of certain states of health. The
construction of the health care services and the priorities which are identified
in their development reflect those views. To the extent that a mechanistic
model of health holds sway, the health care services will give priority to
such matters as surgery, the immunological response to transplanted organs,
chemo-therapy and the molecular basis of inheritance. Medicine comes to
be structured according to a scale of values associated with such a model.
The most sought-after posts will be those at the heart of the model, and
medical education and medical careers are similarly influenced. Medicine
is not, we know, monolithic, as developments in paediatrics, obstetrics,
psychiatry and rehabilitation, and research in the social aspects and in
prevention, indicate. However, once a conception of disease finds embodi-
ment in the structure of a service, major changes become more difficult to
introduce. All professions tend to become over-committed to existing
practice and their receptivity to the need for change is liable to become
weak. The medical, nursing and other professions are no different in this
respect. We have to face the uncomfortable fact that society cannot look
to the professions working within the health services for an account of

illness and health which is always as detached or as full as it might be. Indeed, particularized conceptions of health and illness (including their stages and severity) are already institutionalized in medical practice and the organization, sub-divisions and administration of services.

Therefore, while the knowledge, experience and views of the health care professions are bound to play a predominant part in the debate, the extension of knowledge about the problems of human health and illness depends also on sources outside the health professions. Under the auspices of the medical and social sciences there needs to be a determined search for evidence of a wide variety of health conditions and their social, environmental and psychological as well as physiological significance.

In the last hundred and fifty years it could be said that the pursuit of health has increasingly been acknowledged to be a social and not merely a technical enterprise. In part this is due to the success of medical science in reducing mortality from infectious disease and thus directing attention towards chronic diseases of complex aetiology, but it is also due to the development of public health services, statistical studies of health, the work of epidemiologists in demonstrating the importance of living standards, protection from hazards and population limitation in improving health, and latterly the work of sociologists on the complex effects of the economy and different forms of social organization, including the family, upon levels of health. (See for example Susser and Watson, 1971; Morris, 1975; McKeown, 1976; Tuckett, 1976.)

Nevertheless the shift in emphasis from a medical to a social model still has some way to go. Although bio-medical research will continue to be vital, there is, in the words of one commentator, a 'need for a shift in the balance of effort, from laboratory to epidemiology in recognition that improvement in health is likely to come in future, as in the past, from modification of the conditions which led to disease rather than from intervention in the mechanism of disease after it has occurred' (McKeown, 1976, p. 179). The sociological contribution is recognized to be, in part, to increase understanding of the social and socio-economic factors which play a part in the promotion of health and the causation of disease and in part to take the natural next step and relate these factors themselves to the broader social structure (see Brown and Harris, 1978).

Some working in medical sociology would emphasize a different perspective. They would argue that their contribution is not only like that of social medicine, to contribute to the understanding of the origins of health and disease in the way people live together in society. 'Disease', they would argue, is a medical, not a sociological concept. Sociology is concerned with the social production of understanding, meanings, knowledge; with social structure and process; and with the behaviour of people. Sociologists will try to understand the failure to seek medical attention for what to the physician is a serious disease episode not in terms of simple irrationality, but in terms of the individual's own (learned) coping mechanisms, social situation, and the meaning which he attaches to his symptoms. Hence there is a lot of interest in the social production of conceptions of health, in inconsistencies between lay and professional conceptions, and in conditions which are generated by different forms of social organization.

While the perspectives adopted in the three fields – medicine, epidemiology and sociology – tend to be different, they are subject to mutual influence and some of the most creative practitioners acknowledge the need to absorb or combine their strengths. Thus, nearly forty years ago Sigerist, a famous American medical historian (following Virchow, a German pathologist, long before), argued that 'The task of medicine is to promote health, to prevent disease, to treat the sick when prevention is broken down and to rehabilitate the people after they have been cured. These are highly social functions and we must look at medicine as basically a social science' (Sigerist, 1943, p. 241).

Choice of indicators of health and ill-health

Conceptions of health may vary in time and according to place, but science demands precision, and different aspects of the meaning of health and ill-health have to be translated into operational terms and applied systematically.

Measures of the 'health' of populations can take many different forms. Among the most familiar are mortality rates, prevalence or incidence of morbidity rates, sickness-absence rates and restricted-activity rates. Each of these indicators poses problems of measurement and has its limitations. For example, undue dependence on mortality rates can induce comparative indifference towards problems of chronic illness. Undue dependence on morbidity rates can discourage interest in congenital and other permanently incapacitating conditions, as well as conditions affecting human well-being which fall outside the conventional classification of 'morbidity'.

Partly because of the problems of measurement, but also because of the need for time-series statistics, we have given precedence to mortality rates. But we wish to call attention to the need for measures of health which combine several factors and which allow the real experiences among the population to be captured. For instance a combined indicator of pain and restricted activity has been proposed (Culyer et al., 1972) and in current Canadian work indicators reflecting social, emotional and physical functioning are being developed (Sackett et al., 1977). Again, the need to relate rather complex indicators of depression to the measure of life events was felt to apply to the community generally and not just those selected for psychiatric treatment (Brown and Harris, 1978).

A distinction is often drawn between acute and chronic sickness, and attempts have been made to relate the utilization of health services to these conditions. But it is clear from GHS reports over the years that the choice of terminology in 'indicator' questions can considerably affect the percentage of the population identifying themselves as having 'short-term' or 'chronic' health problems. Moreover, whatever method is adopted for distinguishing acute from chronic sickness we would also want to call attention to the dangers of treating any two sets of people so identified as distinct (Morris, 1975). Acute and chronic conditions in some patients are difficult to distinguish. Since the evidence suggests that the poorer groups are at greater risk of chronic sickness and disablement, there are dangers of distorting conclusions being reached about the characteristics of the 'acute' sick if all those with chronic sickness are first excluded from any analysis.

Disablement is also an important related concept. While interpretation of the concept of disability varies, it has been identified increasingly in recent years (as in the GHS surveys) with restriction of activity, which includes self-care, household management, and occupational and social activities. Parallel with this trend has been a greater emphasis on treating severity of disablement irrespective of cause or sex or age. Most local authorities have made returns since 1975 which have sought to distinguish the numbers of the physically handicapped according to severity of handicap. Non-statutory bodies are pressing for even wider application of this principle. 'All disabled people: the old, young adults and children; the mentally and physically handicapped, those disabled at home as well as at work or in war; and those disabled from birth, after an accident, or a long illness must be treated alike. It is not the origins or type of disablement or age which should count.' This statement is made on behalf of a large number of organizations of and for disabled people (*Disability Rights Handbook for 1980*, 1979, p. 48) which are concerned to call public attention to the consequences for individuals of the effects of disablement rather than its origins or type. Surveys of public opinion seem to endorse such statements (*Help for the Disabled*, 1974).

Concepts of inequality

The distribution of health or ill-health among and between populations has for many years been expressed most forcefully in terms of ideas on 'inequality'. These ideas are not just 'differences'. There may be differences between species, races, the sexes and people of different age, but the focus of interest is not so much natural physiological constitution or process as outcomes which have been socially or economically determined. This may seem to be straightforward, but the lengthy literature, and widespread public interest in the subject of inequality, show that factors which are recognizably or discernibly man-made are not so easy to disentangle from the complex physical and social structure in which man finds himself. Differences between people are accepted all too readily as eternal and unalterable. The institutions of society are very complex and exert their influence indirectly and subtly as well as directly and self-evidently. For some the concept of inequality also carries a moral reinforcement, as a fact which is undesirable or avoidable. For others the moral issue is relatively inconsequential. For them differences in riches or work conditions are an inevitable and hence 'natural' outcome of the history of attempts by man to build society, and they conclude that the scope for modification is small and, besides other matters, of little importance.

Central to the development of work on inequality has been the development of concepts of 'social class': that is *segments of the population sharing broadly similar types and levels of resources, with broadly similar styles of living and* (for some sociologists) *some shared perception of their collective condition*. This too has been controversial and there remains considerable controversy within sociology about the origins and relative importance of class in relation to social inequalities and social change.

The problems of choosing indicators of inequality

Traditionally inequalities have been portrayed through a characterization of class obtained by ranking occupations according to their social status or prestige. Of course, a variety of other factors may be said to play a part in determining class: income, wealth, type of housing tenure, education, style of consumption, mode of behaviour, social origins and family and local connections. They are interrelated and none of them should be regarded as sufficient in itself. But historically occupation has been selected as the principal indicator, partly because it has been regarded as more potent than some alternatives, but partly because it was the most convenient for statistical measurement and analysis. Occupation not simply designates type of work but tends also to show broadly how strenuous or unhealthy it is, what are the likely working conditions – for example whether it is indoors or outdoors and whether there is exposure to noise, dust or vibration – and what amenities and facilities are available, as well as level of remuneration and likely access to various fringe benefits. Pay will also determine family living standards and, while members of a family will not be exposed to some features of the working conditions experienced, there are others which may affect them indirectly, like the risk of intermittent unemployment, or the stress of disablement and of shift work.

Throughout this report we shall employ occupation as a basis of class because of its convenience. In particular we shall use the Registrar General's categories as follows:

I. Professional (for example accountant, doctor, lawyer) (5 per cent)*

II. Intermediate (for example manager, nurse, schoolteacher) (18 per cent)

III N. Skilled non-manual (for example clerical worker, secretary, shop assistant) (12 per cent)

III M. Skilled manual (for example bus driver, butcher, carpenter, coal face worker) (38 per cent)

IV. Partly skilled (for example agricultural worker, bus conductor, postman) (18 per cent)

V. Unskilled (for example cleaner, dock worker, labourer) (9 per cent).

But in doing this we should also be aware of its limitations. *We believe an effort should be made to make this classification in the rankings of occupations as objective as possible, by taking into account current and lifetime earnings, fringe benefits, security, working conditions and amenities.* Our intention is to shift attention from the more elusive subjective rating of 'prestige' or 'general standing' of occupations that have been traditionally used, to their material or environmental (and more measurable) properties. *Second, it would be desirable for the term 'occupational class' to be used rather than 'social class' when the current occupation of the individual is used as the basis of the classification* (and we shall do this throughout the report when we use this definition of class). *Third, it will become increasingly important to use the married man's occupation in combination with the married woman's occupation in analysing various health conditions and experiences,* for example infant and child mortality. *Fourth, the need for a 'social class' measure for analysis of the health of the family unit as a whole or of individual members of the family unit will become increasingly important.* One possibility is using the current occupations of both parents, together with information, where it can be obtained, about the main occupations of the husband's father and the wife's father. We return to these possibilities in Chapter 7.

---

* The percentages are of the total number of economically active and retired males.

Finally, use of occupation as an indicator of social class has become so widespread in Britain in recent decades that the pre-occupations of some pioneer health statisticians have been forgotten. Some, however, were particularly concerned to relate health experience to riches or poverty (for example, Stevenson, 1928). Efforts should be made to restore this tradition, and not only because of the difficulties of taking occupation as a reliable indicator of a family's social class. The growth of absolute levels of resources, the spread of employer welfare benefits in kind and of social service benefits, and the increase of owner-occupation among the working classes makes a measure of 'resources' all the more important. The term 'resources' seems to be more appropriate than 'income' because of the present-day impact of wealth and both employer welfare and social service benefits-in-kind upon living standards. Considerable sums are spent each year on official annual surveys – including the Family Expenditure Survey (FES), the General Household Survey (GHS) and the National Food Survey. The FES provides the best measure of income, and although some information is collected about employer welfare and social service benefits it is incomplete and rather rough. Valuable data about the distribution of health are collected in the GHS, and although the information collected about income has, since 1979, been the same as in the FES, it is not supplemented by information on other resources. The development of a more adequate measure will not be easy, and the Royal Commission on the Distribution of Income and Wealth took a very cautious view in some of its reports about the possibilities of linking income and wealth in surveys (see especially Reports Nos. 1, 4 and 5). However, its Seventh Report took a more positive view about the need to develop joint distributions of income and wealth as a priority (p. 160) and about the desirability of sample surveys of personal wealth holdings.

We recommend that in the General Household Survey steps should be taken (not necessarily in every year) to develop a more comprehensive measure of income, or command over resources, through either (a) a means of modifying such a measure with estimates of total wealth or at least some of the most prevalent forms of wealth, such as housing and savings, or (b) the integration of income and wealth, employing a method of, for example, annuitization. (Questions of improvements in our knowledge about health in relation to inequalities are also taken up in Chapter 7.)

Summary

In examining the state of health of a population it is necessary to remember there are different meanings of 'health' which have different implications for action to improve health. On the one hand 'health' can be conceived as the outcome of freeing man from disease or disorder, as identified throughout history by medicine. On the other hand, it can be conceived as man's vigorous, creative and even joyous involvement in environment and community, of which presence or absence of disease is only a part. While there are many indicators of health and ill-health, including mortality rates, morbidity rates, sickness-absence rates and restricted activity rates, we concentrate most attention in this report, mainly for practical reasons, on mortality rates.

Different meanings are also given to the term 'inequality'. Interest tends to be concentrated on those (substantial) differences in condition or experience among populations which have been brought about by social or industrial organization and which tend to be regarded as undesirable or of doubtful validity by groups in society. Inequality is difficult to measure and trends in inequalities in the distribution of income and wealth, for example, cannot yet be related to indicators of health, except indirectly. Partly for reasons of convenience, therefore, occupational status or class (which is correlated closely with various other measures of inequality) is used as the principal indicator of social inequality in this report.

Chapter 2

The Pattern of Present Health Inequalities

Inequalities in health take a number of distinctive forms in Britain today. This chapter examines the pattern of inequalities according to a number of criteria: the relationships between gender and mortality, race and mortality, regional background and mortality, plus a range of measures of ill-health. But undoubtedly the clearest and most unequivocal – if only because there is more evidence to go on – is the relationship between occupational class and mortality. This will be the main theme of the next chapter.

Occupational class and mortality

Every death in Britain is a registered and certified event in which both the cause and the occupation of the deceased or his or her next of kin are recorded. By taking the actual incidence of death among members of the Registrar General's occupational classes and dividing this by the total in each occupational class it is possible to derive an estimate of class differences in mortality. This shows that on the basis of figures drawn from the early 1970s, when the most recent decennial survey was conducted, men and women in occupational class V had a two-and-a-half times greater chance of dying before reaching retirement age than their professional counterparts in occupational class I (Table 1, p. 57). Even when allowance is made for the fact that there are more older people in unskilled than professional work, the probability of death before retirement is still double.

What lies behind this gross statistic? Where do we begin to look for an explanation? If we break it down by age we find that class differences in mortality are a constant feature of the entire human life-span (see Fig. 1). They are found at birth, during the first year of life, in childhood, adolescence and adult life. At *any* age people in occupational class V have a higher rate of death than their better-off counterparts. This is not to say that the differences are uniform; in general they are more marked at the start of life and, less obviously, in early adulthood.

At birth and during the first month of life the risk of death in families of unskilled workers is double that of professional families. Children of

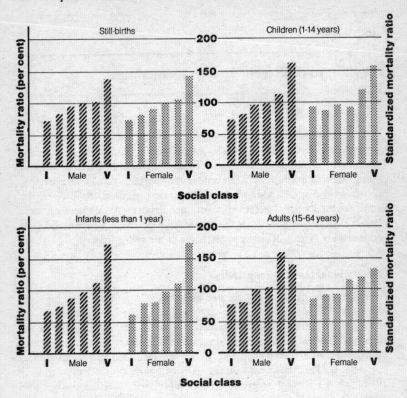

Figure 1. *Mortality by occupational class and age. Relative mortality (%) is the ratio of rates for the occupational class to the rate for all males (or females). (Source:* Occupational Mortality 1970–72, *HMSO, 1978, p. 196)*

skilled manual fathers (occupational class III M) run a 1.5 times greater risk.

For the next eleven months of a child's life this ratio widens still further. For the death of every one male infant of professional parents, we can expect almost two among children of skilled manual workers and three among children of unskilled manual workers. Among females the ratios are even greater.

If we measure this against different causes of death – Fig. 2 – we find that the most marked class gradients are for deaths from accidents and respiratory disease, two causes which we will show later to be closely related to the socio-economic environment (see Chapter 6). Other causes, associated

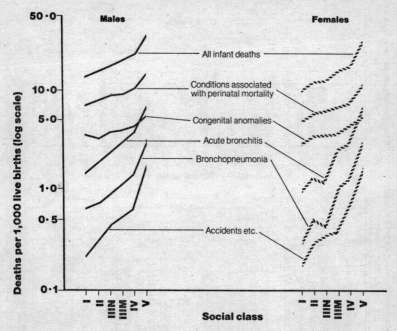

Figure 2. *Infant mortality by sex, occupational class and cause of death.* (*Source: Occupational Mortality 1970–72, H M S O, 1978, p. 158.*)

with birth itself and with congenital disabilities, have significantly less steep class gradients.

Between the ages of 1 and 14 relative class death rates narrow, but are still clearly visible. Among boys the ratio of mortality in occupational class V as compared with I is of the order of 2 to 1, while among girls it varies between 1.5 and 1.9 to 1.

Once again the causes of these differences can be traced largely to environmental factors. Accidents, which are by far the biggest single cause of childhood deaths (30 per cent of the total), continue to show the sharpest class gradient. Boys in class V have a ten times greater chance of dying from fire, falls or drowning than those in class I. The corresponding ratio of deaths caused to youthful pedestrians by motor vehicles is more than 7 to 1. Trailing somewhere behind this, but also with a marked class gradient, are infectious and parasitic diseases, responsible for 5 per cent of all child-hood deaths, and pneumonia, responsible for 8 per cent of the total. Most other causes of death show less clear evidence of class disadvantage (Fig. 3).

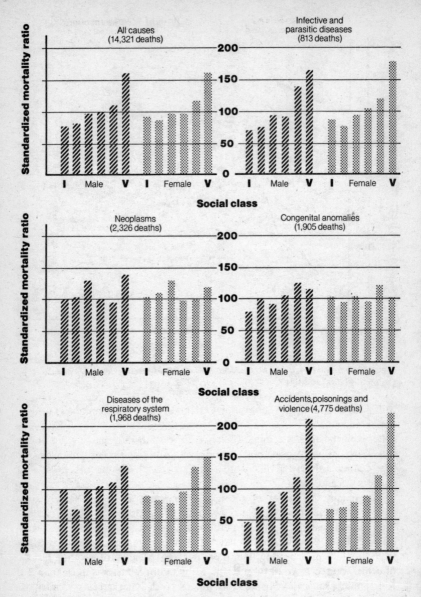

Figure 3. *Class and mortality in childhood* (*males and females 0–14*). (*Source:* Occupational Mortality 1970–72, *H M S O, 1978, p. 160.*)

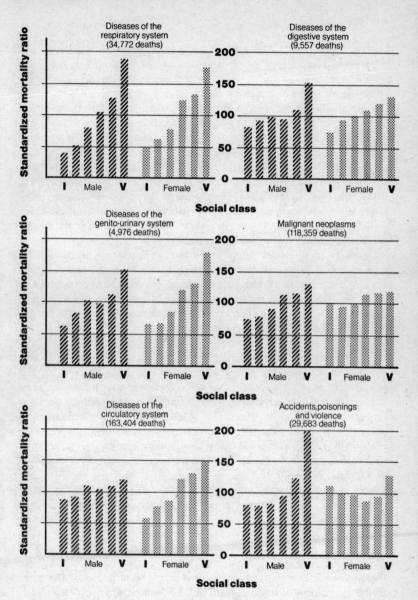

Figure 4. *Occupational class and mortality in adult life (men and married women 15–64), by husband's occupation.* (*Source:* Occupational Mortality 1970–72, *H M S O, 1978.*)

Among adults, taken in this context to be people aged between 15 and 64, class differences appear to narrow further, but the overall statistic conceals a large difference for those in their twenties and thirties and a relatively small one for adults nearer pension age.

As in childhood the rates of death from accidents and infectious disease show steep class gradients, but equally an extraordinary variety of non-infectious diseases like cancer, heart and respiratory disease also show marked class differences (Fig. 4). This will be discussed further in the next chapter when we come to describe *trends* in the pattern of death rates.

Finally, as pension age is reached, class differences in mortality diminish still further, but by this age classification by occupational class becomes less meaningful. Information about occupation and cause of death recorded on death certificates for people over 75 is sometimes imprecise or inaccurate, particularly in the case of widows who, dying in their seventies or later, may still be classified according to the last occupation of husbands who may have died many years earlier. Again, there is some movement late in working life from skilled to unskilled occupations which is not reflected in the occupation reported at death. A minority of men, dying in their sixties, are recorded with the skilled occupation held for most of their working life rather than the unskilled occupation they may have had in the last five or ten years of that life.

Occupational class may therefore be a weak indicator of life-style and life chances over lengthy periods. Bearing this in mind, data about the mortality of men aged 65 to 74 in 1970/72 showed that there were very large differences between some groups of manual and non-manual workers. For example, the mortality ratio for former miners and quarrymen was 149, gas, coke and chemical makers 150, and furnace, forge, foundry and rolling mill workers 162, compared with administrators and managers with a ratio of 88 and professional, technical workers and artists with a ratio of 89 (OPCS, 1978, p. 107).

Now let us look at some other criteria for dividing the population which have a bearing on any attempt to describe the 'structure' of health among the population.

Sex differences in mortality

The gap in life expectancy between men and women is one of the most distinctive features of human health in the advanced societies. As Table 1 indicates, the risk of death for men in each occupational class is almost twice that of women, the cumulative product of health inequalities between the sexes during the whole lifetime. It suggests that gender and class exert

Table 1: *Death rates by sex and social (occupational) class (15–64 years) (rates per 1,000 population, England and Wales, 1971)*

Social (occupational) class	Males	Females*	Ratio M/F
I (Professional)	3.98	2.15	1.85
II (Intermediate)	5.54	2.85	1.94
III N (Skilled non-manual)	5.80	2.76	1.96
III M (Skilled manual)	6.08	3.41	1.78
IV (Partly skilled)	7.96	4.27	1.87
V (Unskilled)	9.88	5.31	1.86
Ratio V/I	2.5	2.5	

* In this table women with husbands have been classified by their husband's occupation, women of other marital statuses are attributed to their *own* occupational class.

Source: *Occupational Mortality 1970–72* (microfiches and 1978, p. 37).

highly significant but different influences on the quality and duration of life in modern society.

It is also a gap in life expectancy which carries important implications for all spheres of social policy, but especially health, since old age is a time when demand for health care is at its greatest and the dominant pattern of premature male mortality adds the exacerbating problem of isolation for many women.

Although attempts have been made to explain the differences between the sexes, comparatively little systematic work exists on the aetiology of the mortality and morbidity differences between men and women and much remains to be disentangled. Women suffer uniquely from some diseases and it would be wrong, for example, to assume too readily that all wives share the same living conditions or even standards as their husbands. Some men have the advantage, for instance, not only of a preferential diet at home but subsidized meals at work. Where both husband and wife are in paid employment, the meals they get in the day, as well as working conditions and the nature of the work, may be radically different. There is a great deal more research to be undertaken to sort out these various influences.

Regional differences in mortality

Mortality rates also vary considerably between the regions which make up the United Kingdom. Using them as an indicator of health, the healthiest part of Britain appears to be the southern belt below a line drawn across

Table 2: *Regional variations in mortality*

Standard region	SMR: standardized for	
	Age	Age and class
Northern, Yorkshire and Humberside	113	113
North-west	106	105
East Midlands	116	116
West Midlands	96	94
East Anglia	105	104
South-east	90	90
South-west	93	93
Wales I (South)	114	117
Wales II (North and West)	110	113
England and Wales	100	100

Source: *Occupational Mortality 1970–72*, p. 180.

the country from the Wash to the Bristol Channel (see Table 2). This has not always been true. In the middle of the nineteenth century, the south-east of England recorded comparatively high rates of death, while other regions like Wales and the far north had a rather healthier profile.

Race, ethnicity and health

Another important dimension of inequality in contemporary Britain is race. Immigrants to this country from the so-called New Commonwealth, whose ethnic identity is clearly visible in the colour of their skin, are known to experience greater difficulty in finding work and adequate housing (Smith, 1976). Given these disabilities it is to be expected that they might also record rather higher than average rates of mortality and morbidity.

This hypothesis is difficult to test from official statistics, since 'race' has rarely been assessed in official censuses and surveys. Moreover it is far from clear what indicator should be utilized in any such assessment – skin colour, place of birth, nationality – and the most significant may depend on the precise issue of interest.

The pattern of social and economic disadvantage experienced by black Britons is connected with occupational class and is reflected in the working of the labour market. But other factors may also be important, and at least amongst adult males the variables of occupational class and race do not compound one another in a linear fashion as far as health is concerned, when place of birth is used as a means of measuring race. The age standardized mortality ratios of immigrant males compares favourably with their British-born equivalents in occupational classes IV and V, but less so higher up the scale in classes I and II (see Table 3). The interpretation of these ratios is made difficult at the higher end of the occupational scale because they are based on small numbers.

In the poorer occupational classes, where the standardized mortality ratio is based on larger numbers of deaths, men born in India, Pakistan or the West Indies seem to live longer than their British-born counterparts. It should be remembered, however, that the percentage of workers in class V among the British-born is less than 7 while the equivalent percentage of those born in, for example, India and Pakistan is 16. In addition, of course, the average British-born male classified as an unskilled manual worker is likely to be older than his foreign-born counterpart and is more likely to have acquired this low occupational status after a process of downward social mobility associated with failing health.

This rather favourable comparison between immigrant and British-born males may also reflect the underlying tendency for migrants to select themselves on the grounds of health and fitness. Men and women prepared to cross oceans and continents in order to seek new occupational opportunities or a new way of life do not represent a random cross-section of humanity. A better comparison for exploring health inequality would ideally involve second- or third-generation immigrants, but these are the very groups that are difficult to trace for statistical purposes. What little evidence that has

Table 3: *Mortality by country of birth and occupational class (S M R) (males 15–64)*

Country of birth	I	II	IIIN	IIIM	IV	V	All
India and Pakistan	122	127	114	105	93	73	98
West Indies	267	163	135	87	71	75	84
Europe (including UK and Eire)	121	109	98	83	81	82	89
UK and Eire (including England and Wales)	118	112	111	118	115	110	114
England and Wales	97	99	99	99	99	100	100
All birth places	100	100	100	100	100	100	100

Source: *Occupational Mortality, 1970–72*, pp. 186–7.

been accumulated, however, does suggest that the children of immigrants do suffer from certain specific health disabilities related to cultural factors such as diet or to their lack of natural immunity to certain infectious diseases (Thomas, 1968; Oppé, 1967; Gans, 1966). Studies based on small samples of immigrant children have pointed to the possibility of higher-than-average morbidity associated with material deprivation, but the evidence is scarce and somewhat inconclusive and needs to be augmented by further research (Hood, et al., 1970).

Housing tenure and mortality

Because of its bearing on our discussion in Chapter 6 of explanations for inequalities in health, it should also be noted that when the population is divided into housing tenure groups – owner-occupiers, private tenants and local-authority tenants – class gradients vary considerably (Table 4). People who live in houses which they own have lower rates of mortality than those who rent their homes from private landlords who in turn have lower rates than those who are tenants of local authorities. Housing tenure is, of course, one possible measure of the accumulation by an individual or family of fixed property or assets; it also says something about familial attitudes and priorities. Here it can be shown that this variable shows a very close relationship with the risk of premature death.

Table 4: *Mortality by tenure and class (S M R) (males 15–64 years)*

Class	Tenure		
	Owner-occupied	*Privately rented*	*Local-authority tenancy*
I	79	93	99
II	74	104	99
IIIN	79	112	121
IIIM	83	99	104
IV	83	100	106
V	98	126	123

Source: Unpublished data, Medical Statistics Division, OPCS, preliminary results of the LS 1970–75.

Illness and class

Morbidity data provide a second way of looking at the pattern of class inequalities in health. Moreover there is a sense in which the extent of ill-health in a social group is a better indicator of its health vis-à-vis another group than is the relative mortality rate. Morbidity data are available from a variety of studies and *ad hoc* surveys and are of two kinds, though both are scant at the national level. The first is based on examination of, or symptom identification in, the social group as a whole or in a properly selected sample. An approach of this kind has sometimes been used in the attempt to assess the prevalence of specific diseases within research studies. Social or occupational class is sometimes noted.

The second kind of data derives from analysis of medical consultation and hospital admission rates. But not only do we have few data of this kind by occupational class, there is the disadvantage that rates reflect not only the incidence of disease but also the process by which an individual defines himself (or herself) as ill, seeks medical attention and has his (or her) definition confirmed or legitimated by medical authority. Since we know that there are class-related differences in the propensity of an individual with a given set of symptoms to go for treatment or attention, as well as in the subsequent medical response (Chapter 4), we recognize that data of this kind cannot be interpreted clearly.

Nevertheless data from both these sources confirms, broadly speaking, the picture which mortality data has already indicated.

An example of the first sort of morbidity data is provided by a survey of the prevalence of chronic bronchitis in Great Britain. Ninety-two GPs, distributed throughout the country, were asked to select similarly sized age/sex-stratified random samples from their practice lists. All were to be aged between 40 and 64. In terms of GP diagnosis, the percentage suffering from chronic bronchitis rose with descending class from 6 per cent in class I to 26 per cent in class V. Bronchitis is diagnosed from symptoms and these can vary from doctor to doctor, but even when a more rigorous 'standard diagnosis' was used, the picture was broadly the same.

GPs have also recorded details of consultations. Results from one study showed that consultation rates for each of a wide range of conditions for males, females and children, classified according to occupational class, are of considerable interest though not easy to interpret (Logan and Cushion, 1960, p. 21). The findings were summarized in the following scheme, where + indicates morbidity above and − below average.

	agricultural occupations	non-manual occupations	manual occupations
psychoneurotic disorders	−	+	−
cardio-vascular disorders	−	+	−
respiratory disorders	−	−	+
gastric disorders	−	−	+
arthritis/rheumatism	−	−	+
injuries	−	−	+

Table 5: *Comparison of distribution of standardized patient consultation ratios (males 15–64, May 1955–April 1956) and standardized mortality ratios (males 20–64, 1949–53) by class: selected conditions*

	SPCR class					SMR class				
	I	II	III	IV	V	I	II	III	IV	V
Respiratory tuberculosis	102	85	105	102	91	58	63	102	95	143
Malignant neoplasms	75	111	94	91	111	94	86	104	95	113
Diabetes mellitus	89	123	100	108	74	134	100	99	85	105
Coronary disease/angina	89	108	102	89	93	147	110	105	79	89
Hypertension	120	127	99	70	89	123	106	103	83	101
Influenza	83	82	103	113	107	58	70	97	102	139
Pneumonia	70	87	90	121	132	53	64	92	105	150
Bronchitis	49	70	99	118	146	34	53	98	101	171
Gastric and duodenal ulcer	48	78	99	88	116	68	76	101	99	134

Source: Logan and Cushion, 1960, p. 16.

Another way of looking at the results is by comparing mortality ratios (by class and disease) with consultation ratios, as in Table 5. If we compare the class gradients on the left-hand side of the table with those on the right-hand side we find that with some exceptions (for instance coronary disease and diabetes) the gradients on the right-hand side are steeper. This suggests more severe sickness or smaller likelihood of treatment with declining class.

This tends to be brought out too in more recent national studies of self-reported illness, like the General Household Survey. Thus, the rates of 'limiting long-standing illness' (as defined in the GHS) rise with falling socio-economic status and are three times as high among unskilled manual males and females as they are among their professional counterparts (see Table 6). Further details are given on pp. 21, 72–3 and 77–9.

Table 6: *Sickness and medical consultation in early adulthood (average rates per 1,000 population 1971–1976)**

Socio-economic group	Limiting long-standing illness		Restricted activity (in two-week period)		Consultations	
	males	females	males	females	males	females†
Professional	79	81	78	89	105	134
Managerial	119	115	74	83	113	137
Intermediate	143	140	83	95	116	155
Skilled manual	141	135	87	86	123	147
Semi-skilled manual	168	203	87	102	131	160
Unskilled manual	236	257	101	103	153	158
Ratio unskilled manual to professional	3.0	3.2	1.3	1.2	1.5	1.2

* England and Wales for 1971–2.
† 1972–6.

Source: *General Household Survey, 1976*, HMSO, 1978.

It will be seen however that the comparable ratios for 'restricted activity' or acute illness are much smaller, and generally resemble the ratios for consultation rates. However, inequalities are smaller in childhood and larger in middle age. Rates of sickness absence from work are also widely unequal. Thus, a special inquiry into the incidence of incapacity for work found marked class gradients for a number of diseases. When the number of employed males beginning a spell of incapacity was expressed per 1,000 in each occupational class, standardized for age, there were, for disease of the respiratory system, 91 in combined classes I and II and 177 in class V. For influenza the figures were 39 and 70, bronchitis 15 and 57 and arthritis and rheumatism 7 and 40 (Ministry of Pensions, 1965).

Summary

There are marked inequalities in health between the social classes in Britain. In this chapter mortality rates are taken as the best available indicator of the health of different social, or more strictly occupational classes and socio-economic groups. Mortality tends to rise inversely with falling occupational rank or status, for both sexes and at all ages. At birth and in the first month of life twice as many babies of unskilled manual parents as of professional parents die, and in the next eleven months of life four times as many girls and five times as many boys, respectively, die. In later years of childhood the ratio of deaths in the poorest class falls to between one and a half and two times that of the wealthiest class, but increases again in early adulthood before falling again in middle and old age.

A class 'gradient' can be observed for most causes of death and is particularly steep for both sexes in the case of diseases of the respiratory system and infective and parasitic diseases.

Other aspects of class than merely occupational category have an impact on health, although few data relating mortality to education and income, for example, are available. This is however illustrated by evidence that in all classes owner-occupiers have lighter mortality than those paying rent.

Available data on (self-reported) morbidity tend to reflect those on mortality, though inequalities between occupational classes are more pronounced, and the gradients more uniform, in the case of chronic sickness than in the case of acute or short-term ill-health.

Chapter 3

Trends in Inequality of Health

For about 100 years mortality rates for both sexes, taken one decade with the next, have declined, even after discounting changes that have taken place in the age structure of the population (Fig. 5). At the same time rates for males have remained markedly higher than for females, and in recent decades the difference has become relatively greater (Fig. 6). In fact since 1946 the excess of male over female deaths has increased at all ages and

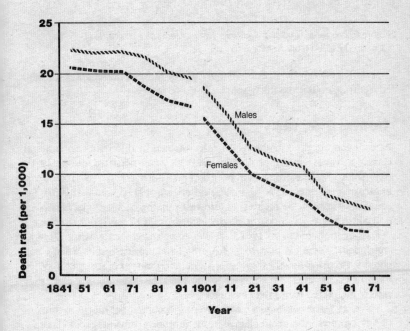

Figure 5. *Death rates, standardized to 1901 population* (*England and Wales*). (*Source: T. McKeown*, The Role of Medicine, *Nuffield Provincial Hospitals Trust, 1976, p. 30.*)

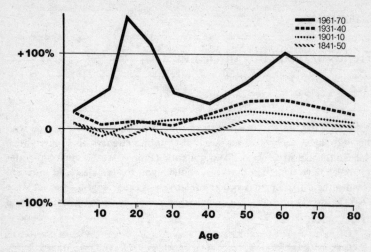

Figure 6. *Percentage excess of male over female death rates by age, 1841–1970.*
(*Source: OPCS,* Trends in Mortality, *1978.*)

especially between the ages of 10 and 30. For most of this chapter we shall
concentrate on the last thirty years.

The trend among men

After a long decline in the death rates of men in different occupational
classes, a sharp change took place in the 1950s which persisted into the 1970s
(see Table 7). The trend can be examined during two recent decades,
approximately the 1950s and 1960s. Between 1949/53 and 1959/63 inequalities between the highest- and lowest-ranking occupational classes in
mortality experience appear to have widened. Some of this is due to changes
in classification, but in his 1961 *Decennial Supplement* the Registrar General
concluded: 'The most disturbing feature of the present results when compared with earlier analyses is the apparent deterioration in social class V ...
Even when the rates are adjusted to the 1950 classification it is clear that
class V men fared worse than average.'

The next *Decennial Supplement*, covering occupational mortality during
1970/72, shows little or no change in the mortality 'advantage' of classes I
and II, but although there was an improvement in the mortality of social
class V relative to other classes, this improvement fell short of restoring the
position the class had reached in 1949/53 (OPCS, *Occupational Mortality,*

Table 7: *Mortality of men by occupational class (1930s–1970s) (standardized mortality ratios)*

Occupational class	Men aged 15–64					
			1959–63 unadjusted		1970–72 unadjusted	
	1930–32	1949–53*		adjusted †		adjusted
I Professional	90	86	76	75	77	75
II Managerial	94	92	81	—	81	—
III Skilled manual and non-manual	97	101	100	—	104	—
IV Partly skilled	102	104	103	—	114	—
V Unskilled	111	118	143	127	137	121

*Corrected figures as published in *Registrar General's Decennial Supplement, England and Wales, 1961: Occupational Mortality Tables*, London, HMSO, 1971, p. 22.

†Occupations in 1959–63 and 1970–72 have been reclassified according to the 1950 classification.

Source: *Registrar General's Decennial Supplement* and *Occupational Mortality Tables* (see above).

Decennial Supplement, 1970–72, England and Wales, 1978, p. 174), and compared with 1959/63 the mortality of class IV relative to other classes had deteriorated.

Behind these relative changes in position (and those looked at in Chapter 2) lie absolute changes in mortality rates for the different classes. If we break the trends down by age group (Table 8) we see that mortality rates for younger men of all occupational classes declined throughout the 1950s and 1960s, but that for men in different ten-year age groups between 35 and 65 in occupational classes III, IV and V, the mortality rate actually increased or stood still, while rates for men in occupational class I and II continued to fall. The inequality between the classes was therefore greater by the beginning of the 1970s, as the bottom half of Table 8 demonstrates, by virtue of changes in the pattern of mortality rates for older men. (The trends among married women revealed by the table are discussed below.)

As before, one way of trying to understand this is to look at the changing causes of death. In 1959/63 more class V men died at every age than in 1949/53 from cancer of the lung, vascular lesions of the central nervous system, arteriosclerotic and degenerative heart disease and motor vehicle

Table 8: *Mortality rates per 100,000 and as percentage of rates for occupational classes I and II (1951–71, England and Wales, men and married women)*

Occupational class	Age	Men: rates per 100,000			Married women: rates per 100,000		
		1949–53	1959–63	1970–72	1949–53	1959–63	1970–72
I and II	25–34	124	81	72	85	51	42
III		148	100	90	114	64	51
IV and V		180	143	141	141	77	68
I and II	35–44	226	175	169	170	123	118
III		276	234	256	201	160	154
IV and V		331	300	305	226	186	193
I and II	45–54	712	544	554	427	323	337
III		812	708	733	480	402	431
IV and V		895	842	894	513	455	510
I and II	55–64	2,097	1,804	1,710	1,098	818	837
III		2,396	2,218	2,213	1,202	1,001	1,059
IV and V		2,339	2,433	2,409	1,226	1,129	1,131
		as per cent I and II			*as per cent I and II*		
I and II	25–34	100	100	100	100	100	100
III		119	123	125	134	125	121
IV and V		145	177	196	166	151	162
I and II	35–44	100	100	100	100	100	100
III		122	134	151	118	130	131
IV and V		146	171	180	133	151	164
I and II	45–54	100	100	100	100	100	100
III		114	130	132	112	124	128
IV and V		126	155	161	120	141	151
I and II	55–64	100	100	100	100	100	100
III		114	123	129	109	122	127
IV and V		112	135	141	112	138	135

Source: OPCS.

and other accidents. Some diseases, like lung cancer and duodenal ulcer, which forty to fifty years ago showed no trend with social class or, like coronary disease, an inverse trend, were by the 1960s producing higher mortality among social class IV and V than I and II. Indeed by 1959/63, forty-nine of the eighty-five observed causes of male death showed higher SMRs for classes IV and V than I and II. (And fifty-four out of eighty-seven applying to women.) For only four causes of death among men, and four among married women, was the class gradient reversed. (See *Registrar General's Decennial Supplement*, 1959/63, op. cit.)

By 1970/72 this position had grown still more marked. For ninety-two causes of death which were picked out for men aged 15 to 64 in the latest OPCS report, the mortality ratios for both classes IV and V were higher than for I and II in as many as sixty-eight, a proportionate increase compared with ten years earlier. For only four causes were mortality ratios for I and II higher than IV and V: accidents to motor vehicle drivers, malignant neoplasm of the skin, malignant neoplasm of the brain and polyarteritis nodosa and allied conditions. (OPCS, 1978, op. cit., Table 4A). The question of course is why should there have been this proportionate increase in the number of causes of death showing a class gradient, a question we shall return to in Chapter 6.

The trend among women

With the exception of the youngest group, the 'spread' of inequality among women has been narrower than for men, as an examination of the lower half of Table 8 illustrates. But between 1949/53 and 1970/72, the 'spread' increased among married women aged 35 to 64, as Table 8 also illustrates. The trend for single and married women aged 15 to 64 in the second of the two decades is given for each occupational class in Table 9. The numbers in class I are small and the figures in the table have been placed in brackets on that account. There are also relatively small numbers of women, especially married women, in class V. With these reservations, it can be seen that the relative mortality of both married and single women in class IV, and of single women at least in class V, deteriorated between 1959/63 and 1970/72.

When causes of death are divided into thirteen broad groups for women aged 15 to 64, there is markedly higher mortality among the partly skilled and unskilled classes (whether defined by their own or a husband's occupation) in the case of infective and parasitic diseases, circulatory diseases, respiratory diseases, diseases of the genito-urinary sytem and, though less markedly, congenital anomalies, diseases of the blood, endocrine and nutritional diseases and diseases of the digestive system.

Table 9: *Mortality of women by occupational class* (*1961–71*) (*England and Wales*) (*standardized mortality ratios*)

		Women aged 15–64			
		Married		Single	
		1959–63	1970–72	1959–63	1970–72
I		(77)	(82)	(83)	(110)
II		83	87	88	79
III non-manual	}103{		92	}90{	92
III manual			115		108
IV		105	119	108	114
V		141	135	121	138

Sources: *Registrar General's Decennial Supplement: 1961*, pp. 91, 503; OPCS, *Decennial Supplement*, 1970–72, p. 211.

In the case of benign neoplasms there is no trend by class, but in mental disorders, diseases of the nervous system, malignant neoplasms and accidents, and poisoning and violence, there was a higher mortality in 1970/72 among classes I and II.

Throughout the 1960s maternal mortality fell by more than a third, but mortality among women in class V was still nearly double that of class I and II.

Infants and childhood mortality

Inequalities in mortality among infants reflect those among adults. Since the 1930s deaths per 1,000 live births have diminished among all classes, but in 1975 inequality was still marked. As the Court Committee (appointed by the government to examine the development of child health services) commented in its report in 1977, between 1950 and 1973 the perinatal mortality rate declined by 45 per cent for those of professional and 49 per cent for those of managerial class, but by only 34 per cent for those of unskilled manual class (Table 10).

Among children (1 year old and above) trends during the 1960s and early 1970s varied with age. There was a small reduction in the class difference between 1 and 4 years of age, especially for girls, little or no change between the ages of 5 to 9 and an increase in the difference between the ages of 10 and 14. For boys aged 1 to 14, mortality ratios for classes IV and V

Table 10: *Trends in infant mortality by occupational class (England and Wales)*

	Ratios of actual to expected deaths of infants			
	1930–32	*1949–53*	*1959–63**	*1970–72†*
I	53	63⎫	73	74⎧ 66
II	73	73⎭		⎩ 77
III	94	97	98	94
IV	108	114⎫	119	128⎧ 111
V	125	138⎭		⎩ 175

	Infant deaths per 1,000 legitimate live births			
I	32	19	—	12
II	46	22	—	14
III	59	28	—	16
IV	63	35	—	20
V	80	42	—	31

*For 1959–63, estimates calculated from C. C. Spicer, and L. Lipworth, *Regional and Social Factors in Infant Mortality*, GRO, Studies on Medical and Population Subjects No. 19, London, HMSO, 1966, by J. Tudor Hart, 'Data on Occupational Mortality 1959–63', *Lancet*, 22 January 1972, p. 192.

† For 1970–72, estimated from OPCS, *Occupational Mortality, Decennial Supplement*, 1970–72, England and Wales, pp. 168 and 216.

in 1970/72 were both higher than for classes 1 and II for twenty-three of thirty-eight observed causes of death, compared with only one cause (asthma) where the ratios were lower. For girls the corresponding figures were twenty-two and nought respectively (OPCS, 1978, op. cit., Table 7E).

The elderly

By 1970/72 the mortality ratios for several groups of manual occupations, including former miners and quarrymen, gas, coke and chemical makers and furnace, forge, foundry and rolling mill workers, had deteriorated relative to the death rate for all men. But we should bear in mind the qualification made in Chapter 2 about the value of occupational class as an indicator of life chances among older people.

Morbidity

It is difficult to trace morbidity data by class for any span of years. The General Household Survey has now been running since 1971, but it is still too early to distinguish reliable trends in health from that source. For example, Table 11, drawn from GHS data, shows that absence from work because of sickness or injury is sharply related to class, but that the precise rates are liable to fluctuation from year to year. The average number of days lost through illness or accident among unskilled manual men was 4.5 times that among professional men in 1971 and 1972 (the data are not given for 1977).

Table 12 is also drawn from GHS data and also shows a class gradient during the 1970s for restricted activity, this time measured in terms of acute sickness, long-stay (chronic) sickness and GP consultations, but the rates are even more uneven from year to year and in some years, for some age groups, there is no perceptible gradient. (However, information published since the report was submitted shows that in 1979 the gradient was marked).

Table 11: *Working males absent from work owing to illness or injury*
(England and Wales 1971)

Socio-economic group	Absent from work due to illness or injury in a two week reference period – rate per 1,000			Average number of work days lost per person per year	
	1971	1972	1977*	1971	1972
Professional	37	21	20	3.9	3.1
Employers and managers	37	39	20	7.2	6.2
Intermediate and junior non-manual	44	48	50	7.6	6.0
Skilled manual	57	56	60	9.3	9.4
Semi-skilled manual	56	68	70	11.5	10.5
Unskilled manual	88	99	60	18.4	17.6
All groups	52	54	40	9.1	8.4

* Rate given only to nearest 10.

Sources: OPCS, *The General Household Survey, Introductory Report*, HMSO, 1973, p. 304; OPCS, *The General Household Survey, 1972*, HMSO, 1975, p. 207; OPCS, *General Household Survey, 1977*, HMSO, 1979, p. 65.

The figures illustrate the problem of drawing conclusions about trends

Table 12: *Rates of long-standing and acute illness and consultations per 1,000 of occupational classes IV and V, as a percentage of class I (1971–6, Britain)*

Sex/class/health indicator	1971	1972	1973	1974	1975	1976
Males class IV						
Long-standing illness	—	158	163	157	160	157
acute sickness	126	133	110	134	102	80
GP consultations	133	132	125	146	129	91
Males class V						
Long-standing illness	—	196	213	218	197	196
acute sickness	155	181	129	150	85	102
GP consultations	143	175	164	147	121	125
Females class IV						
Long-standing illness	—	274	214	182	197	176
acute sickness	105	128	115	115	134	95
GP consultations	—	108	150	110	123	114
Females class V						
Long-standing illness	—	320	276	204	253	246
acute sickness	107	141	113	122	128	94
GP consultations	—	117	150	120	107	102

Source: Reports of the General Household Survey.

in self-reported sickness for some major sex/age groups, if not for the population as a whole, during a short span of years.

Conclusion

When examining indicators of health for different occupational or socio-economic classes for a span of years, any changes that may be taking place in the relative size of particular classes may be as important as any changes in the inequality between classes in assessing trends in the overall health of the population. Some commentators have pointed out that while inequalities in health between the unskilled manual class and other classes may not have diminished, or may even have increased, that class has become smaller and therefore there has still been an 'improvement' in the distribution of health. This change has been regarded as compensation for the lack of any closing of the gap *between* classes.

Two comments should be made. The first is that changes in occupational classification have caused commentators to believe that the reduction of class V since 1931 has been greater than it has. (See Appendix, Tables 1 and 2). In fact, as attempts to adjust census findings show, the fall in the proportion of men in class V has been small since 1961 and in absolute numbers has not fallen at all.

The second is that relatively poor health experience applies to other manual classes and especially class IV and that though this class too has fallen in proportion to the population, it continues to make up, together with class V, more than a quarter of the economically active male population. Mortality indicators for class IV, relative to other classes, have shown some deterioration between the early 1960s and the early 1970s, but perhaps the most important general finding is the lack of improvement, and in some respects deterioration, of the health experience of *both* class V and IV relative to class I, as judged by mortality indicators, during the 1960s and early 1970s.

The more specific conclusions, underlying this finding, are as follows. (These conclusions apply to England and Wales. Scottish experience has been rather similar, though certain differences are noted in the text.)

1. Mortality rates of males are higher at every age than of females and in recent decades the difference between the sexes has become relatively greater.

2. For men of economically active age there was greater inequality of mortality between occupational classes I and V both in 1970–72 and 1959–63 than in 1949–53.

3. For economically active men the mortality rates of occupational class III and combined classes IV and V for age groups over 35 either deteriorated or showed little or no improvement between 1959–63 and 1970–72. Relative to the mortality rates of occupational classes I and II they worsened.

4. For women aged 15–64 the standardized mortality ratios of combined classes IV and V deteriorated. For married and single women in class IV (the most numerous class) they deteriorated at all ages.

5. Although deaths per thousand live births in England and Wales have diminished among all classes, the relative excess in combined classes IV and V over I and II increased between 1959–63 and 1970–72.

6. During a period of less than a decade maternal mortality fell by more than a third. Although that of class I fell less sharply than other classes inequality between the more numerous class II and classes IV and V remained about the same.

7. Among children between 1 and 4 years of age, there has been a small reduction in the class differential (especially for girls), for children aged 5 to 9 little or no change, but for children aged 10 to 14 an increase in the differential. For boys aged 1–14, mortality ratios for classes IV and V in 1970–72 were *both* higher than for classes I and II for twenty-three of thirty-eight causes of death, compared with only one cause (asthma) where the ratios were lower. For girls the corresponding figures were twenty-two and nought respectively. There is evidence that as rates of child death from a specific condition decline to very low levels class gradients do disappear. The gradual elimination of death from rheumatic heart disease over the post-war period provides evidence of this (Morris, 1959).

Chapter 4

Inequality in the Availability and Use of the Health Service

One of the fundamental principles of the NHS is to 'divorce the care of health from questions of personal means or other factors irrelevant to it' (Cartwright and O'Brien, 1976). Yet a number of studies have revealed significant social inequalities in the availability and use of health services. In 1968 Richard Titmuss argued, on the basis of evidence then available, that: 'Higher income groups know how to make better use of the Service: they tend to receive more specialist attention; occupy more of the beds in better equipped and staffed hospitals...' Subsequent studies, many of which we shall refer to, have cast further light on the issue and added to the evidence.

Unequal usage will never be more than a partial explanation of the overall inequalities in standards of health. Several commentators have shown, and we shall go on to show this later, that differences in health between sections of the population may be far more a function of 'variations in the socio-demographic circumstances of the population than the amount and type of medical care provided and/or available' (Martini, Allan, Davison and Backett, 1977). Nevertheless, any inequality in the availability and use of health services in relation to need is in itself socially unjust and requires alleviation. This remains true whatever the relative importance of health care in comparison with other areas of social policy.

Moreover, since equal access has always been a fundamental principle of the NHS, the extent to which it has been achieved is a matter of considerable interest. In sorting out the evidence we have found it useful to look separately at GP consultation rates, hospital care, preventive services and services for the disabled and infirm. This is partly because such a distinction reflects the availability of information and the foci of research, and also because, as we shall show, while some uncertainty remains as to the existence of inequalities in the first two cases, there are no grounds for doubt in the case of preventive services in particular.

GP consultations

There is no simple interpretation of the evidence linking class with rates of consultation with general practitioners. The GHS is the best source of information, but the trend, while clear enough for the sample of males and females in general, does not apply to males aged 0 to 14 or females aged 0 to 14, and is uneven for some other age groups. GHS results have fluctuated from year to year and the consulting rate (and even more the average number of consultations) has not generally shown as marked a class gradient, as have the measures of morbidity discussed in earlier chapters. (See tables on pp. 21 and 63 above.)

For most years covered by the GHS the number of people consulting a doctor, and the average number of consultations, has tended to increase with falling class. However, for some years the figures are uneven and the rate for classes III, IV and V is lower than for classes I and II. This may partially miss the point. It may be that the proper basis for comparing rates of consultation is not one of simple population but of the *need* for care. One study, for example, using the GHS data, divided the number of GP consultations by the number of restricted activity days, each in a two-week reference period, for each occupational group (defined a little differently from the occupational classification referred to earlier). The 'use/need ratios' clearly declined in going from socio-economic class I to class V (Brotherston, 1976). Table 13 shows use/need ratios calculated on the basis of the GHS for 1974/6 which similarly show an overall pattern of decline from socio-economic group 1 to group 6. The table shows that the observation that the poor use GP services more is reversed once 'usage' is corrected for 'need'.

Another study used aggregated 1971 and 1972 GHS data and also found statistically significant trends in consultation rates/morbidity, where the 'morbidity' measure was rate of chronic sickness or rate of sickness absence

Table 13: *'Use/need ratios' by social group (Great Britain, 1974–6)*

Socio-economic group	Males	Females
1	0.23	0.23
2	0.21	0.24
3	0.20	0.22
4	0.18	0.22
5	0.20	0.20
6	0.17	0.19
All	0.19	0.22

from work or school, but a non-significant trend in the case of acute sickness (Forester, 1976). The study showed that in proportion to reported sickness and sickness absence from work, the semi-skilled and unskilled in fact made less use of G P services than did other groups.

A weakness of this method of relating use to need derives from the fact that many of those with restricted activity may not visit a G P but may visit a hospital out-patients' department, whereas others may visit a G P for reasons different from restricted activity. In other words, comparison of these rates may not be purely indicative of differences in receipt of care when sick.

At the same time, comparison of *rates* of consultation, even when related to need as shown by mortality or morbidity data, is not a wholly adequate conceptualization of inequality in care. Several studies have shown that middle-class patients tend to have longer consultations than working-class

Table 14: *Morbidity and G P attendance indicators for socio-economic groups: semi-skilled and unskilled as a percentage of professional*

	Males					
	1971	1972	1973	1974	1975	1976
Long-standing illness						
semi-skilled	—	158	163	157	160	157
unskilled	—	196	213	218	197	196
Limiting long-standing illness						
semi-skilled	272	203	233	179	174	222
unskilled	371	290	333	274	244	292
Acute sickness (restricted activity)						
semi-skilled	126	133	110 —	134 —	102 —	80 —
unskilled	155	181	129 —	150	85 —	102 —
Acute sickness (days per person)						
semi-skilled	—	169	168	169	130	122
unskilled	—	268	206	215	121	196
GP consultations: persons consulting (rate per 1,000)						
semi-skilled	122	132	121	146	122	91
unskilled	128	157	145	141	111	111
GP consultations (rate per 1,000)						
semi-skilled	133	132	125	146	129	91
unskilled	143	175	164	147	121	125

	Females				
Long-standing illness					
semi-skilled	—	274	214	182	197	176
unskilled	—	320	276	204	253	246
Limiting long-standing illness					
semi-skilled	245	303	257	213	259	248
unskilled	298	355	332	246	346	348
Acute sickness (restricted activity)					
semi-skilled	105	128	115—	115	134	95—
unskilled	107	141	113—	122	128	94—
Acute sickness (days per person)					
semi-skilled	—	205	137—	117	136	127
unskilled	—	238	148	122	129	133
GP consultations: persons consulting (rate per 1,000)					
semi-skilled	—	113	147	110	118	116
unskilled	—	112	141	123	111	115
GP consultations (rate per 1,000)					
semi-skilled	—	108	150	110	123	114
unskilled	—	117	150	120	107	102

Source: Reports of the GHS 1971–6.

patients and that more problems are discussed during this period. One study also found that middle-class patients were able to make better use of the consultation time, as measured by the number of items of information communicated and the number of questions asked (Cartwright and O'Brien, 1976). Moreover, even though working-class patients tended to have been with the same practice for longer, the doctors seemed to have more knowledge of the personal and domestic circumstances of their middle-class patients. An earlier study found, for example, that middle-class patients were more likely to be visited by their GP when in hospital than were working-class patients (Cartwright, 1964). For cultural reasons, then, and also because there is a tendency for the 'better' doctors to work in middle-class areas (as we shall see), the suggestion must be that middle-class patients appear to receive a better service when they do present themselves than their working-class contemporaries.

The data are limited and further analyses remain to be carried out, but what is available suggests that the level of consultation among partly skilled and unskilled manual workers does not appear to match their need for health care (see Table 14). With certain exceptions,* the socio-economic or class differences in ill-health are larger than the corresponding class differences in GP attendance (rates for persons consulting and total number of consultations). If we were to combine different measures of chronic and acute ill-health and compare 'need' with 'care received' (on the basis of some principle of weighting), there would be no exceptions for any year.

Hospital services

There is no regular source of class-related information on use of hospital services comparable with that obtained on GP consultation rates, even though questions on hospital attendance are asked in the GHS. In the case of hospital in-patients, the percentage concerned (about 2 per cent) is too small for any class breakdown of GHS data to be statistically meaningful. Attendance at out-patients is higher, and although since 1972 these rates have not been published on a class basis, some information is available. This suggests that there are no systematic class gradients in out-patient attendance for either males or females.

Data given in the 1972 GHS report does however seem to suggest that men in occupational class V aged 15–64 do have particularly high rates of attendance, which drop off after retirement. Referring to this 'relatively much greater use of "out-patients" by unskilled males than by males of other groups', the report indicated that it did not distinguish between attendance at out-patient casualty departments and other ancillary services. But the decline in rate at retirement at least suggests that 'the higher rates amongst unskilled males of working age than amongst males of other groups may reflect a rather particular use of out-patient facilities related to their greater risk of exposure to accident or injury compared with other groups'. Though later data do not show this discontinuity at retirement, the possibility of this special use of hospital out-patients is a matter of interest.

Such little evidence as is available on hospital in-patient care describes not the proportions of various social groups spending time in hospital but the social composition of the groups admitted. For England and Wales admission rates on an occupational basis are available only prior to 1963 (from HIPE), after which date they ceased to be centrally collected (mainly owing to doubts about their quality). The older data, however, suggest that the rate of usage of hospital beds rises with declining class. In Scotland, an analysis of hospital admission rates and duration of stay found clear

---

* The relative consultation rates of semi-skilled and unskilled groups exceed the relative rates of restricted activity in the cases in the table marked with a dash, though in most of those instances they no longer do so when *days* of restricted activity are taken.

upwards trends in both with declining class. Moreover SHIPS (Scottish Hospitals In-Patient Survey) does continue to code social class and more recent figures confirm this class gradient, both in admission rates (given by SDR in Table 15) and length of stay (given by SBDR).

Table 15: *Hospital standardized discharge ratios (SDR)*
and standardized bed-day ratios (SBDR) by occupational class (Scotland, 1971)

	SDR		SBDR	
Class	Males	Females	Males	Females
I	79.5	95.9	63.7	92.5
II	80.9	98.0	73.3	93.6
III	94.0	90.4	93.9	91.0
IV	115.1	107.4	116.4	106.7
V	141.4	161.1	151.7	153.9

Source: Scottish Hospitals In-Patient Survey.

Preventive and promotive services

Although neither administrative returns nor the GHS provide information on the utilization of community health and preventive services by social or occupational class, there is a substantial body of research on which to draw, and it is well established that those in the manual classes make considerably less use of them than do those higher up the occupational scale. Moreover, the ambiguity which surrounds the relation of utilization to 'need' in the case of GP consultations is not encountered here. Assessment of morbidity, or need for care, is not at issue in comparing rates of attendance for ante-natal care (though this may be more essential for those put at risk by social factors), cervical screening, radiography or immunization of children.

In the case of family planning and maternity services substantial evidence shows that those social groups in greatest need make least use of services and (in the case of ante-natal care) are least likely to come early to the notice of the service. A study published in 1970 found clear class gradients in the proportion of mothers having an ante-natal examination, attending a family planning clinic and discussing birth control with their GP (Cartwright, 1970). Unintended pregnancies were also more common among working-class women. A second study, in 1973, appears to confirm these findings (Bone, 1973). It found that women from the non-manual classes make more use of family planning services than those from the manual classes. This is true both for married and unmarried women. Scottish data also show that late ante-natal booking is more common in poorer social groups, although the situation seems to be improving in all classes (Table 16). (They further suggest that late attendance for ante-natal care is an effective predictor of subsequent infant morbidity and mortality within families (Brotherston, 1976).)

Table 16: *Late ante-natal booking. Percentage of married women in each occupational class making an ante-natal booking after more than twenty weeks of gestation (Scotland 1971–3).*

Occupational class	1971	1972	1973
I	28.4	27.2	27.0
II	35.3	32.3	29.8
III	36.3	33.4	30.6
IV	39.3	37.8	35.3
V	47.1	44.2	40.5

Source: Brotherston, 1976. Data from Scottish Information Services Division.

Similar class differences have been found in attendance at post-natal examinations (Douglas and Rowntree, 1949), and immunization, ante-natal and post-natal supervision and uptake of vitamin foods (Gordon, 1951). Among slightly older children the National Child Development Study (1958 birth cohort) found substantial differences in immunization rates in children aged 7, as well as in attendance at the dentist (Table 17).

These patterns are further confirmed in studies of screening for cervical cancer, even though working-class women are much more likely to die from it. A study in Greater Manchester, for instance, showed that while women from classes IV and V accounted for over one third of all women living in the study area, they made up only about one sixth of women who had a smear test done.

Further studies show that working-class people make less use of dental services (Gray et al., 1970; Bulman et al., 1968) and of chiropody (Clarke, 1969) and receive inferior dental care (Sheiham and Hobdell, 1969). Many of these studies are admittedly old, and their findings cannot necessarily be accepted as still valid. Nevertheless, taken together, and in the absence of later evidence to the contrary, a clear relationship between social class and use of preventive services seems to have been demonstrated.

Table 17: *Use of health services by children under 7 by occupational class of father (Great Britain, 1965)*

	I	II	IIIN	IIIM	IV	V
Per cent who had never visited a dentist	16	20	19	24	27	31
Per cent not immunized against						
smallpox	6	14	16	25	29	33
polio	1	3	3	4	6	10
diphtheria	1	3	3	6	8	11

Source: Second Report of the NCDS.

Table 18: *Percentage of old persons of different occupational class who receive or feel the need for chiropody treatment (Great Britain, 1962)*

Source of chiropody treatment	Occupational Class					
	I	II	IIIN	IIIM	IV	V
	%	%	%	%	%	%
Public or voluntary service	2	6	6	9	8	8
Privately paid	20	18	14	8	9	8
Non-professional or none, need felt	6	8	13	11	13	10
Non-professional or none, no need felt	72	68	67	72	71	74
Total	100	100	100	100	100	100
Number	82	557	396	1,193	1,040	457

Note: A further 42 persons were classed in armed services occupations, 10 had no occupation and 290 were unclassifiable.

Source: Townsend and Wedderburn, 1965.

Care of the infirm and disabled

There is little information on class inequalities in the care received by the infirm and disabled, though we now enter that awkward and neglected area where health care shades into the variety of other forms of social service provision. That is, to make comparisons of the care or services received by those who are disabled or infirm (including the aged infirm and the long-term chronic sick) would necessarily be to consider not only health care in the strict sense, but social work support, delivery of meals, home help, sheltered housing, mobility aids, sheltered work and rehabilitation etc., all or many of which may be crucial to the well-being of an infirm or disabled person.

But the slight, and unfortunately somewhat old, empirical evidence available does indicate that class inequalities are to be found here. A study of the elderly in residential homes and in geriatric and psychiatric hospitals carried out some years ago found not only that the manual and non-manual elderly were likely to be in different kinds of institution (the latter less commonly in hospital), but a gap in the standard of living and care available in institutions catering principally for one or the other group (Townsend, 1962). A second national study of people aged 65 and over found disparities

Table 19: *Percentage of old persons of different occupational class who were receiving public or private domestic help, or who said help was needed (Great Britain, 1962)*

Source of domestic help	Occupational class					
	I	II	IIIN	IIIM	IV	V
	%	%	%	%	%	%
Local authority	1	2	4	6	4	4
Privately paid	42	27	12	5	3	2
Other (e.g. family) or none, but need felt	10	7	6	6	6	4
Other (e.g. family) or none, no need felt	47	64	78	83	87	90
Total	100	100	100	100	100	100
Number	81	555	396	1,188	1,033	447

Source: Townsend and Wedderburn, 1965.

in receipt of a number of services. Both publicly provided chiropody services and domestic help, for instance, fail fully to compensate for unequal ability to purchase such services (Townsend and Wedderburn, 1965). (See Tables 18 and 19.)

Of equal concern is the difference in attitude between old people of different social classes. Table 19 shows that 90 per cent of those in class V neither receive domestic help (from outside their family) nor feel the need of it. Among the elderly who are incapacitated 'nearly half those in Social Classes I and II ... already had privately paid or local authority domestic help, and nearly half the others said they needed help. But only a sixth of those in Social Class V who were severely incapacitated had such help already and only a fifth of the remainder felt the need for it' (Townsend and Wedderburn, 1965, p. 46). While we cannot tell if these differences still exist, the study shows all too clearly the way in which norms and values associated with class may influence subjective perceptions of need.

In considering the needs of the disabled, aged infirm and chronic sick, not only is it difficult clearly to distinguish needs for strictly medical services from needs for other supportive services, but it is similarly difficult to distinguish needs related to the condition 'itself' (i.e. medically defined) from those relating to its social and economic consequences. In this context it may be helpful to look at the circumstances of the long-term sick, that is those receiving sickness, invalidity and industrial injury benefits for periods of between a month and a year (Martin and Morgan, 1975). This shows not only that the sample of benefit recipients as a whole contained a much higher proportion of semi-skilled and unskilled manual workers, which is to have been expected, but that the longer the spell of sickness, the higher the proportion of unskilled workers. Moreover, the longer the period of incapacity the less likely the sick person is to be able to return to the same type of work with the same employer as before, though skilled manual workers are more likely to have their jobs kept open for them than are semi-skilled or unskilled workers. Unsurprisingly also, receipt of sick pay from the employer is also related to duration of invalidity and to level of job (defined by occupational group).

Clearly therefore in considering the needs of the disabled, long-term sick and aged infirm, financial problems and (in some cases) problems of subsequent re-employment are both pertinent and class-related. The implication of this for policy (which we take up in Chapter 9) is that the equalization of provision of health and social services is not justifiably separable from the equalization of the social and economic consequences of long-term invalidity or sickness.

The interaction of geographic and social disparities

It has been known for a long time that there are differences in the health services available in well-to-do and poor areas. In 1957 a study of the social aspects of prescribing found that the average total cost of drugs per prescription was higher in wealthier areas (Martin, 1957). More recently an analysis of health expenditure at the regional level also found a positive correlation between the percentage of the population in professional and managerial socio-economic groups and both community health expenditure and hospital revenue expenditure, and a negative correlation between expenditure and proportion of population in unskilled and semi-skilled occupations (Noyce, Snaith and Trickey, 1974). The authors concluded: 'There are no regions of above-average spending which are not also high socio-economic status regions. Indeed, if one knew no other facts it would be possible to explain two thirds of the variation in community health expenditure by a knowledge of what proportion of the population in each region were managers, employers, or professional workers.'

In 1971 Tudor Hart (a general practitioner working in a poor area of Wales) contrasted the availability of medical care in poor industrial areas of high need and affluent salubrious areas of lower need in memorable terms. He wrote:

In areas with most sickness and death, general practitioners have more work, larger lists, less hospital support and inherit more clinically ineffective traditions of consultation than in the healthiest areas; and hospital doctors shoulder heavier caseloads with less staff and equipment, more obsolete buildings and suffer recurrent crises in the availability of beds and replacement staff. These trends can be summed up as the inverse care law: that the availability of good medical care tends to vary inversely with the need of the population served. (Tudor Hart, 1971)

An analysis of data in 1976 on need for and provision of child health services for each of the fifteen pre-1974 hospital board regions of England and Wales showed how, in particular, regional provision of GPs and health visitors is negatively correlated with a number of indicators of need (including still-birth rate, level of infant mortality and birth rate to teenage mothers) (West and Lowe, 1976). There are indeed very few positive correlations; midwives alone seemed to be relatively well distributed throughout the regions. The authors go on to suggest: 'When data becomes available for area health authorities even greater differences between need and provision will probably be uncovered between areas than between regions' (cf. Morris, 1975, pp. 53, 77). In the meantime it has at least been established that *variations* in expenditure (Rickard, 1976) and in the provision of services

(Buxton and Klein, 1975; Jones and Masterman, 1976) are greater at the sub-regional than at the regional level. This, of course, is the level at which it matters to people. It is extremely difficult to know for sure what this means for small typically working-class areas in comparison with typically middle-class areas. One recent study does give some indications though. It looked at three areas of council housing, one in Newham (east London) and two in the Midlands, one solidly middle class, the other a council estate with a history of social problems. Unlike Newham, which has long suffered from severe deprivation of the environment, both Midlands areas were situated in 'a socially mixed county, with a teaching hospital, and an attractive environment: a highly desirable county in which to work, with no reputation for recruitment problems in general practice.' Questions covered morbidity (GHS questions were used) and experiences in seeking help from the GP. Although much was found to be common to the two working-class areas, differentiating their inhabitants from the middle-class residents of the third area, this was not the whole picture. Indeed, the principal conclusion of the study is as follows:

The provision of health care and the subjective experience of seeking that care are all partly determined by the socio-economic structure of society on an area basis, so that *a working-class person is at a greater disadvantage if he lives in a predominantly working-class area than if he lives in a socially mixed area.* The data ... are consistent with a theory of structural determination of need and demand for health care from an area, operating both through environmental and social conditions on the level of health, and through the social pressures and life experiences that further affect demand, particularly in the case of childhood illness. The level and quality of available medical manpower, relative to need and demand, is likely also to be strongly affected by the environment and social class composition of an area through the operation of the market for recruitment. (Skrimshire, 1978)

It is likely that similar conclusions would follow from a consideration of race or ethnicity. However, information on use of services by ethnic groups is sparse. One study has referred to hesitation in seeking ante-natal care among immigrants and their difficulties in securing adequate dietary information (Coombe, 1976), and there is evidence of some lack of appreciation among health services staff of the special needs of some immigrant groups, as well as a clear lack of adequate facilities in some of the areas in which they have been obliged to concentrate.

Conclusion

Generalization about inequality of utilization is made difficult partly because of sampling errors in the case of national surveys and of partial information in the case of local studies, and because of the (as yet unresolved) problem of relating utilization to need.

Inequalities appear to be greatest (and most worrying) in the case of the preventive services. Severe under-utilization by the working classes is a complex result of under-provision, of costs (financial, psychological) of attendance, and perhaps of a life-style which profoundly inhibits any attempt at rational action in the interests of *future* well-being. Such factors are not, in this case, outweighed by the costs of present disruption of normal social functioning. We have also seen, however, how services provided on an 'outreach' basis can serve to reduce at least some of the costs of attendance, with beneficial results.

The situation is not clear-cut in the case of GP attendance, partly because attendance rates cannot be compared with any precise measure of need. Excepting, for some years, children, more of those in lower than in higher socio-economic groups consult a doctor, and their total consultations are, relatively, greater. But on most of the health indicators their need for care is greater still. It is hard not to conclude that poorer groups make relatively low use of GP services, irrespective of the separate question of the *adequacy* of the services to which they typically have access.

Middle-class parents are, however, more likely than working-class parents to seek medical attention for their children. Since the (direct) costs of attendance may be presumed similar, this may imply that working-class *adults* are likely to be typically *more* sick than are middle-class ones before help is sought. Moreover, we have seen also that middle-class patients typically receive better care from their GP – a consequence, once more, of both interpersonal and ecological factors.

Hospital out-patient departments are used more by the working class than by the middle class. In the case of Accident and Emergency departments there is evidence of some use in place of the GP, access (as to the GP) being on the basis of self- (or 'lay') referral. It has been suggested that this preferred use of out-patients in treatment of 'traumatic' conditions (suffered at work or in the home) is principally a result of their greater availability: they are open twenty-four hours a day, no appointment is needed and availability of diagnostic aids is certain.

In the case of in-patient departments too, evidence suggests greater use by the working class. It may be noted that, since admission is generally on the basis of GP referral, a higher proportion of working-class patients than of middle-class patients consulting a GP must be subsequently admitted to hospital. This in turn must imply that more working-class patients have illnesses requiring hospital admission, or that the working-class patient seeing his GP is *typically* sicker and/or that he or she is seen as less likely to receive adequate care at home. And indeed, evidence from a survey of the elderly suggests that this is so: public provision of domiciliary services seems not fully to compensate for differential ability to purchase such services.

It is hard to resist the conclusion that this pattern of unequal use is explicable not in terms of non-rational response to sickness by working-class people, but of a rational weighting of the perceived costs and benefits to them of attendance and compliance with the prescribed regime. These costs and benefits differ between the social classes both on account of differences in way of life, constraints and resources, and of the fact that costs to the working class are actually increased by the lower levels and perhaps poorer quality of provision to which many have access.

Class differentials in the use of the various services which we have considered derive from the interaction of social and ecological factors. Differences in sheer availability and, at least to some extent, in the quality of care available in different *localities* provide one channel by which social inequality permeates the NHS. Reduced provision implied greater journeys, longer waiting lists, longer waiting times, difficulties in obtaining an appointment, shortage of space and so on. A second channel is provided by the structuring of health care *institutions* in accordance with the values, assumptions and preferences of the sophisticated middle-class 'consumer'. Inadequate attention may be paid to the different problems and needs of those who are less able to express themselves in acceptable terms and who suffer from lack of command over resources both of time and of money. In all cases, for an individual to seek medical care, his (or her) perception of his (or her) need for care will have to outweigh the perceived costs (financial and other) both of seeking care and of the regime which may be prescribed. These costs are class-related.

It is the interaction of these two sets of factors which produces the inequalities documented in this chapter.

Chapter 5

International Comparisons

The success or otherwise of comparable developed countries in altering patterns of health inequality is an inevitable yardstick against which to measure the British performance and is also a possible pointer to what should or should not be done here. Accordingly we shall now attempt to set the British experience in an international context and in a limited way to explore what has been happening elsewhere. We start by looking at overall national levels and trends and go on to look at the different experiences of inequalities in health. Inevitably there are cultural and social (structural) variables which make any such comparisons complex and subject to a variety of interpretations. Nevertheless the success of some countries in raising health standards makes it an essential input into our analysis of the British experience. Once again mortality data are the most available indicator of relative levels of health, and in particular infant mortality, because infancy remains one of the most vulnerable periods of human life and infant mortality has long-term consequences, has been accepted as an important index of a country's achievements in the health field.

Levels of health and changes over time

International comparisons over the last two decades highlight a number of points about the relative success or otherwise of British health policy (see Tables 20 and 21).

1. In 1975 England, Wales and Scotland (in particular) experienced significantly higher perinatal mortality rates than those of the four Nordic countries and the Netherlands. France and Germany had broadly similar rates to the British.*

2. The overall decreases in perinatal mortality rates between 1960 and 1975

---

*More recent data show that by 1978 Scotland had caught up with England but that the conclusion otherwise holds. Rates of perinatal mortality in 1978: England 15.4; Wales 16.8; Scotland 15.4; Sweden (1977) 10.1; Norway (1977) 13.2; Denmark (1977) 10.6; Finland (1977) 11.0; Netherlands (1977 provisional) 12.9; France (provisional) 14.7; W. Germany (1977) 14.9.

Table 20: *Perinatal and infant mortality in Europe*

	Perinatal mortality per 1,000 live births				Infant mortality per 1,000 live births			
	1960	1975	% Decrease 1960–75	Annual % decrease 1971–5	1960	1975	% Decrease 1960–75	Annual % decrease 1972–5
England & Wales	33.5	17.9*	46.5‡	4.1	21.8	14.2*	34.3‡	4.5
Scotland	38.1	18.5*	51.3‡	5.1	26.4	14.8*	44.0‡	5.4
Sweden	26.2	11.1	57.7	7.3	16.6	8.3	50.0	7.7
Norway	24.0	14.2	40.8	5.1	18.9	11.1	41.3	2.0
Denmark	26.5	12.7*	52.1‡	5.5	21.5	10.3*	52.0‡	3.9
Finland	25.3	13.9†	45.0§	5.9	21.0	11.0†	47.6§	1.4
Netherlands	25.6	14.0	45.3	4.3	16.5	10.6	35.7	3.1
France	31.8	19.5†	38.7§	4.8	27.4	11.1	59.8	10.2
W. Germany	36.3	19.4	46.5	4.8	33.8	19.7	41.6	4.5
(E. Germany)	—	(17.6)	—	—	—	(15.9)	—	(3.4)
USA	29.4	20.7	29.2	—	26.0	16.1	38.1	4.3

* 1976 † 1974 ‡ 1960–76 § 1960–74

Sources: 1960–72 data: *Health Care – the Growing Dilemma*; 1975 data: WHO and *World Health Statistics*, 1978, Vol. 1; 1975, France: *Eurohealth Handbook*, 1978.

Table 21: *Adult mortality in Europe: deaths per million*

	Men				Women			
	35–44		45–54		35–44		45–54	
	1964	1975	1964	1975	1964	1975	1964	1975
England and Wales	2,471	2,095*	7,330	6,985*	1,778	1,468*	4,382	4,298*
Scotland	3,245	2,817*	9,322	8,876*	2,029	1,896*	5,473	5,412
Sweden	2,205	2,343*	5,223	5,736*	1,444	1,372*	3,546	3,056*
Norway	2,327	2,012*	5,664	6,009*	1,299	947*	2,938	2,955*
Denmark	2,128	2,420*	6,126	6,865*	1,695	1,579*	4,000	4,529*
Finland	4,427	4,171†	?	10,748†	1,746	1,430†	4,413	3,537†
Netherlands	2,043	1,859*	5,811	5,897*	1,336	1,159*	3,421	3,159*
France	3,400	3,388†	8,200	8,288†	1,830	1,552†	4,145	3,681†
W. Germany	2,919	3,016	7,724	7,504	1,942	1,601	4,461	4,164
USA	3,836	3,469	9,643	8,563	2,315	1,908	5,227	4,563

* 1976 † 1974

Sources: 1966–9 data: McKinsey, *Health Care*; 1975 data: *World Health Statistics, 1978*, Vol. 1.

show that as a percenfage of the 1960 rate, England and Wales, and Scotland in particular, performed more than averagely well. However, if we then look at the annual percentage decrease over the more recent period (1971–5) it appears that the result for England and Wales at least was no longer satisfactory, and improvements were not up to those being achieved in any of the other countries.*

3. Infant mortality rates (deaths in the first year of life) reflect socio-environmental factors to a greater degree than perinatal rates. In 1975 the Nordic countries and the Netherlands once again showed the lowest rates, but France had also joined them. There is then a significant jump to England, Wales, Scotland, Germany (East and West, the former being substantially lower than the latter) and the USA.

4. The decreases in infant mortality recorded between 1960 and 1975, as a percentage of the 1960 rates, show England and Wales to have done substantially less well than Scotland and, indeed, than any other country. By far the highest rate of improvement was obtained in France. In contrast to the perinatal rates, however, the relative performance of England and Wales, and Scotland in particular, was more creditable in the more recent period. Between 1972 and 1975 only France and Sweden recorded higher average annual rates of decrease.

5. The picture for adult mortality is somewhat less clear. Certainly so far as younger men are concerned, the 1975 rate for England and Wales compares favourably with several other countries and even with three of the four Nordic ones. Moreover the general improvement recorded over the period 1964 to 1975 (or 1976) was not paralleled in some of the countries with the lowest rates (Sweden, for example, showing rising mortality among men). In the case particularly of women aged 45–54, however, the data offer little comfort.

How are we to explain the differences? One way is through comparison of the relative importance of causes of death. If Sweden is compared with England and Wales, taking rates of infant death for a number of major causes, it becomes apparent that perinatal factors and respiratory conditions are major contributors to the poorer British rate.

If the difference between the two national rates is 5.9 per 1,000 live births, 2.8 of these are accounted for by various perinatal factors and 1.4 by respiratory conditions and pneumonia (Table 22). In other words it is not

* This conclusion does not hold for the most recent period. Rates of improvement since 1975 have been similar to those of, for example, Finland, France and W. Germany.

difficult to see how both factors impacting before and during birth *and* those which relate principally to the environment and care of the infant have their effect. The difference in death due to congenital abnormality is relatively slight and the fact that in Sweden, with its excellent record in perinatal and infant death, the congenital abnormality death rate remains comparable with the situation in England and Wales has led some commentators to the view that there may here be an 'irreducible minimum' beyond which progress is, given present knowledge, unlikely on this particular front (see for example Pharaoh and Morris, 1979).

Table 22: *Mortality rates under 1 year per 1,000 live births, for selected causes* (*1976*)

	Sweden	England and Wales	difference
Infections	0.26	0.43	0.17
Acute respiratory conditions	0.04	0.57	0.53
Pneumonia	0.13	1.02	0.89
Accidents	0.08	0.35	0.27
Various anoxic and hypoxic conditions of pregnancy	1.43	2.96	1.53
Other causes of perinatal mortality	1.07	2.30	1.23
Congenital abnormality	3.03	3.45	0.42

Another approach to an explanation might be through a comparison of levels of provision of health care in different countries (Table 23). Differences in numbers of doctors per head of population are not, however, extreme, and West Germany, which throughout the 1960s and early 1970s was the most generously endowed, shows up relatively poorly in the mortality tables. The supply of nurses accords a little better with mortality. But the importance of medical care provision, however expressed, has to be considered in relation to socio-environmental variables which are the principal determinants of relative levels of, and changes in, the health of nations.

For instance a comparison of health services in England, Sweden and the USA found that although Sweden put greater emphasis on child health and the USA on the health of old people (both spent similar proportions of GNP on health care) and that there were differences in access between income groups, the main conclusion was that: 'The dominant reason why

Table 23: *Availability of health care: physicians, nurses and hospital beds in Europe per 10,000 population*

	Physicians			Nurses		General (non-psychiatric) hospital beds	
	1960	1971	1975	1960	1975*	1960	1971
England and Wales	10.5	12.7⎫	11.0	20.8†	37.5	46.0	40.7
Scotland	11.8	15.6⎭		22.0	48.2	47.8	49.4
Sweden	9.5	13.9	16.2§	28.6	71.1	—	69.4
Norway	11.8	14.6	18.3¶	28.1	73.6	55.8	46.1
Denmark	12.3	—	17.9‡	37.7	80.4	59.7†	60.1
Finland	6.4	11.1	13.3§	33.8	81.9	41.9	46.8
Netherlands	11.2	13.2	15.9¶	—	32.2	45.0†	53.6
France	10.0	13.9	14.6	18.6	50.2	55.5†	60.5
W. Germany	14.9	17.8	19.2	22.0	35.9	65.3	66.8
USA	13.4	15.4	—	27.9	63.7	41.4	46.7

* breaks in series: data not comparable around break † 1959 ‡ 1968 § 1974 ¶ 1976

Sources: McKinsey, *Health – The Growing Dilemma*, New York, 1974; 1975 physicians' data: *Eurohealth Handbook*; 1975 nurses' data: WHO *World Health Statistics*, 1978, Vol. III.

the Swedish mortality rates are lower than in any state in the United States is a high minimum standard of living for everyone and a cultural homogeneity ... Health services are, of course, also a factor in the low mortality rates, but the elimination of poverty in the United States in the sense true for Sweden would be more likely to bring mortality rates closer to Sweden than a policy limited to health services only' (Anderson, 1972, p. 158).

One factor which can probably be eliminated as an explanation of the relatively poor British showing is the degree of regional disparity in medical services. Indeed, in so far as broadly aggregated data give an accurate picture, the regional disparity of physicians is more equitable in England (Table 24).

Inequalities in health: the international experience

While in the UK mortality and morbidity statistics are routinely presented by social class, the same is not true of other countries. It may be that social class is a less politically salient dimension of social stratification than in

Table 24: Regional variations in number of physicians per thousand population: highest and lowest areas

	England		France		Germany		Netherlands	
Average	1.06		1.47		1.74		1.36	
Highest (H)	1.31	(N.W. Thames)	2.18	(Paris)	2.97	(W. Berlin)	2.10	(Utrecht)
Lowest (L)	0.91	(Trent)	0.98	(Basse Normandie)	1.41	(Nieder-Sachsen)	0.92	(Friesland)
Ratio H/L	1.4		2.2		2.1		2.3	

Sources: England, France, Germany: A. Maynard in *Social and Economic Administration*, 12, 1, 1978; Netherlands: Compendium Gezondheitsstatistiek Nederland, Centraal Bureau voor de Statistiek, 1974.

the UK and other dimensions are more important, but whatever the reason, health inequality data are more commonly presented on a geographic or, as in the USA, ethnic basis. Certainly in those Nordic countries made up of industrialized densely populated southern regions and cold rural northern regions with sparse and declining populations this is not surprising. One result, though, is that international data expressing the extent of health inequalities are not readily presented on a comparable basis. Moreover, where social or occupational groupings are used these are not strictly comparable with the groupings used in Britain by the Registrar General. Additionally, the overall social class compositions of countries are far from identical. Nevertheless, though the data we have collected relate variously to regional, industrial, occupational or income groups, they do permit some attempt at answering the question: are the health inequalities in England and Wales which we have illustrated encountered also in Europe and the USA? The best way of dealing with our somewhat disparate data is to make country-by-country comparisons with England and Wales.

Denmark

Denmark has lower perinatal and infant mortality rates than England and Wales and has succeeded in reducing the latter but not the former by more than we have. Their rate is also more evenly divided among the social groups. While in England and Wales neonatal mortality rates in class V are twice those in class I, with regular class increments in between, in Denmark the difference is significantly less: 5.7 neonatal deaths per 1,000 live births in 1974 in the top social group against 9 per 1,000 in the bottom (Table 25). The neonatal mortality rate for unskilled workers in Denmark has also fallen by the same percentage as for the country as a whole, which it has not in Britain.

Table 25: *Denmark: neonatal mortality rate by occupation per 1,000 live births*

	1970	1972	1974
Self-employed	10.9	8.1	5.7
Salaried employee	9.9	9.8	7.5
Skilled worker	10.1	8.9	8.1
Unskilled worker	13.5	11.3	9.0
Other/unknown	11.1	10.2	8.8
All	11.0	9.7	8.0

Source: *Medicinisk Fødselssatistisk*, Copenhagen, 1974.

Table 26: *Finland: age-adjusted mortality indices (1970) by social group per 10,000 adults*

		Male	Female
I	Higher administrative or clerical employees, comparable employers, and people with academic degrees	78	95
II	Lower administrative or clerical employees, and comparable employers	95	100
III	Skilled and specialized workers	92	102
IV	Unskilled workers	148	103
V	Farmers	87	96

Source: S. Naytia, 'Social Group and Mortality in Finland', *British Journal of Preventive and Social Medicine*, 31, 4, 1977, p. 23.

Table 27: *France: rates of infant, neonatal and post-neonatal death by socio-professional group of father (per 1,000 legitimate live births)*

	1956–60			1970–72		
	Infant	Neo-natal	Post-neonatal	Infant	Neo-natal	Post-neonatal
Liberal professions; higher and middle cadres	17.0	12.4	4.6	11.6	8.7	2.9
Employees	24.9	19.7	8.2	14.7	10.8	3.9
Industrial and commercial proprietors	25.4	17.4	8.0	15.0	11.2	3.8
Skilled workers	28.1	17.7	10.4	26.2	11.4	4.8
Farmers	31.2	20.8	10.4	15.2	11.4	3.8
Specialized workers	32.9	19.6	13.3	19.0	13.2	5.8
Agricultural workers	35.3	21.0	14.3	19.8	14.0	5.8
Labourers	44.8	23.1	21.7	25.7	16.5	9.2
All	29.6	18.4	11.2	15.9	11.4	4.6

Note: Certain categories of workers, which fall within the range shown, are not given.

Source: Dinh Quang Chï and S. Hemery, 'Disparités régionales de la mortalité infantile', *Économie et statistique*, 1977, 85, pp. 3–12.

Finland

Finland is a country which, though enjoying low rates of perinatal and infant mortality, suffers from very high rates of adult mortality, far above those of England and Wales. The existence of regional disparities in adult Finnish mortality is well known, but there are also differences between social groups (Table 26).

France

The classification system in France suggests at first glance greater inequalities than in Britain, but in fact it seems the relativities are broadly comparable. There are pronounced differences in infant mortality rates both between social groups and regions. During the period 1956/60 and 1970/72,

Table 28: *France 1968: mortality rates among economically active men aged 45–64 (unstandardized) (per 100,000)*

I	Higher cadres (administrators etc.)	699
II	Industrialists, liberal professions, large commercial proprietors	919
III	Middle cadres (including teachers, medical/social service personnel, army, police)	928
IV	Artisans and small shopkeepers	1,225
V	Farmers	1,117
VI	Employees (including service workers, clergy)	1,392
VII	Qualified workers	1,589
VIII	Agricultural workers	1,520
IX	Other workers (including miners)	1,169
	All	1,189

Note: The French data shown in Table 28 refer to men aged 45–64 (unstandardized for age), excluding those classified in the census as 'inactive' (16 per cent of the total, and with a very much higher mortality rate) and excluding three regions of France in which a very high proportion of deaths are attributed to unspecified or inadequately specified causes. If those classified as 'inactive' are included, the overall rate rises from 1,189 to 1,443. Thus, though the classifications within I, II and III on the one hand and VII, VIII and IX on the other do not correspond to those in Great Britain, the picture of distinctly higher mortality rates in the latter group is comparable with the British.

Source: Derrienic et al., 1977.

the ratio between infant mortality in the most favoured group (liberal professions) and the least favoured (labourers) fell slightly from 2.6 to 2.2 (Table 27). There was no change in the ratio of neonatal rates (first month), which remained at about 1.9. In the case of post-neonatal death rates, however, the least favoured social group has improved its relative standing very strikingly, the ratio falling from 4.7 to 3.2. This latter change is in marked contrast to Britain and seems to imply a greater levelling of socio-environmental factors closely implicated in post-neonatal death than has taken place here.

Among adults the difference between the most and least favoured social groups in terms of mortality is slightly more than a factor of two, a figure roughly comparable with the UK (Table 28).

From a regional point of view a factor of two separated the area of France enjoying the lowest infant mortality rates in 1970/72 from the highest. While Île de France, including Paris, had a figure of 13 per 1,000 legitimate live births, Corsica had a figure of 24.6 per 1,000. In 1956/60 these two regions also ran first and last and in the intervening years there has been no change in the ratios separating them.

The interaction between socio-economic and regional disparities can be shown by the cross-tabulation of infant mortality rates by occupation and region simultaneously. One study showed that for the group 'liberal professions and higher and middle cadres', the infant mortality rate in 1970–72 ranged from 10.2 in Haute-Normandie and Rhône-Alpes, to 17.6 in Corsica; but that in two areas (Franche-Comté, Languedoc-Roussillon) 'industrial and commercial proprietors' actually had lower rates. Similarly, for 'labourers', the range was from 18.3 (Pays de la Loire) to 33.4 (Franche-Comté); but once more in two areas (Corsica and Aquitaine) the group 'specialized workers' showed up less well. In terms of the ratio mortality rates between 'labourers' and 'liberal professions ...' there was also a considerable range, from 1.4 (Corsica and Aquitaine) to 2.7 (Brittany).

West Germany

In the German case it is necessary to use regional disparities as an indicator of the existence of health inequalities. On this basis, and using infant and neonatal mortality as an indicator, the German experience shows up as being less favourable than that in England and Wales (Table 29).

Both rates, but particularly the infant mortality rate, show substantial variation. The same is true for England and Wales. The range in infant mortality rates for the German *Länder* is from 17.9 (Baden-Württemberg) to 25.9 (Bremen): a difference of 8.0 or 40 per cent of the lower figure. The

International Comparisons   101

comparision may be made with the RHAs of England and Wales. The
lowest infant mortality rate here (1975) is Oxford (12.68 per 1,000 live
births), the highest Yorkshire (17.93) – a difference of 5.2 or about 40 per
cent of the lower figure (OPCS, DH3, no. 2, 1977).

Table 29: *West Germany 1974: infant mortality and early neonatal mortality rates,
by Land*

Land	Infant mortality rate	Early neonatal mortality rate
	per 1,000 live births	
Schleswig-Holstein	18.0	10.5
Hamburg	19.0	11.2
Niedersachsen	21.9	13.5
Bremen	25.9	12.1
Nordrhein-Westfalen	23.2	14.3
Hessen	21.5	13.3
Rheinland-Pfalz	22.3	12.6
Baden-Württemberg	17.9	11.4
Bayern	20.4	13.2
Saarland	25.6	15.7
W. Berlin	18.7	9.3
All	21.1	13.0

Source: Statistisches Bundesamt, 1974.

Netherlands

Here too social class or occupation categories do not seem to be employed
in analyses of inequalities in health: provincial differences are, however,
available. Table 30 shows variation in adult mortality rates between the
Dutch provinces, standardized for age.

Once more, comparison may be made with OPCS statistics giving SMRs
by English and Welsh RHAs (OPCS, DH5, no. 2, 1977). The range in
SMRs among males is from 87 (Oxford), 88 (East Anglia) to 113 (North-
West) and 111 (Northern); for females the range is distinctly smaller, from
92 (Wessex) and 93 (East Anglia) to 108 (Northern) and 110 (North-West).
Allowing for the different bases on which the two sets of figures are given,
the ranges from lowest to highest do not seem very different. The superior
performance of the Netherlands seems, rather, to be reflected in the distribution of provinces within this range. There are more nearer the lower end
than the higher.

Table 30: *Netherlands 1971: age-standardized adult mortality per 10,000 population*

Province	Males	Females
Groningen	88.8	71.6
Friesland	84.9	71.9
Drenthe	88.0	76.8
Overjssel	89.7	73.1
Gelderland	93.6	77.4
Utrecht	93.8	70.5
Noord Holland	94.5	73.0
Zuid Holland	92.4	71.4
Zeeland	80.9	68.5
Noord Brabant	95.5	79.4
Limburg	101.4	82.7
All Netherlands	92.8	74.3

Source: Centraal Bureau voor de Statistiek, 1974.

Norway

Like the Netherlands, Norway distinctly surpasses England and Wales in its rates of perinatal, infant and adult mortality. Norwegian statistics give standardized mortality rates for the twenty Norwegian counties, in relation to the national average, for adult males and females. The picture differs somewhat between the two groups. In both cases, however, the highest rates are found in Finnmark (the most northerly and very sparsely populated part of the country): 122 for men and 118 for women (1969–72). In the case of men the next highest rate is found in the Oslo area (the industrialized capital in which over 10 per cent of the population live); whereas in the case of women it is in Troms (a county also many hundreds of miles into the Arctic circle). These rates are 111 and 110 respectively. The southern regions of more moderate climate which are not industrialized have much lower mortality rates. Leaving aside Finnmark, the range for men is 85–111 and for women 95–110. However, if Troms also is omitted, the range for women falls to 95–104, the figure for Oslo being 99 (less than the national average). Clearly, in the case of Norway climatic factors render such comparisons of uncertain value.

Also available are morbidity data, more or less comparable with those given in the GHS, on an income basis. These data suggest something of an income gradient in morbidity among single persons and among the older members of multi-person households, though not among 16–49-year-olds.

Table 31: *Norway 1975: morbidity* by age and income: percentage of all in each group*

annual income	persons in multi-person households						single persons, ages over 16
			Age				
	0–6	7–15	16–30	30–49	50–66	67+	
under 15,000 kr	35	31	36	52	74	80	78
15,000–29,999 kr	29	30	44	54	76	78	75
30,000–49,999 kr	33	36	45	54	72	78	58
50,000–79,999 kr	31	34	42	52	65	77	58
over 80,000 kr	24	32	39	48	60	67	—

* 'Morbidity' is defined as persons sick on 1 October and/or at least one day of restricted activity in the period 1–15 October.

Source: Central Bureau of Statistics, Oslo, 1977.

Sweden

Sweden has the lowest perinatal and infant mortality rates in the world and, moreover, is succeeding in continuing to reduce them. The Swedish situation in this respect is of particular interest.

Early in the century Sweden suffered from substantial differentials in infant death rates, on both a geographical and an income basis. Thus, among legitimate infants born in Stockholm between 1918 and 1922, the infant mortality rate in families with an income over 10,000 S Kr was 14.3 per 1,000, in families with an income of less than 4,000 S Kr it was 48.9 per 1,000.* Professor Sjolin of Uppsala University writes of this differential: 'Today the difference is probably completely erased, but there are no recent studies to confirm it' (Sjolin, 1975). The decline in regional differentials is shown by Fig. 7, which compares rates for the three most northern and relatively poor counties with two southern counties (Uppsala, Göteborg). By 1971, Sjolin writes, the northern county of Vasternorrland had the lowest rate of infant mortality among all the Swedish counties (8.2).

Moreover, Sweden seems also to have eliminated socio-economic differ-

* Rietz Acta Paediat, **9**, quoted by Sjolin.

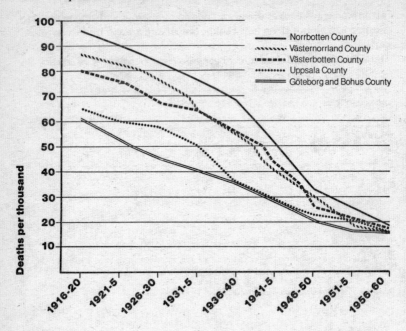

Figure 7. *Infant mortality in five Swedish counties, 1916–60.* (*Source: Sjolin, 1975.*)

ences in height and age of maturity among children. A study in 1976 found no such differences in a sample of 740 Swedish urban school children followed from age 9–17 (Lindgren, 1976). (By contrast, Rona, Swan and Altman (1978) found that social class remains an important determinant of children's height – between ages 5 and 11.5 years – in England and Scotland. Moreover, within each of the class-groups children with *unemployed* fathers were shorter.)

The reduction of inequalities

Several recent studies in the USA have attempted to focus on the question of *changing* inequalities. In particular there have been attempts to assess the effect of the poverty programmes of the 1960s on health inequalities, measured by adult and infant mortality rates and morbidity/utilization of the health services rates (Lerner and Stutz, 1977; Chase, 1977; and Wilson and White, 1977).

Taken together they indicate that the medico-social programmes of that period were associated (since causality cannot be assumed) with reductions in infant mortality differentials, though not adult mortality differentials, and with improved utilization of medical services by the poor relative to the non-poor, but again not with reductions in differentials in morbidity. In so far as this is an accurate picture, it might conceivably be seen as indicative of the feasibility of influencing the various indicators of 'health inequality' with which we are concerned.

So far as policies designed specifically to reduce the overall incidence of perinatal and infant mortality (and the associated morbidity among survivors) are concerned, the experience of France and Finland is particularly significant.

A study in France has attempted an analysis of the effect of laws promulgated in 1970/71 requiring all pregnant women to attend at least four pre-natal consultations (at three, six, eight and nine months) and requiring examination of all newborn infants by a doctor in the first week of life. The law also recommended pre-natal consultation with a doctor qualified in obstetrics and additional consultations for those assessed as 'at risk' (Rumeau-Rouquette et al., 1977). The study took a representative sample of about 1,000 pregnancies in the Rhône-Alpes region in July 1972 and in June 1975, and looked at both the effect on the patterns of usage of services and the outcome. Overall, the proportion of women having less than four consultations fell from 14.4 per cent to 10.6 per cent, and the number with an obstetrician responsible for pre-natal surveillance rose from 56.6 per cent to 69.3 per cent. At the same time, however, there was a rise in the average educational level of the mothers, in the standard of housing, in the use of contraception and in the percentage of mothers working, and a fall in the percentage of mothers who already had two or more children. So far as outcome was concerned, it was found that the distribution of birth-weights was unchanged, but the rate of 'anomalies or pathologies at birth' fell from 23.8 to 15.6 per cent.

The adequacy of pre-natal surveillance as a function of various 'class' factors showed a complex pattern of change. In 1972 inadequate surveillance (a total of less than four consultations or first consultation after three months) was associated with immigrant status (mother or father), no post-primary education (mother or father), number of children and manual employment of father. By 1975 the association with educational level of mother and number of children had both fallen considerably. There was no clear change on the basis of manual/non-manual employment of the father.

In Finland success in reducing perinatal and infant mortality rates has been attributed in particular to a reduction in the hazards of child-birth for larger babies (over 2,500 g birth-weight) and a reduction in the proportion of babies born at below 2,500 g, even though there has been no improvement in the survival chances of the reduced number of fragile babies (Wynn and Wynn, 1974). A study of perinatal mortality in Sweden reaches similar conclusions (Geijerstam, 1969). In reducing the incidence of low birth-weight, nutrition seems to be crucial, and it is perhaps worth noting that ante-natal clinics in Finland typically recommend the consumption of 1–1½ litres of milk per day by the pregnant woman – considerably more than is recommended in England. There is, of course, a typically large difference in the consumption of dairy products between England and Finland – among all income groups – a fact which may show up both in perinatal and adult mortality rates (though in opposite senses).

High rates of attendance for ante-natal care are also characteristic of the Nordic countries and are generally agreed to be importantly related to low rates of mortality and morbidity. In Finland, a 1944 law required the establishment of at least one maternal health centre in each local authority area. At that time, according to the Wynns, 31.3 per cent of pregnant women who subsequently gave birth were registered: by 1968, 99.3 per cent were registered at one of the health centres. (The figure for Sweden is also over 95 per cent.) Moreover, by 1968 91.2 per cent were attending for first examination by the end of the fourth month of pregnancy. By contrast, it seems likely that only about 50 per cent of women have registered by this stage in England and Wales, and in some areas the figure is undoubtedly very much lower.

In addition in Finland all women deemed to be at risk by virtue of, for example, a previous failed pregnancy or hypertension are referred from the health centre to the ante-natal department of a major central hospital, for either one or more consultations. This accounts for about one quarter of all the women. It is part of a broader policy of disbanding domestic deliveries and concentrating child-birth in major specialized centres.

In emphasizing the importance of surveillance from an early stage of pregnancy, both Finland and France have made use of financial incentives to improve ante-natal take-up.

In Finland, only mothers who go for examination to a doctor, midwife or maternal health centre within the first four months of their pregnancy can receive the maternity grant. In 1974 this could be taken as a cash grant of 80 FMK (£10) or in the form of a baby 'kit' (which the Wynns estimated to be worth double) which most took. The view is that this relatively modest grant served as the necessary inducement at times and among groups of low income. Attendance now is simply taken for granted by all. It might also be noted that travel to the health centres is subsidized.

In France, maternity grants were initially seen as an instrument of population policy. Between 1946 and 1975 they were paid only where (1) a baby was conceived within two years of marriage, or (2) the mother was less than 25 years old, or (3) the interval between births was not more than three years (Doguet, 1978). Today, the grants, which form part of a rather complex French 'family policy', are seen specifically as a means of reducing perinatal mortality and birth handicap. To this end the total grant of 1,620 francs (£190) is paid in three instalments: at the end of three, six months and eight months of pregnancy, dates judged to be of significance for the detection of anomalies, and with proof of attendance at ante-natal examinations necessary. A fourth examination, in the ninth month, is also required according to a law of 1971.

A recent secondary analysis of survey data relating to 11,000 1972 births shows that among French-born mothers (where the father also was born in France) 14 per cent had three or less ante-natal examinations and 9 per cent attended for their first examination after three months of pregnancy. These figures rose to 27 per cent and 16 per cent for non-French (migrants) (and to 35 per cent and 16 per cent for the North African-born in the migrant group). However when those mothers who were French-born but were *also* both married to a manual worker and had received no post-primary education were considered alone, they also rose to 20 per cent and 12 per cent (Kaminski et al., 1978). Thus, although there are both class and ethnic differences in this respect in France, like those in Britain, the overall rate of attendance seems to be distinctly better.

In both France and Finland financial incentives also play a part in ensuring post-natal medical examination. In Finland, the maternity health centres are informed of all births to mothers registered with them. Within forty-eight hours of returning home, the mother is visited by a midwife, who has the duty of ensuring that the child is registered at a child health centre. Today, over 90 per cent of children are registered within one month of birth. The proportion of those registered within the first year rose from 84.7 per cent in 1957 to 94.2 per cent in 1969.* Each child is seen ten to eleven times in the first year (twice by a doctor), and then twice a year between the ages of one and six by health centre staff. The Wynns point to the important contribution made by these staff beyond the assessment of purely medical well-being. They teach parents about nutrition, the care of minor ailments,

* This is higher than in Britain, where the National Child Development Survey found a figure of about 80 per cent. Official statistics show that of children born in England in 1974 90.1 per cent attended a child health clinic in 1976. However, in some AHAs the figure is very much lower: for example, Birmingham 71.2 per cent, Camden/Islington 70.6 per cent, Salford 68.2 per cent, Cornwall 62.4 per cent.

dealing with behaviour problems and the importance of mental stimulation of the child. It appears that parents increasingly go there for advice on all aspects of child behaviour. The third maternity allowance instalment is only paid after attendance at the post-natal medical examination.

In France, there exists a post-natal allowance of 2,130 francs (about £240), paid in three instalments. For the first, the child must be examined within the first week of life, for the second within the ninth month and for the third within the twenty-fourth month.

As well as these incentives, it is important to note that in Finland, when an appointment at the health centre is missed, a midwife or health visitor visits the home. This is felt to be very important and is, of course, made possible by very much more generous staffing levels. Also regarded as important to Finnish practice is the accountability for coverage required of Finnish public health services.

Today it is clear from the experience of both of these countries that a deliberate policy of attempting to ensure that ante-natal and child health services have a 100 per cent take-up yields major benefits for perinatal and infant mortality rates. It is not possible unambiguously to conclude that the financial incentives used in Finland and France are themselves directly responsible for the improved rates of attendance and consequent reduction in death and, inevitably, in perinatal morbidity. But irrespective of this, the 'outreach' capacity of the Finnish system (following up all missed appointments, etc.) must be stressed. So too, in our view, must the importance of adapting the functioning of these health centres to the needs and the difficulties of those whose attendance must be secured.

It is worth noting, also, that the obligations upon women in France to attend ante-natal care in force since 1971, intended to increase coverage, form part of a broader attack on handicap of perinatal origin (Wynn and Wynn, 1976). Other measures include the improvement in equipment and staffing of major obstetric departments; the establishment of more I C Us for newborn infants; and the regulation of minimum standards of equipment, staffing, size etc. binding on all establishments with maternity units, whether public or private. This latter has led to the closure and amalgamation of many small units. Moreover, it now appears that concern in France is not with coverage of ante-natal care (which is adequate) but with the poor quality, and often perfunctory nature, of the examinations given. Also, the striking reduction in 'class' differential in post-neonatal mortality rates suggests some levelling in social, economic and environmental conditions. It is noteworthy that, between 1956–60 and 1970–72, this reduction has been much greater than the (negligible) reduction in the class differential in neonatal rate – implying a greater relative levelling of environmental conditions than in obstetric care.

Conclusions and summary

Comparison of the British experience with that of other industrialized Western countries, on the basis of commonly used overall mortality rates, shows that British perinatal and infant mortality rates are distinctly higher than those of the four Nordic countries and of the Netherlands, and comparable with those of Western Germany. The rate of improvement in perinatal mortality enjoyed by Britain over the period 1960–75 was as good as that of most other countries, though the rate of gain is *now* poor. Moreover in the case of infant mortality all comparable countries have done better, especially France. Adult mortality patterns, especially in the younger age groups, compare reasonably with other countries.*

Why, then, might it be that infant mortality in particular presents so dismal a picture? Analyses quoted earlier suggest that infant death rates are associated with a number of characteristics of socio-economic and health systems. Low infant death rate seems clearly to be associated with per capita GDP, and there is some evidence for an association with an egalitarian income distribution. (In other words distributional aspects of society – and the extent of income inequalities – may be related to national performance in the infant mortality rankings.) So far as health policy is concerned, it seems that extent of provision of nurses and midwives, and of hospital beds, are more important than provision of physicians. Not unrelated, it seems that a relative emphasis upon preventive, ante-natal and child health services within health policy is required. International comparison here may thus have implications for policy.

It is possible, of course, that the superior performance of Sweden, Netherlands etc. might be attributed to difference principally in the extent of internal inequalities. Thus, if the perinatal mortality rate for all England and Wales were equal to that of social classes I and II, or the infant death rate equal to that obtaining in Oxford RHA, there would be little difference between these countries and ours. The second question, then, is whether the inequalities in health between social classes and regions, found in Britain, also exist elsewhere.

* It has, however, recently been noted that whereas the death rates among men aged 45–54 from coronary heart disease in Australia, Canada, Finland and America are now *declining*, those in England and Wales have merely *stopped rising*. The reasons for decline remain to be explained (Morris, 1979).

Briefly, the evidence – although disparate and not permitting comprehensive comparison – suggests that they do. The evidence relating to France and Germany (in the first case on an occupational basis, in the second on a regional basis) indicates disparities broadly corresponding to those of Britain. Finland also seemed comparable. So too did the Netherlands, at least in terms of the total range of regional inequality noted. Only in the cases of Norway and Sweden did a significantly smaller inequality appear to obtain. Moreover, in both these cases the extent of regional inequality (at least on the index of adult male mortality rate) seems to have fallen consistently over the years. American evidence on changing inequalities suggests an improvement in the case of infants and access to medical services, but not in adult mortality or morbidity.

If the evidence for changes in the extent of inequalities is slight (and in the American case ambiguous), that for the success of specific policies designed to reduce inequalities is slighter still. Clearly, as the study by Rumeau-Rouquette et al. showed, various dimensions of comparison can produce discrepant results, and changes in extraneous variables may often interfere. Of course, this study also suggested that reductions in inequality of access to, or utilization of, pre-natal care can come about.

None of the results quoted enables us to deal with the question of the relative importance of inequalities in provision or utilization of health services on the one hand and other forms of inequality on the other in determining inequalities of outcome. (Although it is noteworthy that provision of physicians is more equal on a regional basis in England than even in the Netherlands.) An aspect of this question is that of the intervention of social class or related factors between morbidity and use of health services. Is it *commonly* the case that working-class or low-income individuals or families have less recourse to the health services when they are sick? There are relatively few studies to draw upon.

One important study was carried out by Purola et al. in Finland in 1964, just prior to the introduction of much expanded health insurance (Sickness Insurance Act), which for the first time covered primary medical care. Methodologically this study, like the General Household Survey, was based on a questionnaire administered to a representative sample of non-institutionalized families (not households). Questions covered self-reported morbidity, use of health services, income etc. The most important conclusion for our present purposes was that the number of consultations with a GP in a given period of time was proportional to income, when number of days of reported sickness was held constant. A similar relationship obtained in the case of the chronic sick. On the other hand, the number of days spent in hospital was not a function of income. Moreover, since it was known that incomes in rural areas were lower than in urban areas, and it had been established that distances to physicians were greater in rural areas and that consultation rates were inversely proportional to distance, the effects of income were examined holding both morbidity and distance constant. The effects of income on GP consultation rates and those of distance were independent of each other (Purola et al, 1968).

The Finnish Sickness Insurance Act was designed to reduce the financial disincentive to making use of physicians' services. It does not appear however that organizational or financial arrangements can wholly compensate for income inequalities in bringing about parity of usage.

An analysis by Salkever of data collected in five countries with very different health systems (Liverpool, Helsinki, Lodz, Baltimore and north-west Vermont, and an area of Saskatchewan) – in the context of a WHO study – throws some light on this (Salkever, 1975). Relating probability of contacting a physician to an index of ill-health (perceived seriousness of condition; days restricted activity; days in bed), according to income, Salkever found first that in all cases except Saskatchewan low-income children fared worse. That is, their reduced utilization was independent of the organization and costs of health care. Among adults, it appeared that the clearest association of low income with low utilization was found in Liverpool. If American and French experiences are any guide, this is one aspect of the cause of health inequality which can be corrected.

Chapter 6

Towards an Explanation of Health Inequalities

Death rates in present-day Europe have reached what appear to be their lowest points in the history of human society. The twentieth century has witnessed a dramatic decline in the rate of infectious disease, as well as the introduction of powerful therapies for its treatment. Common causes of death like TB and diphtheria, often linked with poverty and material deprivation, have greatly diminished, though they have been replaced by new diseases, some of which have been linked in particular studies with affluence and material abundance. On that account inequalities in health might have been expected to diminish. But the evidence which we have presented in earlier chapters suggests that this has not been the case. In this chapter we ask why occupational class continues to exert so significant an influence on health in Britain.

There are a number of approaches to an explanation, though none in our view provides a wholly satisfactory answer. Indeed, the variable of occupational class is in itself multifaceted, and its influence probably varies according to age or stage in the life-cycle and according to the natural history of disease.

Theoretical approaches

Theoretical explanations of the relationship between health and inequality might be roughly divided into four categories:

1. Artefact explanations.
2. Theories of natural or social selection.
3. Materialist or structuralist explanations.
4. Cultural/behavioural explanations.

In some respect each one of these approaches sheds light on the observed relationships between class and health in present-day Britain. We shall first describe and discuss in general terms the four approaches and then go on, by reference to the problems of different age groups, to show that any satisfactory explanation must build essentially on the ideas of the cumulative dispositions and experience of the lifetime, and of multiple causation.

The artefact explanation

This approach suggests that both health and class are artificial variables thrown up by attempts to measure social phenomena and that the relationship between them may itself be an artefact of little causal significance. Accordingly, the failure of health inequalities to diminish in recent decades is believed to be explained to a greater or lesser extent by the reduction in the proportion of the population in the poorest occupational classes. It is believed that the failure to reduce the gap *between* classes has been counterbalanced by the shrinkage in the relative size of the poorer classes themselves. The implication is that the upwardly mobile are found to have better health than those who remain, or that their health subsequently improves relative to the health of those they join. We would make two comments. One is that informed examination of successive census reports shows that the poorer occupational classes have contracted less sharply than often supposed (see Appendix, Tables 1 and 2). The other is that indicators of relatively poor progress in health apply to much larger sections of the manual occupational classes than just those who are 'unskilled' (see p. 68, for example).

Natural and social selection

Occupational class is here relegated to the state of dependent variable and health acquires the greater degree of causal significance. The occupational class structure is seen as a filter or sorter of human beings and one of the major bases of selection is health, that is, physical strength, vigour or agility. It is inferred that the Registrar General's class I has the lowest rate of premature mortality because it is made up of the strongest and most robust men and women in the population. Class V by contrast contains the weakest and most frail people. Put another way, this explanation suggests that physical weakness or poor health carries low social worth as well as low economic reward, but that these factors play no causal role in the event of high mortality. Their relationship is strictly reflective. Those men and women who by virtue of innate physical characteristics are destined to live the shortest lives also reap the most meagre rewards. This type of explanation has been invoked to explain the preponderance of individuals with severe mental disorders in social class V (a thesis which was reviewed critically in, for example, Goldberg and Morrison, 1963). It is postulated that affected people *drift* to the bottom rung of the Registrar General's occupational scale.

Similar selective processes are thought to occur with other forms of disease even though the extent of drift may not be so great and there is little actual evidence of it.

Materialist or structuralist explanations

The third type of explanation emphasizes the role of economic and associated socio-structural factors in the distribution of health and well-being, and, because it is frequently misunderstood, requires fuller exposition. There are several separate strands of reasoning within it which can be ordered more or less according to the extent to which the primary causal significance is assigned directly or indirectly to the role of economic deprivation. Amongst explanations which focus on the *direct* influence of poverty or economic deprivation in the production of variation in rates of mortality is the radical Marxian critique. With the benefit of a century's hind-sight the validity of much of this nineteenth-century theory of the relationship between health and material inequality has been accepted today, especially for the earlier phase of competitive industrial capitalism (Stedman-Jones, 1971; Thompson, 1976). Exploitation, poverty and disease have virtually become synonymous for describing conditions of life in the urban slums of Victorian and Edwardian cities, as they are today for the shanty towns of the under-developed world.

But can it be so readily applied to contemporary health experience? Can the premature mortality of the working class still be directly attributed to subsistence poverty and exploitation? It is true that a relationship between material deprivation and certain causes of disease and death is now well established, but then so is the capacity of the capitalist mode of production to expand the level of human productivity and to raise the living standards of working people. Economic growth of the kind most readily associated with the European style of industrialization has in itself been credited with the decline in mortality from infectious disease during the nineteenth and twentieth centuries (cf. McKeown, 1976; Powles, 1975). Today death rates for all age groups in Britain are a fraction of what they were a century ago and many of the virulent infectious diseases have largely disappeared (cf. Morris, 1975; OPCS 1978), and the 'killer' diseases of modern society – accidents, cancer and heart disease – seem less obviously linked to poverty. Against this background, the language of economic exploitation no longer seems to provide the appropriate epithet for describing 'Life and Labour' in the last two decades of the twentieth century. Through trade-union organization and wages council machinery it is now argued that labour is paid its price and, since health tends to be conceptualized in optimum terms as a fixed condition of material welfare which, if anything, is put at risk by affluent living standards, it is assumed by many that economic class on its own is no longer the powerful determinant of health that it once was.

The flaw in this line of reasoning is the assumption that material subsistence needs can be uniquely and unambiguously defined in terms independent of the overall level of economic development in a society. People may still have too little for their basic *physiological* as well as social needs. Poverty is also a relative concept, and those who are unable to share the amenities or facilities provided within a rich society, or who are unable to fulfil the social and occupational obligations placed upon them by virtue of their limited resources, can properly be regarded as poor. They may also be relatively disadvantaged in relation to the risks of illness or accident or the factors positively promoting health.

It is worth illustrating how this can happen. New types of industrial process can introduce entirely new risks for the workforce or the population in the area. Certain forms of building or construction or town planning can introduce new hazards for adults as well as children. Changes in distances from work, type of participation in the local community and in leisure can alter the balance for many people in their access to health services as well as their knowledge about health. People living alone who have a fall, or people who have a heart attack, face different problems in different communities. Warnings about undesirable food and other products (inflammable clothing and furniture, for instance), as well as the latest information about the means of obtaining a healthy diet, may or may not be communicated, depending on the social circumstances. Many other examples of how new problems of health arise in a changing society might be given. The material deprivation of some sections of the population can paradoxically grow even when their income increases, relative to changing structures and amenities.

How far might differences in access to resources help to explain this? How unequal is the distribution of wealth in Britain? Historically the structure of living standards has been slow to change. Personal wealth is still concentrated in the hands of a small minority of the population, as reports of the Royal Commission on the Distribution of Income and Wealth have shown.

The question whether the richest men and women in Britain have maintained their economic position at the expense of less well-endowed citizens eludes a categorical answer. The Royal Commission has referred to the 'remarkable' stability of the unequal distribution of income over the past two decades (see also Appendix, Table 4). Moreover there is no doubt that the proportion as well as number of the population dependent on a subsistence or near-subsistence income from the state has grown. For some groups, and especially manual groups, relative lifetime resources will have been reduced. Earlier retirement, unemployment and redundancies, single-parent status and disablement, as well as the proportionate increase in the elderly population, all play some part in this development. For recent years Table 32 shows the tendency for those at the lowest relative income standards to increase in number and proportion.

Table 32: *Numbers of persons in poverty and on the margins of poverty* (*Family Expenditure Survey*)

Income relative to supplementary benefit	Britain (000s)			
	1960*	1975	1976	1977
Under supplementary benefit standard	1,260	1,840	2,280	2,020
Receiving supplementary benefit	2,670	3,710†	4,090†	4,160†
At or not more than 40 per cent above standard	3,510	6,990	8,500	7,840
Total	7,740	12,540	14,870	14,020
Per cent of population	14.2	23.7	28.1	26.6

*From B. Abel-Smith and P. Townsend, *The Poor and the Poorest*, Bell, 1965, pp. 40 and 44. The data are for the UK and are on a household rather than an income unit basis. It should be noted that this column is based on national assistance scales, not supplementary benefit scales.

†Drawn separately from a supplementary benefit sample inquiry with people drawing benefit for less than three months excluded. In the FES, such people are categorized according to their normal income and employment.

Sources: For 1960, Abel-Smith and Townsend, 1965, pp. 40 and 44. For 1975–7, DHSS (SR3), Analyses of the FES.

There is therefore a paradox: while we would not wish to assert that the evidence is consistent and complete, the proportion of the population with relatively low lifetime incomes (in the widest sense of 'income') seems to have increased in recent decades, just as the proportion assigned to classes IV and V seems to have decreased, though the latter continue to comprise more than a quarter of the population. While economic growth has improved the access of both groups to income and other resources, other groups have gained in proportion, and since neither facilities nor knowledge is a finite commodity, those with relatively low incomes (in increasing numbers) have remained relatively disadvantaged.

So it has been with health. Occupational classes IV and V may in time catch up with the contemporary levels achieved by I and II but by that time the latter groups will have forged even further ahead. There is nothing fixed about levels of physical well-being. They have improved in the past and there is every likelihood that they will improve in the future. But class inequalities persist in the distribution of health as in the distribution of income or wealth, and they persist as a form of relative deprivation.

Unfortunately the opportunity for examining the association between income and health is restricted by lack of information and the role played by material factors in creating the pattern of health and ill-health which can be found in the population is complex. Occupational class is multifaceted in 'advanced' societies, and apart from the variables most readily associated with socio-economic position – income, savings, property and housing – there are many other dimensions which can be expected to exert an active causal influence on health. People at work, for instance, encounter different material conditions and amenities, levels of danger and risk, degree of security and stability, association with other workers, levels of self-fulfilment and job satisfaction and physical or mental strain. These dimensions of material inequality are also closely articulated with another determinant of health – education.

Two other related theoretical approaches should be mentioned. Each is concerned with the effect of macro-economic variables – levels of production, unemployment etc. – on health. First an American social scientist, Harvey Brenner, making use of time-series data trends in the US economy and fluctuations in rates of mortality, purports to show that recessions and wide-scale economic distress have an impact on a number of health indicators, including foetal, infant and maternal mortality, the national mortality rate – especially of death ascribed to cardio-vascular disease, cirrhosis of the liver, suicide and homicide rates – and on rates of first admission to mental hospitals (Brenner, 1973, 1976 and 1977).*

In fitting the data on economic trends, essentially unemployment, to health indicators, Brenner suggests there is a delayed effect of between two and five years, choosing the lag to obtain the best fit. By doing this he purports to be able to estimate both the initial impact of recession on the dependent variable as well as the cumulative impact over the space of several years. He also posits time lags of varying numbers of years between economic changes and changes in various health indicators (on a purely empirical basis) and in doing so claims to establish the direction of causality in a temporal sequence as well as suggesting the length of time involved. A major

* Studies of this kind were actually carried out by Morris and Titmuss in the 1940s, in an attempt to examine the effects of the violent economic fluctuations of the 1920s and 1930s upon a variety of health and mortality indicators (see, for example, Morris and Titmuss, 1944a, 1944b).

problem with such research, even if validated, is, of course, the causal mechanism. *How* does unemployment increase mortality? Brenner makes use of the somewhat ill-defined concept of 'stress' to link the two.

The second approach, in opposition to Brenner's, is concerned to disprove the common assumption that economic growth leads to an increase in general levels of health. In advanced capitalist societies, it is argued, profit is realized through hazardous, punishing and physically stressful work. Time-series data on employment and death rates are here presented in such a way that high rates of mortality appear to follow on from low rates of unemployment and high levels of prosperity (Eyer, 1975, 1977a, 1977b). In periods of high unemployment this is supposed to be the combined result of weakened institutionalized pressures to consume, relief of workers from stressful work routines, an increase of social solidarity (unlikely as this may seem), the added stimulation of supportive relationships and networks, and in general a more varied and more elevated meaning for human existence.

Cultural/behavioural explanations

A fourth approach is that of cultural or behavioural explanations of the distribution of health in modern industrial society. These are recognizable by the independent and autonomous causal role which they assign to ideas and behaviour in the onset of disease and the event of death. Such explanations, when applied to modern industrial societies, often focus on the individual as a unit of analysis emphasizing unthinking, reckless or irresponsible behaviour or incautious life-style as the moving determinant of poor health status (cf. Fuchs, 1974). What is implied is that people harm themselves or their children by the excessive consumption of harmful commodities, refined foods, tobacco and alcohol, or by lack of exercise, or by their under-utilization of preventive health care, vaccination, ante-natal surveillance or contraception. Some would argue that such systematic behaviour within certain social groups is a consequence only of lack of education, or individual waywardness or thoughtlessness. Explanation takes an individual form. What is critical, it is implied, are the personal characteristics of individuals, whether innate or acquired – their basic intelligence, their skills obtained through education and training, their physical and mental qualities, and their personal styles and dispositions. Others see behaviour which is conducive to good or bad health as embedded more within social structures – as illustrative of socially distinguishable styles of life, associated with, and reinforced by, class.

Tables 33, 34 and 35 provide the kind of data sometimes used to illustrate a cultural/behavioural type of explanation. Certain styles of living, like a diet strong in carbohydrates, cigarette smoking and lack of participation in sporting activities, are known to cut across class. It is implied that there are individual or, at most, sub-cultural life-styles, rooted in personal characteristics and level of education, which govern behaviour and which are therefore open to change through changes in personal activities or educational inputs. However, data of the kind illustrated in these tables are not easy to interpret. For one thing, the observations are themselves only indicators which are subject to qualification if their meaning is to be put into context.

Table 33: *Household food consumption by income group (oz./person/week)*
(Great Britain, 1979)

Income group	Food				
	white bread	brown, including wholemeal bread	sugar and preserves	potatoes	fresh fruit
A	17	5.3	11	39	25
B	22	4.5	12	40	20
C	26	4.3	13	48	16
D	29	4.3	15	48	15

Gross weekly income of head of household: A = £145+; D = less than £56 per week.

Source: Adapted from *Household Food Consumption and Expenditure*, HMSO (see Morris, 1979).

Table 34: *Cigarette smoking by socio-economic group (males and females aged 16 +)*
(1980)

SEG	Current smokers %	
	Men	Women
Professional	21	21
Managerial	35	33
Intermediate non-manual	35	34
Intermediate manual	48	43
Semi-skilled manual	49	39
Unskilled manual	57	41
All	42	37

Source: *General Household Survey*: OPCS Monitor, 28 July 1981.

Table 35: *Active leisure pursuits by males: ratio of participation rates, non-manual to manual workers, by age (males aged 16 or over engaging in each activity in the four weeks before interview) (Great Britain, 1977)*

	Age group		
	16–29	*30–59*	*60+*
Squash/fives	4.4	6.9	*
Athletics (incl. jogging)	3.3	3.3	*
Rugby	2.9	*	*
Golf	2.8	3.2	4.9
Badminton	2.8	2.8	*
Cricket	2.4	1.7	*
Tennis	2.4	4.1	*
Table-tennis	1.7	3.1	*
Swimming outdoors	1.6	2.1	*
Walking (more than 2 miles)	1.6	1.8	1.7
Bowls (indoor)	1.4	1.3	1.1
Bowls (outdoor)	1.4	1.4	1.6
Playing football	1.1	1.6	*
Swimming (indoor)	1.1	2.2	*
Dancing	0.9	1.1	1.2
Gymnastics/yoga/keep fit	0.9	2.1	*

* Ten or fewer participants in either manual or non-manual group.

Source: *General Household Survey*, 1977.

Thus, a balanced diet, or balanced physical activity, to promote health is easy neither to define nor measure. People who eat one type of food to excess may make up for that disadvantage in some other respect. And manual workers who are spectators rather than active sportsmen include those who have to exert physical strength and agility in their everyday jobs.

Again, the data can be interpreted in other ways than in relation to level of knowledge or education, or personal responsibility. Commercial advertisements are planned to 'educate' tastes, and the education provided in schools is not always calculated to prepare young people to ward off influences upon their consumption and behaviour which may be undesirable for health. Moreover, access to good food and sports facilities depends also on the area in which people live and the resources they can command, and not only their personal characteristics or behaviour, or education. But, in emphasizing these reservations we must also call attention to the *cumulative* importance of those contributions to personal behaviour made by genetic endowment of attributes, the influence of family upbringing and practices and the evolution of modes of self-management which contribute to wide differences in health achieved by different members of the same occupational or socio-economic class.

The interpretation of level of personal knowledge or education as a causal factor in health illustrates our theoretical problem. It is on the basis of success or the lack of it at school that children are selected for manual and non-manual work and, as we have seen, this occupational distinction plays an important part in measured health status differentials. But we can go further. Bernstein has argued that distinctive patterns of child rearing and socialization, such as those which tended to differentiate between working-class and middle-class families, produce quite different linguistic capacities which are in turn correlated with quite different intellectual approaches to the social world (Bernstein, 1971). The working-class child is rendered at a particular disadvantage on account of these differences because of the *fit* which exists between middle-class norms of socialization and the dominant structure of the educational system. The outcome of this is that children from middle-class homes enter the school system already equipped with the appropriate mode of communication and, as a result, they have more successful educational careers and leave school with a greater facility to manipulate their social and economic environment (which of course includes health services) to personal advantage. These ideas carry the variable of education far beyond the simple idea of the transmission of knowledge and skills. They imply that the educational system tends to be substantially developed and maintained in conformity with the class system or with that pattern of differential material advantages or disadvantages, and social opportunities or obstacles, which govern both the place taken in the system by the individual child and the chances of that child having a successful career within the system. On this reasoning, level of education becomes difficult to treat as intrinsically independent of class.

More theoretically developed as the basis for cultural/behavioural explanations is the 'culture of poverty' thesis – which has much in common with the idea of 'transmitted deprivation'. As originally proposed by Oscar Lewis, an anthropologist who studied poor communities in Central America and, later, migrant groups in New York, the 'culture of poverty' was intended to apply only to market-organized social structures with poorly developed public systems of health, welfare and income maintenance (cf. Lewis, 1967). Starting from a distinct cultural anthropological perspective, Lewis argued that human existence in any given environment involves a process of biological and social adaptation which gives rise to the elaboration of a structure of norms, ideas and behaviours. This culture over time acquires an integrity and a stability because of the supportive role it plays in helping individuals to understand and cope with their environment but, through its influence on socialization practices and the like, it also comes to have an important autonomous influence in the social consciousness of individuals. The integrity of the culture ensures its autonomous survival even when the material base from which it emerged has changed or been modified. It is for this reason that people cling on to outmoded ideas or old-fashioned practices which do not seem to accord with the changed material realities of modern existence. The 'culture of poverty' thesis has been widely criticized by British social scientists (Holman, 1978, Chapter 3; Rutter and Madge, 1976; Townsend, 1979, pp. 65–71).

Consider, for example, the diffusion of the acceptance of the idea of family planning, which is generally agreed to have been first adopted by the professional classes (Banks and Banks, 1964), from whence it diffused to poorer classes. On the basis of the 'culture of poverty' thesis this should not have happened or, at least, there should have been more evidence of stiff resistance to the adoption of the practice. However, the fact that family planning has spread rapidly to all classes is one strand of historical evidence which is felt to cast doubt on the 'culture of poverty' thesis. The implication of that example is that the beliefs and values of poorer sections of the population are less autonomous, and more dependent upon conventional or orthodox beliefs and values, than has been assumed by proponents of the thesis. Instead social scientists have felt it right to place emphasis on the material circumstances of families and their access to the means of contraception in explaining class variations in the readiness or otherwise to adopt new methods of family planning. While recognizing the force of many of their criticisms we believe it is difficult to settle questions of interpretation like that of family planning one way or the other. We are aware that even if it is difficult to make a case for separately identifiable sub-cultures that does not dispose of the possible role of cultural variations in contributing to any overall explanation of variations in health.

Choosing between such complex and sometimes competing approaches, when applied to evidence as complex as that which we have assembled, is a daunting task. We must make clear our belief that it is in some form or forms of the 'materialist' approach that the best answer lies. But there can be little doubt that amongst all the evidence there is much that is convincingly explained in alternative terms: cultural, social selection and so on. Moreover, it may well be that different kinds of factors, or forms of explanation, apply more strongly, or more appropriately, to different stages of the life-cycle. This possibility has guided the presentation of our data.

Birth and infancy

Today the greatest risk at child-birth is among mothers who are older and who have already had several children. Such cases, of course, were more prevalent in Victorian society, where knowledge about birth control was scanty and where rather different ideologies about family size existed. In recent years the percentage of mothers in classes IV and V having a fourth or fifth child has decreased, but remains higher than in classes II and III. It could therefore be that higher rates of still-birth or perinatal death are a consequence of differences in maternal age and 'parity' (family size) between the classes. But class inequalities in rates of death at birth and throughout the first year of life are found even when parity and maternal age are held constant (Morris and Heady, 1955; Morris 1975). While age and parity exert an important influence on the risk of all still-births, the significance of these variables is much more evident among the wives of semi-skilled and unskilled manual workers. The risk of still-birth for the wives in professional and managerial households is lower no matter what their age or their previous record of pregnancies. (Similarly for perinatal death rates: at all ages and parities, the class differential remains.)

Rates of post-neonatal mortality differ somewhat – class differences are generally greater among young mothers under the age of 25 – but overall the broad pattern remains the same. The inescapable conclusion is that occupational class differences are *real* sources of difference in the risk of infant mortality.

Equally importantly, there are similar differences in the class incidence of low birth-weight which, as we shall see, can have, except under the most advantageous conditions, long-term implications for the health and development of the young child.

There are a number of explanations for this situation. Several studies have pointed to the importance of the mother's health, and the quality of obstetric care received, and there can be no doubt, on the basis of the evidence we have presented so far, that these are class-related (Hellier, 1977; Doll, Hill and Sakula, 1960).

Other explanations tend to be more complex. Studies over the last twenty years suggest that genetic factors play a 'predisposing' role in giving rise to congenital defects, with adverse environmental factors acting as a trigger (Lawrence, Carter and David, 1968; Janerich, 1972).

Work in the 1950s ascribed class differences in infant mortality to selective processes in mating and marriage (Illsley, 1955). Tall women married above their father's occupational class, short women below it, and these physical characteristics of women were then associated with different rates of infant mortality, the taller mothers having lower rates of infant death. The study concluded that higher-class men appeared to be recruiting as wives the most effective child-bearing women.

'Transmitted nutritional deprivation' offers another variant on the theme of selection (Baird, 1974). It suggests the existence of a vicious cycle of nutritional deprivation which leads to low birth-weight and congenital mal-formation. This cycle is difficult to break because, the evidence suggests, it originates in the nutritional deprivation of the mother not at the time of giving birth but *at the time of her own birth.* By this account, perinatal death and low birth-weight are seen as caused, in part, by the effects of nutritional deprivation upon the reproductive capacity of the mothers of the infants. These explanations are based upon data accumulated on the childbearing population of Aberdeen over many years, and they offer valuable insights into the mechanisms and processes whereby social class differences in mortality are produced and perpetuated.

If the relative importance of factors such as these in determining rates of perinatal death, and of handicap among survivors, is controversial, the situation is somewhat clearer in the *post-neonatal period.* When we look at causes of death in infancy which exhibit the steepest class gradients, there is much evidence to suggest that the important causal variables are contained within the socio-economic environment. The causes of death which are most likely to be associated with the nutritional status of the mother have the shallowest of gradients, while respiratory disease and accidents show steep class gradients. These observations lead us directly to consider the role of material deprivation on the life chances of the infants, and to the hypothesis that any factors which increase the parental capacity to provide adequate care for an infant will, when present, increase the chance of survival, while their absence will increase the risk of premature death. The most obvious of such factors fall within the sphere of material resources: sufficient house-hold income, a safe, uncrowded and unpolluted home, warmth and hygiene, a means of rapid communication with the outside world, for example a tele-phone or car, and an adequate level of manpower – or womanpower (two parents would normally provide more continuous care and protection than one). In addition to these basic material needs must be added other cognitive and motivational factors which are not independent of the distribution of material advantage. Those factors would include knowledge, certain skills and resources in verbal communication and a high level of motivation to provide continuous and loving care. When all these factors are present the infant's chance of survival is very good indeed. When some or even many of these are absent, the outlook is less propitious. Moreover, it should not be forgotten that these very same factors play a part in determining the development of the infant's own cognitive/linguistic and other skills. Competences acquired at this stage of life can profoundly influence later intellectual (and hence educational) achievement.

Table 36: *Causes of death from accidents of children aged 1–14 years* (*1968–74*)

Type of accident (or violence)	Total age 1–14 years	
	Number	%
Total accidents and violence	10,877	100.0
All accidents	10,204	93.8
Motor vehicle collision with pedestrian	3,656	33.6
Other motor vehicle collisions	1,199	11.0
Other transport accidents	619	5.7
Accidental poisoning	276	2.5
Falls	625	5.7
Fires	904	8.3
Drowning	1,401	12.9
Inhalation of food or other object	343	3.2
Accidental suffocation	375	3.4
Blows, cuts, explosions etc.	460	4.2
Accidents caused by electric current	150	1.4
Other accidents	196	1.7
Total violence	673	6.2
Suicide	33	0.3
Homicide	417	3.8
Injury undetermined whether accidentally or purposely inflicted	223	2.1

Source: OPCS.

Childhood: 1–14 years

The most important causes of death amongst all children aged 1 to 14 are, in descending order, accidents (with a small number of deaths also due to poisoning and violence – see Table 36), respiratory disease, neoplasms, congenital abnormalities and infections. Among 1- to 14-year-olds, and this we wish to stress, *almost all* the differences in mortality between occupational classes I and V are due to accidents, respiratory disease (bronchitis and pneumonia) and to a much lesser extent congenital abnormality. Among older children, deaths from accidents remain highly class-related, though deaths from respiratory disease become less so.

It follows that one approach to explaining this situation is to unravel those aspects of the social situations responsible for respiratory disease and for accidents. There are a number of epidemiological studies which help us to do this.

A study in 1966, for instance, found that the principal correlate of respiratory symptoms was the extent of air pollution in the child's area of residence (Douglas and Waller, 1966). But there was no tendency for working-class children to be more concentrated in high-pollution areas and social class had a small independent effect.

A more recent study in the mid-seventies took 2,000 children living in Harrow (which consequently did not permit consideration of a range of air pollution levels) and concluded: 'Illnesses occurred much more commonly in infants born to families which had several other children already, and in those families where the parents had respiratory disability or were smokers' (Leeder, Corkhill, Irwig, Holland and Colley, 1976). When all variables were taken together the most important proved to be: (i) bronchitis/pneumonia in siblings; (ii) parent smoking (affecting air inhaled by children); (iii) number of siblings (and likelihood of infection); (iv) parental history of asthma/wheeze. Class had no effect independently of these factors; but both smoking and family size are clearly related to class.

A third study of over 11,000 children aged 6 to 10 in a number of urban environments looked more directly at the interplay of social class and physical environment (Colley and Reid, 1970). It concluded that at the equivalent levels of air pollution children of occupational classes IV and V were much more likely to suffer from respiratory diseases than their counterparts in occupational classes I, II and III. Air pollution in short was an exacerbating factor. More directly, it reaffirmed that a past family history of respiratory disease is closely associated with a chronic cough in the 6- to 10-year-olds. It also once more found a clear class gradient in respiratory disease.

The general implication seems to be that the class gradient in bronchitis is largely a consequence of parental smoking, family size (and the increasing likelihood of infection by siblings), and a parental history of lung disease (which may also to some degree genetically place the child at risk). Parental history of lung disease is, of course, as shown independently, a function of type and severity of occupation. Environmental pollution is also implicated, and may be a particular danger for those children made vulnerable through other factors.

The second condition responsible for much of the gradient in child mortality is accidents. Among child pedestrians, for example, the risk of death from being hit by a motor vehicle is multiplied by five to seven times in passing from class I to class IV; for accidental death caused by fires, falls and drowning, the gap between the classes is even greater. These substantial differences demonstrate the non-random nature of these events. While the death of an individual child may appear as a random misfortune, the overall distribution clearly indicates the *social* nature of the phenomena. How is it to be explained?

Accidents have two primary causes: either environmental hazard, or dangerous behaviour reflecting carelessness, adventure or irresponsibility. These primary causes involve both material and cultural factors and indeed a full explanation of inequalities in the risk of death in childhood implicates each of them.

To begin with, the class pattern of accidents has to be seen in the light of the great differences in the material resources of parents, which may place significant constraints on the routine level of care and protection that they are able to provide for their children. Children of parents in occupational classes IV and V are amongst the poorest members of their age group in the population. Their opportunities to play safely within sight or earshot of their parents are less than those of their better endowed peers higher up the social scale. Furnishings, including forms of heating in the home, are likely to be less safe, as are the other domestic appliances which they encounter.

Differences in the material resources of the household also mean that the children of semi-skilled and unskilled workers are more likely to be thrown on to their own devices during holidays and out of school hours, which alone would be sufficient to increase the probability of their being involved in an accident.

It is impossible to escape the conclusion that in the context of childhood the most straightforward of material explanations is capable of providing a simple chain of causation by which the pattern of health inequality is illuminated. Households in occupational classes IV and V simply lack the means to provide their children with as high a level of protection as that which is found in the average middle-class home. This can mean both material and non-material resources. A study in Camberwell in south London, for example, concluded that one of the reasons for the greater prevalence of accidents in working-class homes is the higher incidence of stressful life events experienced by mothers. Such women lack the means to resolve the recurrent setbacks which dominate their domestic lives and are less well equipped to provide continuous and vigilant protection: 'The mother's psychiatric state and the presence of a serious long-term difficulty or a threatening life event were related to increased accident risk to children under 16. These factors were more common among working-class children, and in so far as they are causal, they go a long way to explain the much greater risk of accidents to working-class children' (Brown and Harris, 1978).

One recent study, valuable because it reports a field survey, focused on a sample of boys of 6 to 7 and 10 to 11 years old from severely deprived large families in Birmingham known to the social services department. Children were compared with a control group of similarly aged children, living in the same area but not under social service department supervision. The study was published in two parts.

In the first Brennan (1973) focused on medical characteristics. She found that both groups of children were below national age norms in height but that the sample children were more so. There was a high degree of visual impairment among both groups but again it was more marked among the sample children. (Moreover of the forty-six sample children who suffered visual impairment only one wore spectacles.) There was a higher degree of hearing loss among the sample children. Finally 78.2 per cent of sample children as against 58.9 per cent of control children were diagnosed as having some illness on clinical examination, far higher than indicated for the city as a whole from school health records, the most important being respiratory disorders, orthopaedic defects, speech defects, skin disorders and chest complaints.

The second study, with a cultural approach (Wilson and Herbert, 1978), also considered the 3–4-year-old siblings of those older brothers, and made extensive use of interviews, observation over a long period and psychological test data. This study vividly illustrates the nature and the effects of severe poverty on family life and on child development. It suggests that ill-health, inhibited cognitive development and behaviour problems are associated in a general 'poverty syndrome'.

Accidents to the children were common: thirty-four out of fifty-six families had experienced severe accidents (one child had lost an eye, sixteen suffered burns or scalding needing skin grafts).

Particularly striking was the extent to which ill-health was found to cluster in families. Of the fifty-six families studied: 'In forty families all, or most, members of the family were reported as having had much illness, or as suffering from defects or conditions which affected their activities. Respiratory diseases were most frequently mentioned, followed by gastric conditions and skin conditions.' Moreover, 'only four among the sixteen fitter families can be truly said to be healthy and obstetric problems were frequently mentioned'.

The authors concluded:

The children, in the process of growing up, have many shared experiences. They live in overcrowded conditions, being members of large families; their homes are inadequate by current standards; the neighbourhoods are rough and disliked by most who have to live in them. They experience poverty, by which we mean that they go short of things considered essential or normal by others around them. Most, if not all, the children have first-hand knowledge of illness, disability, accidents and mental stress expressed in a variety of symptoms. (p. 104)

The objective is survival, the operative unit is the family. The needs of individuals must take second place. Decisions were made at family level and related to the main wage earner or recipient of benefit rather than to the needs of individual children. (p. 186)

Finally there is considerable evidence that material deprivation affects physical development in young children and that ill-health contracted in childhood can dog an individual for life. Several studies, for example, have pointed to the effect of nutritional deprivation not only on physical growth, but also on the brain and nervous system. Some of the evidence is circumstantial, but laboratory experiments on animals suggest that malnutrition during the period of rapid brain growth – the first six months after birth – can affect the size and number of brain cells in several ways that can never later be compensated for (Birch and Gussow, 1970; Eichenwald and Fry, 1969). The implications for children from poor families in modern Britain who have a meagre diet are unclear, but few would disagree with the view expressed in an official publication that 'a hungry child is unlikely to be alert during lessons' (DHSS, *Eating for Health*, 1978).

Poor physical development also renders children susceptible to illness, and several reports have suggested that this may then persist. A study of 1,000 Newcastle families illustrates how repeated respiratory infections in the first five years, if inadequately treated, can lead to some degree of disability at the age of 15 (Miller, Court, Knox and Brandon, 1974).

Studies such as this – there are many more – suggest, as one government inquiry put it, that inadequately treated bouts of childhood illness 'cast long shadows forward' (the Court Report). Working-class children are more likely to suffer from them and less likely to be adequately treated for them.

Adult life

Among adults, as we have already seen, health differences between occupational classes have remained or have even widened. The phenomenon is principally one of relative deprivation – the maintenance of big differences in life chances against the dynamic background of a growing economy.

Explanations for this continued inequality have taken a number of forms. The twentieth century has witnessed and will continue to witness a series of revolutionary changes in the structure of occupations. To date these changes have resulted in some contraction of the size of the semi- and unskilled manual labour force and an expansion in non-manual occupations (see Appendix, Table 1). These changes have given rise to alterations in the age composition of each occupational class, older workers tending to be found in the contracting areas – though not as emphatically as some people suppose – and younger and more recent recruits to the workforce in the expanding area. Besides making comparisons between the occupational classes over time somewhat difficult, these shifts in the occupational structure in themselves offer an analytical solution to the continuing pattern of health inequality, for it is argued that the higher death rates of social class IV and V are, at least in part, a reflection of the older age structure of these occupational groups. The same argument has been used conversely to explain, to a small extent, the relatively low death rates of social class I.

In any event, Fig. 8, on the relationship between age and occupation for some of the major causes of death, shows that for all causes except malignant neoplasms class gradients are steepest in early adulthood and most shallow in the decade before retirement. The artefact explanation does not throw light on these observed patterns of fatal disease incidence amongst younger men.

These same distinctive trends also highlight the limitations of the thesis that the health gap is caused by age-related processes of social mobility. Occupational drift throughout the span of working life may help to contribute to class differences among the over-fifties but it cannot be said to be the cause of class inequalities between the ages of 15 and 45 years.

The limitations of these explanations especially among the male workforce of 45 years and under leads to a consideration of the direct role of material life on the production of health differentials. The most obvious starting point is the division between manual and non-manual occupations. Men engaged in manual occupations routinely confront a much higher degree of risk to

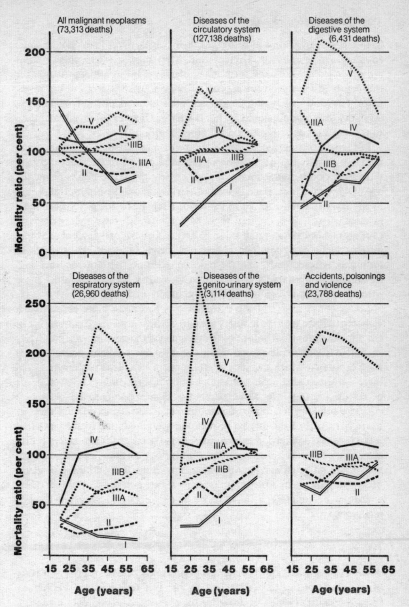

Figure 8. *Mortality ratios by occupational class, age and cause of death* (*men 15–64, England and Wales*). (*Source:* Occupational Mortality 1970–72, *H M S O, 1978, pp. 44–5.*)

health and physical well-being in their work than their non-manual counterparts. These risks are manifold. They may result in direct loss of life either suddenly in the form of accidents or in an attenuated manner through long-term exposure to dust or poisonous substances in the work-place. The same eventualities may also entail, antecedently, physical injury, disability and chronic illness. (This is why in Chapter 9 we pay attention to the importance of improving working conditions.)

But significant as occupation is, it is not a sufficient explanation. The influence of material deprivation in the aetiology of modern degenerative diseases is poorly understood, especially when applied to adults below the age of 45. In the past, poverty was an obvious antecedent in mortality, but its influence in deaths traced to cancer or circulatory disease, for example, is less clear-cut. It is thought these causes of death have their origins in over-indulgence rather than poverty and in behaviour which abuses and misuses the human body. The modern diet, rich in fats and with its emphasis on highly refined foods, and the modern sedentary patterns of work and leisure, are prime targets in the search for causes, as is, at a rather more specific level, the mass consumption of tobacco products.

Let us consider one of these. Smoking is becoming more class-related. Tobacco and the tobacco industry are part of the material and cultural life of Britain – an important source of tax income for the government, still freely permitted in public places and backed up by a multi-million pound advert-ising campaign which includes sports sponsorship. This is changing, and there is a slow swing against smoking, but not surprisingly the avant garde of cultural change are drawn from the higher occupational classes. If cigarette smoking is a major contributory cause of deaths due to cancer or heart disease, then the uneven response in the population to the news that it is dangerous is likely, in future years, to make class differentials in health even wider than they are at present. This raises questions, of course, about the social and economic factors which explain the fact and the prevalence of smoking in the first place and whether these, independent of individual education or counselling, have to be given priority in reducing the dif-ferentials.

Old age

After retirement the appropriateness of mortality rates as a proxy measure of standards of health is increased by the fact that health may literally become a matter of life and death for the over-65s. The bodies of men seem to exhibit the effects of wear and tear sooner than those of women and those of manual workers sooner than those of non-manual, and the manifestations of degeneration in disease become more frequent. What has to be remembered is that these outcomes are the end product of inequalities in the use made of, and the demands upon, the human body earlier in the lifetime and the kind of environment in which human beings have been placed.

This interpretation suggests that inequalities in health are the direct reflection of inequalities in the social division of labour. In the collective effort of social production, some workers' bodies wear out first. But inequalities in health at the end of the lifetime also emanate from the distribution of rewards associated with the social division of labour. Old age is a time of poverty, albeit poverty expressed in the form of relative deprivation, which among Britain's aged can mean material scarcity in very real terms, as deaths from hypothermia among the old reveal in severe winters. A recent DHSS report estimated malnutrition at 7 per cent among a sample of the elderly who were studied (DHSS, 1980, p. 3). In old age the relationship between income and the capacity to protect personal health is stronger perhaps than at any other time in the life-cycle, and in general it is likely that individuals who are well endowed through generous or index-linked pension schemes will lead the healthiest, the most comfortable and the longest lives after retirement. These material fortunes or misfortunes of old age are closely linked with occupational class during the working life. To have secure employment and an above-average income when one is at work is to be better able to provide for one's retirement. It is in this way that continuity in the distribution of material welfare is sustained, and inequalities in health perpetuated, from the cradle to the grave.

Conclusions

Several conclusions can be drawn from this look at different stages in the human life-cycle. First, while cultural and genetic explanations have some relevance – the latter is particularly important in early childhood – more of the evidence is explained by what we call 'materialist' or 'structural' explanations than by any other.

Secondly, some of the evidence on class inequalities in health can be understood in terms of specific features of the socio-economic environment: features such as accidents at work, overcrowding and smoking, which are strongly class-related in Britain. Since such features are recognized objectives of various areas of social policy we feel it sensible to offer them as contributory factors, to be dealt with in their own right, and not to discuss their incidence further in social-structural terms. The same is true of other aspects of the evidence which we feel show the importance of health services themselves. Ante-natal care, for example, is important in preventing peri-natal death, and the international evidence presented in Chapter 5 suggests that much can be done through improvement of ante-natal care and of its uptake. The international evidence also suggests the importance of preventive health within health policy, despite studies, to which we alluded earlier, which suggest that few of the differences in mortality either between nations, or between British regions, can be explained in terms of health care provision. But beyond this there is undoubtedly much which cannot be understood in terms of the impact of such specific factors. Much, we feel, can only be understood in terms of the more diffuse consequences of the class structure: poverty, work conditions (and what we termed the social division of labour) and deprivation in its various forms in the home and immediate environment, at work, in education and the upbringing of children and more generally in family and social life.

It is this acknowledgement of the complex nature of the explanation of health inequalities – involving access to and use of the health services; specific issues in other areas of social policy; and more general features of class, material inequality and deprivation – which informs and structures the recommendations we make in Chapters 8 and 9.

Chapter 7

The Need for More Information and Research

The scope and quality of national statistics relating to health and mortality in Britain are exceptionally good. Our task in compiling this report would have been much more difficult in most, if not all, other European countries. We have drawn on routine birth and death statistics, statistical returns collected for administrative and management purposes such as the hospital in-patient enquiry (HIPE), annual surveys like the GHS and the National Food Survey, the three national birth cohort studies and specific research projects.

Nevertheless there are gaps and imperfections which we feel necessitate either the initiation of further research or modification of the regular instruments of data collection.

There is a real need for continuing assessment of the development of children from birth to at least through primary school. It needs to be undertaken in relation to occupational class and must include surveillance of the nutrition of children. Studies of the kind we have in mind were in fact initiated in 1971, when the availability of school milk was reduced and the price of school meals raised, under the auspices of the Committee on Medical Aspects of Food Policy (COMA), and are still being carried out. Some of the findings of this work are discussed in Chapter 9, where we present our recommendations for policy relating to school meals and milk. The feasibility of surveillance of this kind has now been demonstrated, and the assessment of children's growth in relation to class and nutrition should become a matter of routine.

We recommend that school health statistics should routinely provide the results of tests of hearing, vision, and measures of height and weight, in relation to occupational class. Authorities might also be requested to report separately on schools in inner city areas, or to differentiate between a wide range of urban/rural locations. *As a first step we recommend that local health authorities, in consultation with education authorities, select a representative sample of schools in which assessments on a routine basis be initiated.* We should also like to see progress towards routine collection and reporting of accidents to children. Such reporting should ultimately distinguish not only between occupational classes and age groups, but also locations of accident

– on the road, at home, in school or elsewhere – and when appropriate the articles or building design features involved in accidents. At present the only national source of information is the HIPE. However, not only does HIPE fail to record occupational class, it also omits the vast bulk of accidents not requiring in-patient admission.

We recognize there are difficulties in working towards a national system of child-accident reporting, which may require the co-operation not only of hospital accident and emergency departments, and the police in the case of traffic accidents, but conceivably of health visitors also. In view of the importance of the topic, *we recommend that representatives of appropriate government departments (Health and Social Security, Education and Science, Environment, Trade, Transport, and the Home Office), as well as of the NHS and of the police, should consider how progress might rapidly be made in improving the information on accidents to children, nationally and locally.*

A further area where a concept of health broader than acute sickness has to be employed is in relation to the distribution of impairment and disability. We would like to see local authorities reporting systematically on numbers of disabled as well as, however crudely, on assessments of the severity of disablement. In the late 1970s local authorities began to classify handicapped people by the self-care criteria (whether they could wash and dress, and look after themselves in an elemental way), but that classification is not yet comprehensive, even for the physically handicapped, and needs to be extended, above all to the mentally handicapped. Social service departments and local officers of the Department of Employment should seek to introduce categorizations of severity, preferably on the basis of limitation of activity. This would permit comparison of priorities between services, as well as between authorities.

We would also like to draw attention to the importance of the National Food Survey, for which the Ministry of Agriculture, Fisheries and Food has responsibility. This annual survey is the principal source of information on the food purchased and consumed and hence the diet of the population, and is therefore of great importance. There are, however, problems relating to the low response rate of the survey. We feel that much could be done, through greater recourse to epidemiological expertise, to transform the survey into a more effective instrument of nutritional surveillance in relation to health.

We recommend that consideration be given to the development of the National Food Survey into a more effective instrument of nutritional surveillance in relation to health, through which various 'at risk' groups could also be identified and studied. We fully recognize that such a development may raise questions about proper responsibility for the survey.

Finally, *the importance of the problem of inequalities in health, and their causes, as an area for further research needs to be emphatically stated. We recommend that it be adopted as a research priority by the DHSS and steps taken to enlist the expertise of the Medical Research Council (MRC), as well as the Social Science Research Council (SSRC), in the initiation of a programme of research. Such research represents a particularly appropriate area for departmental commissioning of research from the MRC.*

A strategy for advance

In our view, the six areas in which further research – leading, it should be said, in some instances to improved or augmented administrative statistics – is essential are:

a. surveillance of the development of children, especially in relation to nutrition and accidents;

b. better understanding of the health effects of such aspects of what can be regarded as individual behaviour as smoking, diet, alcohol consumption and exercise;

c. the development of area social condition and health indicators for use in resource allocation;

d. health hazards in relation to occupational conditions and work;

e. better measures of the prevalence and course of disability, and the degree of its severity.

f. study of the interaction of the social factors implicated in ill-health over time, and within small areas.

The importance of each of these derives from its relevance to our overall strategy of developing new policy.

In order to study the dynamics of child health – the process by which ill-health and educational under-achievement (whether a consequence of handicapping conditions, absence from school or cultural factors) develop together and so perpetuate the link between health and social class – it is necessary to turn to longitudinal studies.

In our view three issues upon which research needs to be brought to bear are:

i. the *interaction* of processes leading to physical and mental disadvantage, handicap and ill-health;

ii. the role which services related to child health play, and might play, in inhibiting the cumulation of disadvantage;

iii. the routes by which some children escape what is for most born into similar conditions an unenviable fate.

Conclusions and recommendations

We have made various recommendations which will improve and extend the quality of class-related health and health service utilization data on a regular basis and enhance knowledge of their interrelationships.

It is argued, in relation to health, that the monitoring of ill-health (itself still so imperfect) should evolve into a system also of monitoring health in relation to social and environmental conditions. Two areas where progress could be made are (i) in relation to the development of children, and (ii) in relation to disability. Certain modifications to community health statistics are proposed:

We recommend that school health statistics routinely provide locally and nationally, in relation to occupational class, the results of tests of hearing, vision, and measures of height and weight. As a first step we recommend that local health authorities, in consultation with education author:ties, each select a representative sample of schools in which assessments on a routine basis be initiated.

We should also like to see progress towards the routine collection and reporting of accidents to children, ultimately distinguishing the age and occupational class of the parents as well as the location and circumstances of accidents. In relation to traffic accidents there should be better liaison between the NHS and the police, both centrally and locally.

We recommend that representatives of appropriate government departments (Health and Social Security, Education and Science, Environment, Trade, Transport and the Home Office), as well as the NHS and the police, should consider how progress might rapidly be made. The Child Accident Prevention Committee, if suitably constituted and supported, might be a suitable forum for such discussions, to be followed by appropriate action by government departments.

In relation to the disabled, we should like to see local authorities reporting systematically on numbers of disabled as well as (however crudely) on assessments of severity of disablement applying to mentally handicapped people, elderly people in residential homes and other groups of handicapped people, as well as the general classes of the handicapped, as at present.

In our view it is the extent to which need is unmet, rather than pressure upon existing services, which should form the basis for planning, and it is this view which has underpinned our recommendations. Turning, then, to the health services themselves, it is clear that systematic knowledge of the use made of the various services by different social groups is extremely scanty. We recognize that the collection and central reporting of occupational data within the context of the various administrative returns pose problems of feasibility and accuracy. Nevertheless we feel that the desirability of such information is such that further thought should be given to how these problems might be overcome, within the context of the current review of health service statistics.

Further, we draw attention to the importance of the National Food Survey as the major source of regular information on the food purchase (and hence nutrition) of the population. *We recommend however, that consideration be given (drawing upon epidemiological expertise within the OPCS and elsewhere) to development of the National Food Survey into a more effective instrument of nutritional surveillance in relation to health, through which various 'at risk' groups could also be identified and studied.*

Beyond this, we feel that the six areas in which further research is needed are:

- surveillance of the development of children, especially in relation to nutrition and accidents;
- better understanding of the health effects of such aspects of behaviour as smoking, diet, alcohol consumption and exercise;
- the development of area social conditions and health indicators for use in resource allocation;
- health hazards in relation to occupational conditions and work;
- better measures of the prevalence and course of disability, and the degree of its severity;
- study of the interaction of social factors implicated in ill-health over time, and within small areas.

Though these issues are in an obvious sense quite distinct, yet they can also be seen as aspects of an overall strategy, and it is this strategy which we particularly wish to commend. Our concern is with the interaction of variables traditionally seen as directly implicated in ill-health (such as smoking behaviour and work conditions) with social variables. It will be necessary to examine the effects upon the health of social groups of a wide range of social and behavioural variables, implying further work both on the development of health indicators and upon the way in which disadvantageous social and environmental conditions may give rise to or exacerbate the effects of patterns of dietary behaviour, leisure behaviour etc.

The importance of the problem of social inequalities in health and their causes, as an area for further research, needs to be emphatically stated. *We recommend that it be adopted as a research priority by the DHSS, and steps taken to enlist the expertise of the Medical Research Council, as well as the*

Social Science Research Council, in the initiation of a programme of research. Such research represents a particularly appropriate area for departmental commissioning of research from the MRC.

While we ourselves have not attempted to develop a research strategy in detail within this report, it is our view that two types of study are needed. First, a study of the interaction of social and environmental variables over time, and their relationship to the (healthy) development of children. The longitudinal approach, as in the existing cohort studies, is appropriate here. Second, a study carried out in a small number of carefully selected places. Such a study would concern itself with the whole range of social conditions relevant for health, as well as patterns of behaviour which may in some senses be damaging to health. Crucial for further progress in the elimination of health inequalities is greater understanding of the interactions of this complex set of variables: social and individual. Such interactions will necessarily have both diachronic and locational dimensions, and the studies we have in mind will be sensitive to, and permit elucidation of, both.

Chapter 8

Planning the Health and Personal Social Services

Any strategy for improving health inevitably involves both the health care system and a range of social policies not immediately related to that system. In this chapter we look at those services which fall under the general administration of the Department of Health and Social Security, while in the next we outline some of the major changes which need to be made in other areas of social policy.

Objectives and principles

We believe the health and social services should adopt a three-fold scheme of priorities:
* Priority for children to have a better start in life.
* Priority for disabled people bearing the brunt of cumulative ill-health and deprivation to improve their quality of life and reduce the need for institutional care.
* Priority for preventive and educational action to encourage good health.
  We shall look at each of these in turn.

1. Priority for children at the start of life

The wide gap in life prospects between babies born of members of different occupational classes – amongst the widest we have found in society – together with the likelihood that the beneficial effects of any reduction in that gap will be carried over into adult life and may lead to savings in health expenditure, demands that action be taken at this stage.

It would be wrong to suppose that improvements in infant and child care could be fully effective without paying heed to the need for improvements in the living standards of their families and the physical constitution and access to health services of their parents. Nevertheless some specific action aimed at this age group is possible. The great majority of 'excess' infant deaths in classes IV and V are attributable to congenital abnormalities and other complications of birth and the period immediately afterwards, and in later infancy

and childhood to accidents, respiratory diseases and gastro-intestinal infections. As we shall go on later to show, this means that special measures
need to be taken to improve the quality of community health services,
especially those devoting resources predominantly to children and those
which reduce risks of ill-health, injury and accidents.

2. Priority for disabled people bearing the brunt of cumulative ill-health and deprivation

It cannot be sufficient to plan only for the next generation or to take steps
to prevent certain health problems arising in the future. The cumulative
deprivations of a lifetime are a potent source of class inequality in health.
Those who are the worst victims of past and current industrial and social
practices, who have been exposed for prolonged periods to bad housing,
poor working and environmental conditions and low incomes, also deserve
services to improve their health and to enable them to cope with disabilities.
As with our first priority area, a marked shift of resources to community
health and welfare services is called for.

3. Priority for the preventive services

Greater equality in health depends upon a high national standard of knowledge about self-care, the care of children and other dependants, and the
pursuit of activities conducive to health which themselves depend on such
factors as high standards of home-keeping, good education and widely diffused recreational and sporting activities. This suggests a coherent national
programme of enormous scope and we can only hope to give illustrations
in this and the next chapter of some of the most important parts of such
a programme. They will include an expansion of health education, selective
screening and strong anti-smoking measures. It is important, however, to
convey at once the relative inexpensiveness of such measures. At the same
time we are deeply conscious not only of the preposterously small part of
NHS resources committed to 'preventive health', but also the lack of understanding by health authorities (and education authorities) of what is good
health practice and how they might contribute to strengthening and supple-
menting such practice.

Planning

We know these concerns are not new, and indeed they are very much within
the spirit of much recent government thinking. At least in theory, the whole

period of the middle and late 1970s saw an emphasis on greater care in the community, as well as a higher priority for children, families with children, for the elderly and for preventive health measures.

Nevertheless at least two disconcerting observations need to be made about government priorities. First, objectives are not clearly defined. A good example is that of 'community care'. The DHSS itself seems to mean different things by this concept at different times. In one overall review of planning the department defined a primary objective for the elderly to be to develop domiciliary provision and encourage 'measures designed to prevent or postpone the need for long-term care in hospital and residential homes' (DHSS, *Social Care Research*, 1978, p. 13). But in the planning document *The Way Forward* in 1977 community care was defined as covering a whole range of provision, including community hospitals, hostels, day hospitals, residential homes, day centres and domiciliary support. Again the 1976 Priorities Document which represented new directions in government policy called for relatively higher growth rates for some services but gave no rationale for the percentage growth rates chosen. This laid them open to charges of arbitrariness.

We believe that a clear statement of what is planned and intended produces a better educated and more understanding public, a more democratic and accountable public service, and above all offers an opportunity to question and clarify any shortcomings there may be in the initial thinking.

There is certainly no mathematically precise or exact way of determining the relative priority of different services, but there is room for the development of more precise analytical tools. Although, for instance, there are problems in conceptualizing and measuring 'need' (Lind and Wiseman, 1978; Smith, 1980) *we consider there is no better alternative conceptual basis for developing a coherent rationale for the allocation of health care resources, and we recommend accordingly*. We shall return later to a discussion of 'need'.

Secondly, some of the changes recommended in the various priority documents are simply not materializing or are materializing so slowly as to be difficult to discern. The latest trends in spending on the personal social services, for instance, give little or no sign of the planned decline in spending on *residential* care, with the corresponding expected increase in *community* care. A summary of local authority planning returns does not bear out the change in emphasis recommended by the DHSS (*Local Authority Personal Social Services Summary of Planning Returns 1976–77 to 1979–80*, 1978.)* Even though the planned changes in the emphasis of spending were modest

---

* Later information, discussed in the Introduction, shows that this statement still applies.

(extremely modest in some cases) the inability to fulfil even these limited objectives is disturbing.

We recommend a shift of resources within the national health service and the personal social services on a larger and more determined scale than so far accomplished towards community care and particularly towards the increased availability of care for young children. We see this as an important part of a strategy to break the links between social class or poverty and health.

What does this mean in practice? Table 37 illustrates what we have in mind. Column one shows actual expenditure on the various components of the health and social services in 1976/7. Column two is a projection of expenditure to 1981/2 and shows how modest the shift in resources sought by the last Labour government was. Column three (alternative 1) illustrates our idea of a more determined shift in emphasis assuming current planned levels of expenditure. This shows savings of £200 million in 1981/2 set against additional expenditure of £200 million (plus £30 million for an experimental action programme we shall explain further on). It doesn't imply a reduction in current levels of expenditure for any services but rather cuts in the anticipated growth (admittedly very small) in some areas. In our view the largest scope for reductions in rates of growth, if not in absolute costs, is in the pharmaceutical services.

Column four (alternative 2) is based on the belief that in fact current planned levels of expenditure, taking into account inflation and demographic changes, are inadequate and will do no more than permit an overall maintenance of existing levels. It follows that any reduction, even in anticipated growth, could end up as a real cut. Column four illustrates therefore how the shift in resources should be brought about on the more optimistic assumption that no service should be financed at a level below that previously forecast for 1981/2 and that additional resources could be made available. On this basis our proposals would require an additional £287 million, plus the £30 million mentioned before.

The setting-out of alternatives in Table 37 reflects a clear division of opinion within the Working Group. While we were completely in agreement on the importance of strengthening community and preventive services, two of us (DB and JNM) were opposed to obtaining the necessary resources by reducing expenditure on the hospital services, believing that these are already straitened by inflation and cash-limits; the others, on what may well be a sound appreciation of the financial outlook, were not so opposed to this. Naturally, all of us would wish to see additional resources.

These recommendations should, however, be thought of as money-saving in two senses. First, by reducing inequality and laying a better basis for the maintenance of health, the incidence of ill-health (and hence the need for

Table 37: *Planned and recommended revenue expenditure on selected services*
(£m.; November 1976 prices)

Services to be given higher priority than at present	1976–7 actual	1981–2 DHSS projection (1978)	1981–2 Alternative 1	1981–2 Alternative 2
1. *Health and Welfare of mothers and pre-school and school children*				
Midwives	24	24	26	28
Family planning	12	15	20	21
Health visiting	47	63	66	70
Day nurseries	33	37	60	63
School health	51	51	60	65
Welfare food	18	19	40	43
Boarding out	20	26	28	30
Sub-total	205	235	300	320
2. *Family practitioner (other than pharmaceutical)*	440	494	514	547
3. *Care of disabled in their own homes*				
Home nursing	81	108	116	124
Chiropody	11	13	13	14
Home help	105	131	160	170
Meals	12	15	20	21
Day care	57	76	90	96
Aids, adaptations	13	14	30	32
Services for disabled	42	40	50	53
Sub-total	321	397	479	510
4. *Other specific preventive measures*	14	17	50	53
Total selected 'higher priority' services	980	1143	1343	1430
Recommended increases (Total 1, 2, 3 and 4)	—	—	+200	+287

Table 37: *Cont.*

Services to be given smaller priority than at present	1976–7 actual	1981–2 DHSS projection (1978)	1981–2 Alternative 1	1981–2 Alternative 2
5. Acute in-patients and out-patients				
6. Mental handicap in-patients and out-patients				
Mental illness in-patients and out-patients				
Residential care for elderly				
7. Pharmaceutical services				
Total selected 'lesser priority' services (5 + 6 + 7)	2992	3295	3095	3295
Recommended decrease 'lesser priority' services (5 + 6 + 7)	—	—	− 200	0
Experimental ten-area programme			(30)	30

health care treatment) could be diminished. Second, by precautionary and supportive action the need for more expensive types of treatment will be reduced. While it may be true that many of those in hospital require additional resources, yet if fewer patients need be admitted or if the duration of stay can be safely reduced, there can still be scope for savings.

Resource allocation

The mid-seventies also saw a commitment to redistributing resources geo-graphically across the country in a more appropriate fashion. There is abundant evidence that some parts of the country have historically had much higher health budgets and consequently more adequate facilities. Since these tend to be the better-off regions, health inequalities are reinforced.

In 1975 the government commissioned a DHSS Resource Allocation Working Party to investigate ways of establishing a formula for distributing resources that corresponded more closely to 'need' rather than historical practice. The working party interpreted its objectives as being to secure through resource allocation equal opportunities of access to health care for people at equal risk. We wish to endorse this objective.

Unlike the parallel priority document (1976) it did seek to establish a mathematically quantifiable definition of need as a basis for determining future resource distribution. This rested primarily on mortality rates, which were taken as a proxy for morbidity rates. The procedure was, essentially, to take the age and sex structure of a population together with the average death rates for people of different sexes at different ages and then to 'weight' a region's population according to its need for various services – hospital, GP, ambulance etc. These services were costed and target revenues set accordingly. The RAWP proposal was that those regions furthest from their targets should have relatively larger growth budgets than those nearer, or, in the case of regions in the south-east of England (the so-called rich regions), already well past it. The more difficult questions of exactly how to redistribute resources more fairly at area and district level were largely ignored.

The RAWP formula was complicated and we were unable to get a complete picture of how its method was being applied around the country. Between 1976 and 1979 at least nine of the fourteen health regions had only partially implemented it. Four had not yet analysed their populations according to average death rates and five had not done this in relation to the particular need for general hospital care. Even among the remaining five, progress appeared to be cautious in moving towards targets for particular services.

We believe there are several points which deserve further attention. First, neither RAWP principles nor RAWP methodology has been consistently applied at area or district level and some of the misunderstandings about it have arisen because of the lack of precise illustrations at health district level of the actual and desirable operation of different services. This leads us to recommend that health authorities should consider increasing the volume of information collected and published regularly for each health district about: (a) health experience (indicators of morbidity, mortality and positive health); (b) rates of usage of health and health-related services (including GP consultations, out-patient attendance, home nursing and health visits and in-patient and residential care); and (c) social and environmental conditions.

Secondly, there has been insufficient thought given to how the concept of need could be enhanced by additional indicators. Are there, for instance, indicators of social deprivation which might be used independently or to supplement death rates in developing a formula for resource allocation?

There is in Britain a long tradition of study of the relationship between social conditions and death rates. While surveys like the General Household Survey do not break down information into sufficiently small areas, census data, although biased towards housing information and quickly out of date, does offer material on a range of deprivation-related factors at local authority and ward level.

One study in 1961 used a variety of census indicators, plus climatic and air pollution indicators, in the attempt to explain differences in adult mortality rates between the larger county boroughs of England and Wales. Multiple regression techniques allowed these authors to show, for example, that 'social conditions' (an indicator combining amount of overcrowding, social class, average educational level etc. was used), air pollution levels and inclement climate were independently associated with mortality rates from bronchitis (Gardner, Crawford and Morris, 1969).

More recently a second study, using 1971 census data together with 1971 mortality rates for children aged 0 to 4 and 5 to 14, sought to relate the death rates for children to social need variables, also at county or metropolitan borough level (Brennan and Lancashire, 1978). It found significant correlations between mortality rates, especially for the younger children, and extent of overcrowding, lack of basic amenities, extent of unemployment among male working population and extent of council house occupancy.

A significant correlation was also obtained with the proportion of unskilled workers, and the authors then examined whether or not social class composition (understood in the restricted sense of the percentage of population in class V), housing variables (density, possession of amenities) and unemployment rate are *independently* related to mortality rates. Calculation of partial correlations (housing variables and unemployment rate held constant) showed that the effects were independent of each other in the case of the under-5s.

Although this kind of analysis cannot be extrapolated to causes of mortality at the individual level, it is important here in suggesting that areas having high unemployment rates, *or* bad housing, *or* a high proportion of unskilled workers, or worse, all three, are likely to have high rates of child mortality especially in the first five years of life. The authors also conclude that the percentage of population in social class V *alone* will inadequately

Table 38: *Highest-ranking local authority areas on each of eight 1971 census and mortality indicators (England)*

1 Households with more than one person per room (per 1,000 households)	2 No. unemployed per 1,000 persons	3 No. unskilled workers per 1,000 economically active	4 Married couples with four or more children per 1,000 families	5 Perinatal mortality rate (average 1974–6)	6 Infant mortality rate (average 1974–6)	7 Adjusted mortality ratio (1976)
Knowsley	Knowsley	Tower Hamlets*	Knowsley	Wolverhampton	Rochdale	Salford*
Islington*	Liverpool*	Southwark*	Liverpool*	Sandwell	Oldham	Tameside
Hackney*	S. Tyneside	Newham*	Manchester*	Liverpool*	Salford*	Gateshead*
Tower Hamlets*	Sunderland	Knowsley	Birmingham*	Gateshead*	Wolverhampton	Liverpool
Lambeth*	Manchester*	Liverpool*	Cleveland	Salford*	Manchester*	S. Tyneside
Kensington/Chelsea	Newcastle*	Cleveland	Sefton	Rochdale	Bradford	Tower Hamlets*
Hammersmith	Cleveland	Humberside	Hackney*	Bolton	Calderdale	Durham
Southwark*	Gateshead*	Salford*	Lambeth*	Manchester*	Kirklees	Bolton
Brent	Hammersmith	Newcastle*	Newham*	Walsall	Walsall	Wirral
Camden*	Tower Hamlets*	Islington*	Salford*	Knowsley		N. Tyneside
			Wirral			
			S. Tyneside			
			Sunderland			
			Lewisham*			

* indicates Inner City Partnership Scheme area

Note: Adjusted Mortality Ratio (AMR) is the local death rate standardized for population age/sex structure and divided by the national rate.

Sources: Columns 1–4 Imber, 1977; 5–6 DHSS/OPCS (unpublished); 7 OPCS *Local Authority Vital Statistics 1976*.

reflect the extent to which social factors pre-disposing to high infant mortality are present in an area. Of course more 'inclusive' measures of class composition remain to be examined in relation to mortality. Table 38 shows which metropolitan districts and non-metropolitan counties show up worst on each of four census social indicators, and three indicators of mortality (using recent mortality data). The frequent appearance of certain areas notably in the north-west and the north-east is apparent. Further work on relationships between indicators of social disadvantage and of mortality is needed.

Third, we do not believe that a more equitable distribution of resources alone, without parallel attention to *how* these resources are to be used, will greatly serve to reduce inequalities in health care, still less in health. In the debate on the RAWP recommendations too much attention has been concentrated on criteria of the need for health care and too little on the effects upon health of allocating resources to one type of service rather than another. We believe that 'need' for health care must govern the definition of priorities and that at the present time the definition of such need shows the case for making a more pronounced shift of resources towards community and preventive health care. This leads us to suggest a possible modification to the implementation of the RAWP philosophy.

At present, the proposal is that weighted populations for each kind of health service are combined on the basis of the share of total revenue which each of these services currently represents, that is 8.8 per cent for community health, 55.9 per cent for non-psychiatric in-patients etc. We believe that this process should reflect not *current* distribution of expenditure but that which is *aimed* at in the planning of services. That is, if community health is a *priority* (and is intended to absorb, say, 10 per cent of total resources, excluding those for family practitioner services, within 5 years' time) then it is this figure which should be used in the combining of weighted populations. *We therefore recommend that the resources to be allocated should be based on the future planned share for different services, including a higher share for community health.*

In saying this we reiterate the Royal Commission's endorsement of the Expenditure Committee's view that: 'the expenditure planning and priority setting of DHSS should be synchronized so as to enable Parliament to examine the relationship between the two' (*Ninth Report from the Expenditure Committee.* Session 1976–7, 1977, p. lvi; and see also *Report of the Royal Commission on the NHS*, 1979, p. 56).

A district action programme

To ensure the vigorous implementation of the three-fold priority programme we outlined at the beginning (p. 141) we also propose the establishment of what we have called a *district action programme*. It would be adopted nation-wide and would involve additional modifications to the present structure of care not so far seriously pursued by government policies. It is a four-point programme.

1. The health and welfare of mothers, pre-school and school children

The under-utilization of the community and preventive health services by poorer groups is well documented. While we cannot assess the *extent* to which this is a consequence of the inequitable provision of services – so that, for example, working-class women might have longer journey times and waiting times in visiting child health clinics – we have known for a long time that under-utilization is associated with organizational and cultural aspects of services. One authority puts the problem as follows:

Under-utilization of ante-natal and child-health services results from inadequacies in the services themselves and particularly from their insensitivity to the uncertainty and conflict of responsibility mothers feel regarding the question of their baby's health. Two particular areas of inadequacy are highlighted by recent research: firstly, inadequacies as regards the organization of ante-natal clinics (timing of clinics and length of waiting, location of clinics, facilities for children and other relatives, etc.) and secondly, inadequacies as regards the actual content of the check-up (lack of individual attention and advice tailored to the individual's needs, lack of privacy, etc.)'. (Graham, 1978)

We recommend that areas and districts should review the accessibility and facilities of all the ante-natal and child-health clinics in their areas, and develop plans to increase utilization by mothers. On the basis of our own experience this must include such reforms as experimenting with evening and weekend opening, the dispersion of ante-natal sessions from hospitals covering large catchment areas to new centres in small areas, and the humanization of ante-natal procedures and settings, especially in clinics in hospitals. One clinic which we visited was described, not unfairly it seemed, as a 'cattle market'.

The DHSS should furthermore publicize factors which explain high utilization in some areas, like Liverpool, and low utilization in others, like Salford. Wherever possible clinics should be established in conjunction with group practice and health centres, in partial fulfilment of the recommendations of the Court Committee. As some commentators have pointed out, relatively few general practitioners are keen to devote more time to practising preventive medicine, and a change in outlook will take a long time to bring about (Alberman, Morris and Pharaoh, 1977, p. 394), but it might be encouraged if more health visiting staff were seconded full-time or part-time to group practice. There is room for experiment, and it is possible for some health visitors to combine territorial and team responsibilities. There is an even more powerful case to be made out for the secondment of social work staff, but in this case knowledge of welfare rights would be a very necessary part of their skills. Ease of access, good facilities, respect for the individual and availability of care and advice throughout infancy and childhood might be the watch-words of any planned development of services.

We should perhaps, at this point, mention the experiments in France and Finland (see Chapter 5), where ante-natal care is supported by financial inducements. We have examined these but we are not convinced that reluctance on the part of mothers to attend clinics is the real key to their under-utilization in Britain. In Finland the establishment of a national network of clinics in 1945 preceded the introduction of payments and may have been the key factor in encouraging high rates of attendance. In France ante-natal payments were introduced many years before the dramatic improvements in the French perinatal mortality rate.

One of the problems we face in Britain is that with the huge proportion of hospital births it can be difficult securing the involvement of GPs at an early stage in the life of a child. There are a number of possible solutions to this. One, already mentioned, is the association of more ancillary staff with primary care teams. We would then urge that the teams should generally be constructed on the basis of two and at most three general practitioners so that some contribution might be made to the vitality and integration of the local community. Another is immunization, where GPs have a much better knowledge of family history and the health and development of a child and are in a much stronger position to know about untoward reactions. In principle we advocate such a policy, though we recognize that for some time to come there will have to be back-up provisions in the community where the medical service is inadequate.

Unfortunately this inadequacy is disturbingly widespread and we were very concerned about the standard of GP service in some poor areas with high mortality. There are single-handed general practitioners who live at a considerable distance from the areas in which their patients reside, have little knowledge of or interest in local culture – which leads them to prescribe or otherwise treat patients inappropriately – who rely for a disproportionately large part of the year, the week or the day on the deputizing services, and take little or no interest in the possibilities of new health centres, group practice or other forms of collaboration among and between health service and social service professional personnel.

Some are considerably older than 65 and others are new to practice in this country and include those who are virtually in transit to other career destinations. There are some who have resorted to work in these areas because they have been unsuccessful elsewhere and are exposed here to less criticism. As the Royal Commission said of declining urban areas, 'Many health professionals are coping courageously and effectively in these areas, but there is evidence in some places that services are inadequate. The G Ps tend to be older and to have large lists. The accepted view today is that a G P will work most efficiently in a group practice or partnership with several other G Ps and there may be some connection between the extent of single-handed practice and low quality of care, although there are many excellent single-handed G Ps. More single-handed practices are found in the inner city areas' (*Report*, 1979, p. 88). For the inner London area, these problems have been well documented in the Acheson Report (London Health Planning Consortium, 1981).

We are aware that some of the best and most dedicated members of the medical profession also work in these areas and that the problems of quantifying the problem are immense. Nevertheless we are in no doubt that the problem is sufficiently serious to demand action. The Royal Commission took a similar view and recommended, among other things, close supervision of deputizing services, a review of controls on the appointment of G Ps, the offer of an assisted voluntary retirement scheme to G Ps, a study of the feasibility of introducing a compulsory retirement age, the introduction of audit or peer review of standards of care and treatment and the development of health centres as a priority in inner city areas.

We accept this, but we would want to go further. *We recommend that the professional associations as well as the Secretary of State and the health authorities should accept responsibility for making improvements in the quality and geographical coverage of general practice, especially in areas of high prevalence of ill-health and poor social conditions. Where the number or scope of work of general practitioners is inadequate in such areas we recommend health authorities to deploy or redeploy an above-average number of community nurses attached where possible to family practices.* The review of coverage must include definitions of desirable standards of practice and keeping abreast of modern methods of practice as well as advancement in medical knowledge, and not only questions of remuneration and inducement. *We further recommend that the distribution of general practitioners should be related not only to population but to medical need, as indicated by S M Rs, supplemented by other indicators, and that the per capita basis of remuneration be modified accordingly.*

One possibility deserving careful consideration is the attachment of additional, newly qualified G Ps to existing group practices and health centres for periods of, say, two to five years. Every effort should be made to provide housing temporarily or permanently within the areas. One problem of the poor areas is that health centres are not yet the main form of medical organization. In Gateshead only a fifth and in Tower Hamlets fewer than a tenth of G Ps are in health centres. Previous studies have demonstrated that a more effective policy deserves to be adopted. 'The NHS has not brought about any dramatic shift in the location of GPs ... Areas which are currently facing the most serious shortages seem to have a fairly long history of man-power difficulties, while those which are today relatively well supplied with family doctors have generally had no difficulty in past years in attracting and keeping an adequate number of practitioners ...' (Butler, Bevan and Taylor, 1973). A separate study of mortality and GP statistics in 1972 and 1973 found a significant lack of correlation between measures of illness and death and the number of GPs, suggesting that the supply of GPs is not matched to health care need (Forster, Frost, Francis and Heath).

We believe the evidence suggests that it is precisely those areas most in need of good medical facilities – judged on the basis of rates of mortality and morbidity – which are often least likely to have them.

Education facilities are another area that causes us concern. With the relative increase in number of one-parent families and increased employment of young mothers with children, the problem of facilities for those without relatives living nearby is considerable. Present plans for the expansion of day nurseries are meagre, and the rate of expansion needs to be larger. Within the proposed Health Development Programme at national level *we recommend the financing of new services for children under 5 from the savings that are being made as a result of the decline in the school population.* This proposal is further elaborated below (Chapter 9, pp. 180–83).

School health services are another neglected but valuable resource. They make it possible, for instance, to monitor the health of children in certain types of family more frequently, and there are possibilities of relating health surveillance to teaching about health and the health service. At the same time there have been a number of suggestions that all health services for children should be more tightly integrated. A Scottish working party expected that 'in the course of time much routine school health work will be carried out by primary care teams but the more specialized aspects such as the assessment of handicapped children will be the responsibility of paediatricians working closely with other professional colleagues' (*Towards an Integrated Child*

Health Service, 1973, p. 101). Like the working party, we recognize that there will have to be different systems of provision of school health care for some time to come, but *recommend that every opportunity should be taken to link revitalized school health care with general practice, and to intensify surveillance and follow-up both in areas of special need and for certain types of family.* For this purpose we take the view that certain assessments can be undertaken by health visitors and social workers, especially where they are already working in association with group practice. Much of this has already been accepted, at least in principle, by Ministers.

One area of school health which requires separate attention is the child guidance system. This has traditionally provided psychiatric care for a relatively small number of maladjusted children on an intensive basis. There is evidence of long waiting lists, misunderstood systems of queueing, and a negative image of the work among parents (Fitzherbert, 1977, pp. 85–96). At the same time there is evidence from surveys in the Isle of Wight and in London (Rutter et al., 1970, 1975) of a very much higher prevalence of maladjustment among children than had been thought, or than could be helped by traditional psychiatric methods. Consequently there is a growing view, which we share, that the emphasis must increasingly be upon preventive methods and upon increasing co-operation between psychiatrists, educational psychologists and teachers. For example, the so-called 'nurture group' pioneered by Marjorie Boxall provides a special therapeutic environment to compensate for inadequate early experience *within* the school from which children are gradually returned to normal classes. Such experiments should be encouraged and evaluated.

For handicapped children Ministers have already accepted in principle the establishment of District Handicap Teams. The teams can help to provide careful diagnosis and continuing help and advice and support to handicapped children and their parents. *We recommend that an assessment which determines severity of disablement should be adopted as a guide to health service priorities, and that this should be related to the limitation of activities rather than loss of faculty or type of handicap.* This procedure would help to equate the provision of services for mentally handicapped as well as physically handicapped children.

2. The care of disabled and elderly people in their own homes

When disablement is understood in terms of functional limitation it becomes possible to rank severity and provide a better guide to the selection of priorities. For example, conventions about the division of clients according to type of handicap, or the conventional categorization of patients as requiring hospitalization, residential care, sheltered housing or domiciliary support, may need to be re-examined. Many people seem to find themselves in a particular category more by chance than for any specific medical reason. Moreover the quality of care provided by the different types of institution, judged by costs, manpower, amenities etc., may bear little relation to need.

We believe disabled people suffer two distinct forms of inequality. One is inequality of opportunity for treatment for those in different types of hospital. *We recommend a review of the distribution of facilities and services between acute and long-stay units and also of the distribution of elderly patients in geriatric, psychiatric and general hospitals.*

The second form of inequality is in opportunities for care, rehabilitation, occupation, privacy and social relations between hospital patients and residents of local authority, voluntary and private homes on the one hand and disabled people living in their own homes on the other. These inequalities have attracted rather less attention than inequalities in services for people in different areas.

Both these forms of inequality require attention. However, we believe the first step in doing this is to clarify the meaning of community care and give much greater emphasis to the tendencies towards that objective favoured in government planning documents.

For instance the Jay Committee, which reported on mental handicap nursing and care in 1979, identified three broad sets of principles which should govern community care: (i) Mentally handicapped people have a right to enjoy normal patterns of life within the community; (ii) Mentally handicapped people have a right to be treated as individuals; (iii) Mentally handicapped people will require additional help from the communities in which they live and from professional services if they are to develop to their maximum potential as individuals.

The Committee concluded:

The mentally handicapped person should have access to the full range of services and facilities available to the general public and specialist services should be provided only where the general services cannot cope with a special need. But where special provisions are required they should offer a wide range of options in the three spheres of day, domiciliary and residential services. Mentally handicapped people in residential care should not be isolated from their neighbourhood or, more importantly, from their families. The staff who care for mentally handicapped residents should be compassionate and caring, but also professionally trained; their role should be to help each mentally handicapped person to develop mentally, physically and emotionally. Residents should live in small family-type groups sharing experiences informally with the staff, making their own decisions and taking necessary risks. (DHSS, Jay Committee, March 1979, p. 140)

In realizing such aims one obstacle in the development of services for mentally handicapped people, as for other groups of disabled people, is that responsibility for sheltered housing, as distinct from residential accommodation, is not the responsibility of the personal social services. As a result residential care is sometimes offered when sheltered housing would be the more rational choice. *We recommend that a Working Group, to include representatives of voluntary organizations concerned with relevant client groups, should be set up to review whether sheltered housing should be a responsibility of social service or housing departments and make recommendations.*

The elderly have also continued to have a poor deal from 'community care'. It has certainly not developed as rapidly as the general policy aims would suggest. The 1976 Priority Document argued:

> The general aim of policy is to help the elderly maintain independent lives in their own homes for as long as possible. The main emphasis is thus on the development of the domiciliary services and on the promotion of a more active approach towards the treatment of the elderly in hospital. But old people who can no longer continue to live independently in the community even with the support of all available health and social services will need long-term residential or hospital care (DHSS, 1976, p. 38).

In practice, evidence of capacities among residents and their subjective preferences is not always given the attention it deserves. *We recommend that clear criteria for admission to, and for continuing residence in, residential care should be agreed between the DHSS and the local authority associations, and steps taken to encourage rehabilitation, and in particular to prevent homeless elderly people from being offered accommodation only in residential homes. Priority should be given to expansion of domiciliary care for those who are severely disabled in their own homes.*

It may even be that, in the light of evidence which emerges, numbers in residential care could be frozen and even reduced, thus freeing additional resources. At times the DHSS has seemed to favour such a policy (for example, DHSS, *Social Care Research*, 1978, p. 13). It is true that in the 1970s the population of residential homes became older. This does of course suggest a rising number who are likely to be substantially incapacitated – though that correspondence needs to be demonstrated – but there still remains considerable evidence that a large fraction of residents, perhaps two fifths or even more, do not require continuous or even substantial 'care and attention' in a residential setting (Table 39). This may not mean that it would be right or practicable to attempt to find alternative accommodation for many present residents, but it does suggest that alternative accommodation must be found in future for those who would otherwise be admitted unnecessarily.

Table 39: *Evidence of capacity of elderly residents in homes for self-care*

Date of study	Scope of study	Percent of residents with capacity for self-care (*local authority residents only unless otherwise specified*)
(i) 1958–9	National sample survey of homes in England & Wales	72% neither bedfast nor requiring help dressing
		59% mobile outside home without assistance
		52% (new residents only) with 'little or no incapacity for self-care'
(ii) 1963	National sample survey of homes in Britain	37% little or no incapacity for self-care
		21% little or no incapacity for self-care *and* household management
(iii) 1969	National survey of homes in Scotland	67% complete capacity for self-care (i.e. able to wash, dress and use toilet)
		48% 'fit', i.e. having complete capacity for self-care plus no impairment or only mild impairment of mobility, mental state and continence
(iv) 1970	National census of homes in England	45% minimally dependent (i.e. continent, mobile without assistance, able to eat and drink without assistance, *and* mentally alert)
(v) 1972	Survey of council homes in eight London boroughs	55% high or very high capacity for self-care
(vi) 1973	64 homes in Cheshire	63% able to wash, dress, feed and go to toilet unaided
		42% no mobility problems, no assistance of any kind required *and* no behavioural problems

Sources: (i) and (ii) Townsend, 1962 and 1973; (iii) Carstairs and Morrison, 1972; (iv) DHSS, 1975; (v) Plank, 1977; (vi) Kimbell and Townsend, 1975.

Moreover we believe the tendency of the residential population to grow and become older reflects in part the social difficulties of elderly people, not just the fact that more of them are 75 and over. Factors such as lagging real incomes, displacement at younger ages from occupations and housing and especially the tendency for women increasingly to outlive men and to live alone all make life more difficult, and services have not developed fast enough to compensate.

Ironically another explanation is to be found in the reduction of the percentage of elderly cared for within the hospital system. For reasons of cost or professional definitions of medical or nursing need fewer elderly are to be found in hospital at any particular date, and the elderly residential population has grown at the same time as the hospital population has diminished. We are not sure this change-over has been entirely beneficial. The most severely disabled sector of the elderly population may now have *less* access to medical and nursing expertise than they used to and there may be less effort put into their rehabilitation.

Residential care is by far the most costly element in the personal social services and deserves a thorough review. In planning an efficient system of care for the elderly we may need to ensure that the minority of people in residential accommodation who are very frail and require close and continuous medical and nursing supervision and treatment for long-term conditions receive it in very small residential nursing hospitals, annexes and even day centres under local geriatricians. On the other hand, sheltered housing may be the best environment for that large fraction of people in residential accommodation whose disabilities are slight or at least not substantial, and perhaps in some instances also of residents whose disabilities are severe. *We therefore recommend that the present functions and structure of hospital, residential and domiciliary care for the disabled elderly should be reviewed in relation to their needs, in order to determine the best and most economical balance of future services.* We believe that such a review is likely to demonstrate the accelerated relative priority that deserves to be accorded to the development of domiciliary services. Strictly, the responses to the consultative document *A Happier Old Age* (DHSS, 1978) provide in some respects the material for just such a review. However, the issue deserves more sustained expert examination and research, especially into the subjective attitudes of elderly patients and consumers of residential and community services, than it appears to have attracted.

Overall, the care of disabled people, many of whom are *elderly* disabled people, requires more co-ordinated action by health and social service authorities than currently exists. The introduction of joint funding has encouraged more collaborative planning. *We recommend that this initiative should be developed and that there should be further central government funding of a more specific kind to encourage joint care programmes.* Within the general category of severely disabled people, sub-categories should be more clearly defined so that both types of authority can comprehend their individual but also joint responsibilities at different stages of chronic illness or disablement. *We further recommend that sums within the joint finance allocation should be reserved for payment to authorities putting forward joint programmes to give continuing care to disabled people – for example, post-hospital follow-up schemes, pre-hospital support programmes for families, and support programmes for the severely incapacitated and terminally ill.* Funding might be based on a percentage or per capita grant. Health and local authorities may be involved in broader types of in-service training and acknowledgement of the need to interchange staff between hospital and day centre, or hospital and home.

Like many policies, a more vigorous community care policy on behalf of disabled people in their own homes will encounter difficulties. Risks are involved in encouraging some people to continue living alone when disabled. Attempts to increase the pattern of social contacts in supplementation of support services for some elderly people living alone have not always met with success, and traditions of individual privacy, quite apart from the constraints of poverty and bad housing, do not make any easier the patterns of supportive social interaction which would better suit disablement in old age. In the long run a choice has to be made between the encouragement of further dependency on the part of disabled people in the hands of different professionals, and the ready availability in the community of support, including greater diffusion of information and expertise, reciprocation of services within the community, self-help, and all the risks of depending on spontaneous and other expressios of good-will among neighbours and generally in the community. This latter option is, of course, a form of 'prevention', for it would help people to deal with their own problems in their own homes and preserve for them the dignity of the status of responsible actors.

Finally, there has been a rapid expansion of the home help service. *In practice many home helps undertake a wide range of responsibilities on behalf of disabled people and we recommend that this should be formally encouraged, with short courses of training, specialization of some functions and with access to mini-bus transport, especially to day centres.*

3. Prevention: the role of government

A consultative document on prevention and health was published in 1976 and reprinted three times within the space of a year. This suggests widespread public interest. As Ministers stated in a foreword to the document, 'the preventive approach should permeate and inform all aspects of the health services'.

This will involve a change of outlook in the DHSS and more determined changes in organization and the allocation of resources. For the attainment of national objectives the distribution of information and knowledge about health and management of illness needs to be less hierarchical and more widely shared. In part this means taking a new view of health education. We have already called for the resurgence of the school health service and the introduction of special forms of teaching in the schools. But the issue is not simply the better instruction of individuals at key periods of their lives. As those concerned with health education are aware, there are at least three distinguishable sets of reasons for health education: (1) 'to produce changes in beliefs and behaviour in order to reduce mortality and morbidity; (2) to influence norms and values governing the use of health services; (3) to produce a general understanding of certain more diffuse "health" issues in order to obtain a population who have a general understanding of health issues and to avoid certain forms of "undesirable" or not directly definable "unhealthy" behaviour' (Tuckett, 1979, p. 4). A balance has to be struck between creating better and safer conditions of work, safer travel, well-regulated manufacture of food products and other goods and the creation of social and occupational conditions minimizing stress, as well as the conventional individual 'do-it-yourself' approach to health education.

While laying stress on the importance of designing and regulating appropriate occupational environmental and social structures, *we recommend that a greatly enlarged programme of health education, with a particular focus on schools, should be sponsored by the government. The D H S S and the D E S, as well as other departments, would be involved, and at the local level health education in schools should be the joint responsibility of A H As and L E As.* Such a programme of health education would include new initiatives to use the media for publicity, a drive to involve young parents in a programme of health education arranged in conjunction with local clinics, and corresponding programmes for those caring for disabled people at home.

However, as we have seen, it is not sufficient to regard preventive medicine as a question of individual initiative and responsibility based upon more information, important though this is. We explained in Chapter 6 (pp. 118–133) how the very possibilities for such initiative and responsibility are themselves a function of social circumstances. We accept, for example, the importance of publicity for, and advice on, the importance of adequate diet and of exercise, for health. Yet, it is not always possible for people to act in what they know to be their own best interest, and there are strong occupational class trends of the familiar kind in recreation and exercise (Morris, 1979, 1980). While the value of exercise must be made clear through the media, *facilities* for exercise are also required. We therefore endorse the view of the House of Commons Expenditure Committee in 1977 (HC 169–i,

1977) that 'The Department of the Environment and local authorities [should] be required to make more adequate provision for physical recreation in any future major developments or redevelopments both public and private, particularly in inner city areas.' We consider also that additional grants for the establishment of facilities for physical recreation should be made available.

Vaccination and immunization are not used as much as they should be and in some cases, polio for instance, the rate of immunization has actually declined. Doctors and others in the NHS must convince members of the public of the importance of these preventive measures. Tougher measures against both smoking and alcoholism are also required. In general we would note that the government's response to the Expenditure Committee report (*Preventive Medicine*) contained in the White Paper *Prevention and Health* (Cmnd 7047, 1977) failed to provide the positive measures we believe necessary. *We recommend that national health goals should be established and stated by government after wide consultation and debate. Measures that might encourage the desirable changes in people's diet, exercise and smoking and drinking behaviour should be agreed among relevant agencies.*

In the case of smoking these measures are clear, and cannot rest upon exhortation alone. An anti-smoking policy must involve new forms of education and counselling but also preventive and stringent control measures. During recent years there has been disturbing evidence of a growing inequality in cigarette smoking between rich and poor sections of the population. Between 1961 and 1980 men in professional occupations reduced their smoking by well over half, whereas unskilled workers reduced their consumption by much less (see Chapter 1 p. 21). We take the view that unequal access to information about the effects of smoking has contributed powerfully to this trend. We recommend the adoption of the following measures, which should be seen not only as priorities in themselves, but as illustrative of the determined action which needs to be taken by government in relation to all necessary elements of a strategy for prevention:

i. *Legislation should be rapidly implemented to phase out all advertising of tobacco and sales promotion of tobacco products (except at place of purchase).*

ii. *Sponsorship of sporting and artistic activities by tobacco companies should be banned over a period of a few years, and meanwhile there should be stricter control of advertisement through sponsorship.*

iii. *Regular annual increases in duty on cigarettes in line with rises in income should be imposed, to ensure lower consumption.*

iv. *Tobacco companies should be required, in consultation with the trades unions, to submit plans for the diversification of their products over a period of ten years with a view to the eventual phasing out of sales of harmful tobacco products at home and abroad.*

v. *The provision of non-smoking areas in public places should steadily be extended.*

vi. *A counselling service should be made available in all health districts, and experiments in methods to help people reduce smoking should be encouraged.*

vii. *A stronger, well-presented health warning should appear on all cigarette packets and such advertisements as remain, together with information on the harmful constituents of cigarettes.*

We appreciate that cigarette smoking has a very strong hold on a large section of the population and that no government can appear to be excessively authoritarian in its measures to eradicate it. None the less, international comparisons have shown that Britain is particularly weak in the policies it has pursued. For example, in 1976 Britain was seventeenth among twenty European countries in provision of non-smoking facilities and bans on smoking in public places (ASH, 1976; and see also House of Commons Expenditure Committee report, *Preventive Medicine*, 1977). We wish to stress the relevance of an anti-smoking campaign to any measures at district or national level to reduce inequalities in health.

4. Screening programmes

In this country, general screening programmes have usually been offered to, and accepted by, special high-income groups such as business executives, in whom compliance tends to be higher than average. The question naturally arises whether extension of such programmes to other groups would carry a high priority. On balance, the cost of population screening and the possible production of anxiety might well outweigh any likely benefits, even where there is a known higher incidence of disease in lower-income groups. A similar view on unselected screening is expressed by the Royal Commission on the National Health Service in para. 5.7 of their report.

Screening for particular disorders suffers from similar weaknesses. However there are exceptions. One is ante-natal screening, and we recommend that steps should be taken to educate women of child-bearing age in the importance of reporting suspected pregnancy at the earliest possible stage so that ante-natal care can be provided early in pregnancy. With early attendance at ante-natal clinics there are practicable programmes for screening for Down's syndrome and neural tube defects in the foetus.

The other exception is screening for hypertension in adults, which is both relatively simple and also becoming a more common practice.

In the light of the present state of knowledge we recommend that ante-natal screening for Down's syndrome and for neural tube defects (especially in high-risk areas) on the one hand, and in relation to adult disease for serious hypertension on the other, should be made generally available.

Before leaving this topic we should make it clear that this action programme is not complete and there is plenty of scope for local and voluntary initiatives. In particular we hope that Community Health Councils might be invited to monitor developments in their areas. What is most important is that standards of health, and knowledge about health, should be raised through face-to-face contacts and local group practices, clinics, day centres and schools.

A programme for ten special areas

What might be called an 'area deprivation' strategy has not so far been formally adopted in health policies although it has been followed up in the policies of other central departments, the Department of Education, the Home Office and the Department of the Environment, in the last twelve years. The concepts of 'Educational Priority Area', 'Community Development Project', 'Housing Action Areas' and 'Inner Cities' have become well known and the idea of 'positive discrimination' has been pursued with enthusiasm though with some loss of clarity and coherence.

We are conscious of both the advantages and disadvantages of different forms of 'positive discrimination'. The term itself can be misleading. It implies or rather tends to be taken to mean that individuals, groups or populations are singled out for preferential or above-average treatment to redress their deprivation. In practice, close examination suggests that new programmes are attempting only to bring services in a small number of places closer to the national standard by exceptional, supplementary action. There have been difficulties in selecting areas of deprivation because of lack of certain kinds of information. And the programmes have rarely been related either to the possibility of putting experimental schemes subsequently into wider practice or integrating them fully into the administration of services in their areas. On the other hand, when money is tight there is some advantage from developing demonstration, experimental and compensatory projects.

The argument is three-fold: (i) *for purposes of demonstration.* When resources are scarce the beneficial effects of adopting additional measures generally can be demonstrated for a few places; (ii) *for purposes of experiment.* When there are doubts about the best methods of developing certain features of services – for example early ante-natal attendance or collaboration in assessment and visiting of disabled or elderly people by the statutory and voluntary services – alternatives need to be tried and evaluated; (iii) *for purposes of developing reasoned priorities*. Comparatively little is known about the relationship between health service inputs and outputs and it is becoming more and more important to discover what additional developments, and rearrangements of service, are most economically related to high standards of health in a population and the reduction of inequalities in health.

We therefore recommend that the government should finance a special health and social development programme in a small number of selected areas, costing about £30 m. in 1981–2 (the figure given in Table 37). The following ten areas have the highest death rate, standardized for population and age/sex structure (see also Table 38, p. 149):

Salford
Tameside
Gateshead
Liverpool
South Tyneside
Tower Hamlets
Durham
Bolton
Wirral
North Tyneside

It should be pointed out that *within* these areas wide variations in mortality rates are to be found. In Gateshead, for example, the ratio of infant mortality in some wards to that in others in the mid-1970s was 3:1, but the wards with highest mortality were also wards with the smallest proportions of population in classes I and II.

We propose that in each of the ten areas experimental programmes within the three priority spheres should be introduced. We envisage that a proportion (say at least £2 m.) of the £30 m. should be reserved for evaluative research and statistical and information units, and that the remaining sum should be divided among the ten areas for development of the types of services listed below.

In order to gain a better sense of the problems to be found in these areas, two, Tower Hamlets and Gateshead, were visited by members of the Working Group. Gateshead is in fact already one of the three beneficiaries of the Comprehensive Community Programme. There is no doubt that the health and personal social services, and especially the community health services, in such areas of high mortality where there are also other indicators of severe health and social problems deserve additional government aid.

It is perfectly true of course that many innovations in service provision on a local basis, such as mobile clinics, are already being attempted in areas like the ten listed above. Many of these may indeed be proving successful in reaching those in particular need (the mobile clinic may well be an example), but these innovations are rarely (if ever) the subject of rigorous experimental assessment. It is this essential element of experimental assessment, the equivalent of the randomized clinical trial of clinical procedures, that we wish to stress, certainly in relation to child health, but also in relation to disabled people. Without this not only can change be on no more than an intuitive basis, but learning by one area from another is inhibited. Although the precise form of the proposals will need to take specific aspects of the local situation into account, and there is inevitably an element of overlap among our three spheres of activity, the following would appear to be among the candidates for action:

Making clinics more responsive to needs

i. Developing clinics in group practice and dispensing with hospital clinics dealing with large populations;

ii. Providing child play facilities;

iii. Combining child welfare and ante-natal clinics;

iv. Providing evening and weekend clinics;

v. Setting up counselling services for mothers, covering pregnancy, infant and child care and family health;

vi. Provision of detailed nutritional counselling to pregnant women by trained nutritionists;

vii. Additional or special clinics for (1) lone and/or young mothers (2) handicapped children.

viii. Experiments to enable mothers to keep in touch with each other independently of ante-natal and post-natal appointments by such developments as Young Family Centres and the provision of facilities to enable mothers and babies to meet together regularly.

Domiciliary services

i. More health visitors to (a) follow up all missed clinic appointments; (b) undergo special training in helping ethnic minorities; (c) provide better services at home for severely disabled people.

ii. Liaison between GPs and health visitors: GPs should notify health visitors of all pregnancies promptly, and all pregnant women should be visited. GPs can be encouraged either in existing partnerships or health centres, or, if single-handed, collaboratively, to set up special maternity and infant care groups (possibly, through notification of first births, for first-time mothers and, through child benefit registrations or schools, for mothers of four or more children).

iii. Active development of community nursing services so that nurses are trained to work in the community as well as hospital and prevent certain hospital admissions as well as provide services for disabled or chronically sick people when discharged;

iv. Planned joint services with: (a) social service departments; (b) voluntary bodies. Schemes should include attachment of social workers to primary care teams and use of voluntary visitors on a 'preventive' basis for the disabled.

v. Special counselling services (including services on income rights, heating and housing problems) for severely disabled (especially elderly and mentally handicapped) people and their relatives.

School health

i. Special programme of assessment of health of school children;

ii. Special health education programme in schools as an integral part of the curriculum.

Food

i. Special welfare food provision on greatly increased scale;

ii. Enhanced (free) school meals programme.

Smoking

Experimental anti-smoking programmes (educational and therapeutic).

Screening

Experimental services aimed specifically at older mothers and middle-aged people.

It should not be supposed that an additional area programme would simply add to existing resource allocation. It would contribute to a better balance between necessary and less necessary services and hence would contribute to the more economical satisfaction of the aims of the health and personal social services.

Conclusion and summary

We have identified three objectives for the administration of health and personal social services and recommend their adoption by the Secretary of State. They are:

i. To give children a better start in life.

ii. For disabled people, to reduce the risks of early death, to improve the quality of life whether in the community or in institutions, and as far as possible to reduce the need for the latter.

iii. To encourage good health among a larger proportion of the population by preventive and educational action.

We believe that if these three objectives are pursued vigorously inequalities in health can be reduced. To fulfil them we recommend a shift in the allocation of resources (Table 37). However, this in itself is not enough. It must be combined with an imaginative, and in part necessarily experimental, approach to the nature and delivery of care. District action programmes, by which we mean general programmes for the health and personal social services to be adopted nationwide and involving necessary modifications to the structure of care, should be developed in each area; and an additional experimental programme should be funded in ten areas of high mortality and adverse social conditions.

We have argued for changes in the planning of the development of health services and especially resource allocation. We believe that allocation of resources should be based on need. We recognize that there are difficulties in assessing need, but we agree that standardized mortality ratios (SMRs) are a useful basis for broad allocation at regional level. At district level, further indicators of health care and social needs are called for. These should be developed as a matter of urgency, and appropriately to reinforce, supplement or modify allocation according to SMRs.

Resources within the National Health Service and the personal social services should be shifted more sharply than so far accomplished towards community care, particularly towards ante-natal, post-natal and child health services, and home help and nursing services for disabled people. We see this as an important part of a strategy to break the links between social class or poverty and health.

In building up revenue targets it is not the current distribution of expenditure between services which should be used, but that which is aimed at in the planning of services. In particular, this process should reflect a higher share of resources for community care.

While we are aware of the problems of conceptualizing and measuring 'need', we consider there is no better alternative conceptual basis for developing a coherent rationale for the allocating of health care and resources, and recommend accordingly.

Our main recommendations for a district action programme can be listed under the three objectives set out above.

(A) *Health and welfare of mothers, pre-school and school children*

i. A non-means-tested scheme for free milk should now be introduced, beginning with couples with their first infant child and infant children in large families.

ii. Areas and districts should review the accessibility and facilities of all ante-natal and child health clinics in their areas and develop plans to increase utilization by mothers, particularly in the early months of pregnancy.

iii. Savings from the current decline in the school population should be used to finance new services for children under 5. A statutory obligation should be placed on local authorities to ensure adequate day care in their area for children under 5, and a minimum number of places (the number being raised after regular intervals) should be laid down centrally. Further steps should be taken to reorganize day nurseries and nursery schools so that both meet the needs of children for education *and* care.

iv. Every opportunity should be taken to link revitalized school health care with general practice, and intensify surveillance and follow-up both in areas of special need and for certain types of family.

Some necessary developments apply to other groups as well as children and mothers.

v. The professional associations as well as the Secretary of State and the health authorities should accept responsibility for making improvements in the quality and geographical coverage of general practice, especially in areas of high prevalence of ill-health and poor social conditions. Where the number or scope of work of general practitioners is inadequate in such areas we recommend health authorities to deploy or re-deploy an above-average number of community nurses, attached where possible to family practices. The distribution of general practitioners should be related not only to population but to medical need as indicated by SMRs, supplemented by other indicators, and the per capita basis of remuneration should be modified accordingly.

vi. An assessment which determines severity of disablement should be adopted as a guide to health service priorities, and this should be related to the limitation of activities rather than loss of faculty or type of handicap.

Although we attach priority to the implementation of this recommendation in the case of disabled children we believe that it must ultimately apply to all disabled people. We are aware that since 1977 most local councils have adopted classification of severity of disablement of people on their registers of the handicapped. We hope that this can be extended to people with all types of handicap and to patients in the health services.

(B) *The care of disabled people in their own homes*

i. A Working Group, to include representatives of voluntary organizations concerned with relevant client groups, should be set up to review: (a) whether sheltered housing should be a responsibility of social service or housing departments, and to make recommendations; and (b) the present functions and structure of hospital, residential and domiciliary care for the disabled elderly in relation to their needs, and to decide the best and most economical balance of future services.

ii. Joint funding should be developed and further funding of a more specific kind should be introduced, if necessary within the existing NHS budget, to encourage joint care programmes. A further sum should be reserved for payment to authorities putting forward joint programmes to give continuing care to disabled people – for example post-hospital follow-up schemes, pre-hospital support programmes for families, and support programmes for the severely incapacitated and terminally ill.

iii. Clear criteria for admission to, and continuing residence in, residential care should be agreed between the DHSS and the local authority associations, and steps taken to encourage rehabilitation and in particular to prevent homeless elderly people from being offered accommodation only in residential homes. Priority should be given to expansion of domiciliary care for those who are severely disabled in their own homes.

iv. The functions of home helps should be extended to permit a lot more work on behalf of disabled people; short courses of training, specialization of functions and the availability of mini-bus transport, especially to day centres, should be encouraged.

(C) *Prevention: the role of government*

i. An enlarged programme of *health education* should be sponsored by the government, and necessary arrangements made for optimal use of the mass media, especially television. Health education in schools should become the joint responsibility of LEAs and health authorities. However, we do not believe that an effective programme of preventive health can be a matter entirely for personal initiative and responsibilities. Commitment on the part of government is required, and has not so far been demonstrated, especially in so far as it involves (as it must) departments other than the DHSS. For example, there has been no major attempt at making more adequate provision for physical recreation in inner city area developments, as recommended by the Expenditure Committee in 1977. Additionally, the decline in recourse to vaccination and immunization (as in the case of polio) is worrying. Doctors and others in the NHS must be encouraged to convince members of the public of the importance of these preventive measures.

ii. *National health goals* should be established and stated by government after wide consultation and debate. Measures that might encourage the desirable changes in people's diet, exercise, and smoking and drinking behaviour should be agreed among relevant agencies.

Legislation, and fiscal and other financial measures, may be required and a wide range of social and economic policies involved. We see the time as now opportune for a major step forwards in the field of health and prevention.

iii. Stronger measures to *reduce cigarette smoking* must be adopted. Our recommendations here should be seen not only as a priority in themselves, but as illustrative of the determined action by government necessary in relation to all essential elements of a strategy for prevention. Measures should include those listed on pp. 162–3.

We have already recommended that steps be taken to increase utilization of ante-natal clinics, especially in the early months of pregnancy. Given early attendance there are practical programmes for screening for Down's syndrome and for neural tube defects in the foetus. In relation to adults screening for severe hypertension is practicable, and effective treatment is available.

iv. In the light of the present state of knowledge we recommend that ante-natal screening for neural tube defects (especially in high-risk areas) and Down's syndrome on the one hand, and in relation to adult disease for severe hypertension on the other, should be made generally available.

Additional funding for ten special areas

We recommend that the government should finance a special health and social development programme in a small number of selected areas, costing about £30m. in 1981–2. At least £2m. of this sum should be reserved for evaluation research and statistical and information units. The object would be both to provide special help to redress the undeniable disadvantages of people living in those areas, and also to permit special experiments to reduce ill-health and mortality, and provide better support for disabled people. Some possibilities have been illustrated particularly in connection with the development of more effective ante-natal services.

Chapter 9

The Wider Strategy

While the health care service can play a significant part in reducing inequalities in health, measures to reduce differences in material standards of living at work, in the home and in everyday social and community life are of even greater importance. We have in mind not simply a general reduction of inequalities in living standards, but a marked relative improvement in the living standards of the poorest people, together with measures to prevent new technologies, new working procedures, changes in styles of urban and rural living and the emergence of new social and political associations from undermining the existing living standards of some groups. Like the strategy we proposed for the health care system, the strategy to be adopted outside that system needs to be comprehensive and interlinked.

We therefore outline how a broad strategy might be made up and make certain specific proposals for inclusion in it. Specifically, we shall first indicate the general need for an anti-poverty strategy and then discuss and recommend selected measures, especially for families with children and disabled people.

A comprehensive anti-poverty strategy

Despite increases in GNP during the 1960s and 1970s successive governments have recognized the wide extent of poverty in the United Kingdom. In 1966 the report of a government survey of retirement pensioners estimated that up to 750,000 elderly people were living below national assistance standards – most of whom were eligible to draw national assistance and were not claiming it (Ministry of Pensions and National Insurance, 1966, p. 20). In 1967 a further report on a survey of families with children estimated that there were 160,000 families with half a million children who were living under the new supplementary benefit scale rates (Ministry of Social Security, 1967, p. iv). Further reports from the DHSS in the early 1970s tended to confirm the large numbers of people with incomes below the scale rates and yet who were in, or were dependants of people who were in, full-time employment.

(See for example, Howe, DHSS, 1971.) In Table 32 (p. 116) we showed, on the basis of DHSS estimates, that in 1977 over 14 million people (or 26.6 per cent of the population) had incomes of below or not more than 40 per cent above the supplementary benefit level (a cut-off chosen in recent government and independent studies). About a third were employed, or were dependants of people who were employed, and about two fifths were on retirement pensions. (Because of the under-representation of elderly, sick and disabled people, the use of a measure of 'normal' instead of 'current' income for people who have been sick or unemployed for less than three months, and the exclusion of those receiving supplementary benefit from the data, numbers with incomes below SB level are underestimated (Townsend, 1979, pp. 275–276 and 908–9).) At these levels of income there is evidence of multiple deprivation in diet, housing and environmental amenities, leisure activities and at work. Because of changes in earnings and numbers of dependants, the movement of people into and out of poverty is considerable, and while there is no hard evidence covering a long span of individual life it may be inferred, from survey or cross-sectional data, data about incomes currently and for the previous year, and New Earnings Survey data followed through for several years, that a very high proportion of manual workers experience poverty, or exceptionally low living standards, for a substantial part of the life-cycle.

There are differences of view about what in fact constitutes poverty. The main question is how far a definition acceptable to the government should depend on needs as assessed in contemporary society and how far on needs as measured by some historical bench-mark. Today's poor in Britain have more purchasing power than the poor of the depression years of the 1930s because of the growth of national prosperity. But they are living in a different kind of society, in which they have, and are held to have, different and often *additional* obligations as workers, parents, householders, friends and citizens. We therefore take the view that any historical standard of need becomes more and more unreal with the passage of time in a changing and especially growing economy even when it is repriced in accordance with rises in the cost of living. An effort has to be made every few years to redefine the standard itself in accordance with changing social conditions. As long ago as 1812 Adam Smith recognized the need for such redefinition, declaring that 'by necessities I understand, not only the commodities which are indispensably necessary for the support of life, but whatever the custom of the country renders it indecent for creditable people even of the lowest order to be without'. One of the last reports from the Supplementary Benefits Commission (*Annual Report for 1978*, 1979) expresses the point as follows: 'Poverty in urban industrial countries like Britain is a standard of living so low that it excludes and isolates people from the rest of the community. To keep out of poverty they must have an income which enables them to participate in the life of the community.'

We believe a comprehensive anti-poverty strategy must fall into two parts. The first is a fairer distribution of resources. Successive governments have supposed that they did not so much have to intervene in the initial production and determination of the structures of wealth and of gross incomes in the first place, as redistribute through taxation a slice of gross income to make up minimum subsistence incomes for the poor. But attempts to raise the relative living standards of the poor have been largely frustrated by growing opposition to progressive taxation as well as the diminution of its practical effects, and the steady growth relative to the employed population, of a dependent population. Different examples might be given of this growth. Between 1951 and 1976 the number of social security beneficiaries, excluding those receiving family allowances, grew from just over 7.5 million to 14.25 million, or by 88 per cent, while the total population increased from 51 million to 56 million, or by only 10 per cent. The government expects the number of social security beneficiaries to grow to over 15.5 million by 1982/3, even on an assumption of no growth in unemployment (*Social Trends*, 1979).

Governments have tried to meet this developing problem by lowering the tax threshold, so that people start paying tax on lower incomes, and shifting the balance from direct to indirect taxation. They have also tried to reduce the growing costs of categories already defined as dependent, as well as meeting the additional costs of new categories, by relying increasingly on the supplementary benefit and other means-tested schemes.

Even this solution, however, has now reached a dead end. In the 1980s either the living standards of the poor will not be maintained relative to the rest of the population as their numbers grow, or if living standards are maintained or efforts are made even to improve them, then radically new methods of financing them from the prosperous sections of the population will have to be devised.

We believe that a new approach to the fairer distribution of resources needs to be developed on the following basis. It starts with a recognition that the dispersion of resources *is* very unequal, and that the long-term objective of reducing by a moderate amount the proportionate share of, say, the top 30 per cent of income recipients would substantially augment the sum redistributed at present to the poor. If the share of disposable income of the top 30 per cent, as given in Report No. 5 (p. 75) of the Royal Commission on the Distribution of Income and Wealth, were only moderately reduced, the sum available for distribution in social security benefits, for example, could be doubled.

It follows that although it will be politically difficult, we shall need to develop greater restrictions on the amount of wealth which may be inherited and accumulated, together with more effective measures to inhibit the growth of top incomes and reduce present differentials in incomes. Quite how this might be done and how it might be democratically agreed and enforced is not something we can cope with here. But we believe it may be desirable to establish national minimum *and* maximum earnings (and family income) as indispensable elements of a nationally approved framework of incomes. Within statutory limits local and industrial or occupational wage-levels might be negotiated. Below we shall recommend certain measures to be included in such a strategy.

The second part of a comprehensive anti-poverty strategy is to encourage self-dependence and a high level of individual skill and autonomy as a basis for creating a more integrated society. We believe that this is possible only by raising the standards and broadening the content of education so that the need for advice or supervision from professionally trained personnel in medicine, nursing, law, housing, child care or administration is less marked and the capacity to undertake a range of skills is greater. This includes improving individual access to information about, and control over, what goes on in the immediate community as well as society generally, and conferring rights to employment and occupation and creating corresponding opportunities for such employment. There are of course possibilities of augmenting formal education and of introducing into the curriculum more studies of such subjects as health and nutrition, and (some believe) political education. Methods of enabling adults to have better access to knowledge, theoretical and practical, are equally important.

Most important, of course, is the right to fulfilling employment. Among a variety of possible measures there are two which deserve special mention. One is the energetic sponsorship of new industrial enterprise, based upon newly emerging technologies. In the face of a world recession in trade and severe foreign competition the nation cannot afford to be timid. The other measure is to expand employment within different branches of community service. Up to the present time the youth opportunities programme and similar schemes have done little more than provide some people who would otherwise count as unemployed with temporary, and ill-paid, employment. There are thousands of other men and women who have been unemployed for many months and whom it costs the state nearly as much to support as it would to employ in useful work.

Within this broad outline there are a number of specific measures which need to be picked out and given priority. In the rest of this chapter we shall develop certain priorities outside the health service which correspond with those picked out for the health care system.

A major concern must be families and children. Top priority must be given to measures which will enhance family living standards and reduce the high risk of children suffering those forms of deprivation and poverty which inhibit healthy development. In drawing this conclusion we are conscious in particular of two facts of the utmost importance:

i. There is evidence of substantial deprivation among young children (for example, Wilson and Herbert, 1978; Bone, 1977) and, after people of advanced age, they run the highest risk of all age groups of being in poverty (Townsend, 1979, p. 285);

ii. Those in middle and late middle life (mostly couples without dependants) have a standard of living, measured in relation to supplementary benefit scale rates, far higher than that of families in which there are young children (Townsend, 1979, Figure 7.1, p. 288). This difference between the young and the middle-aged appears to have grown more marked in recent years, partly because the rearing of children has been completed after the first twenty or twenty-five years of adult life by more married couples in each succeeding cohort, but partly because more married women have re-entered employment, non-manual occupations with strongly defined incremental pay scales have grown disproportionately, and more of the middle-aged have had access to cheap housing, through the completion of mortgage repayments or a relative fall in the real value of repayments, because of inflation. The implication for policy is therefore both that a need exists to direct more resources towards children and that checks might be placed on the tendencies for people in middle life without dependants to attract an undue share of additional national resources, so that adequate measures for young children might with less difficulty be financed. A complex programme covering financial well-being, education, nutrition and housing must be developed. In this chapter we have selected some principal measures to give effect to such a programme.

A policy for families and children

It is our view that *the abolition of child poverty should be adopted as a national goal for the 1980s*. We recognize that this requires a redistribution of financial resources far beyond anything achieved by past programmes, and is likely to be very costly. We recognize also that with the growth in national income it will become easier to find the resources for such an anti-poverty strategy.

The recommendations which we make below are presented as a modest *first step* which might now be taken towards such an objective.

1. Child benefit

The history of child benefit has proceeded through two stages and is now entering a third. The first was the campaign to establish family allowances, culminating in the Family Allowances Act 1945. History demonstrates the different motives of the participants in the campaign.

> Family allowances were supported in the early days as a means of reducing inequalities between rich and poor, and between men and women. To socialists and feminists these were worthy ends in themselves but were not regarded as legitimate ends for government social policy until the Second World War. Broader support from Liberals and Conservatives was forthcoming only when family allowances became linked with other problems: a declining birth rate, poverty and malnutrition among children, the maintenance of work incentives and the need to curb inflation. These problems were established concerns of government and thus, by association, the legitimacy of family allowances was enhanced. (Land, 1975, p. 227)

The government agreed to pay 25p (less than the 40p recommended by Beveridge) per week for every dependent child excluding the first.

The second was the re-kindling, in the mid 1960s, of a campaign to extend family allowances to the first child in the family and simultaneously increase the real value of all family allowances, partly in exchange for the phasing-out of child tax allowances. This stage culminated not so much in the Child Benefit Act of 1975 as the completion of its phasing-in during the two years from April 1977 up to the budget of 1979.

Yet throughout this entire period government support for family allowances was never more than luke-warm. (For the recent history see *The Great Child Benefit Robbery*, 1977; Land, 1978; Field, 1978.) Between 1946 and 1978 pensions and other major social security benefits were increased on seventeen occasions: family allowances were increased only six times. This poor record must have some bearing on the relatively large numbers of wage-earning families found in national surveys and by statistical comparison with other countries to be living in poverty or on its margins, and on such indicators as the failure of infant mortality rates to decline as rapidly as those in some other countries.

Over the last half-decade the position has not substantially altered. Improvements introduced in the last years of the 1970s have done little more than restore the levels of the late 1960s, and inflation continues to eat into these 'improved' rates.

The importance of a properly endowed child benefit programme to the future health of the children of this country cannot be exaggerated. In its report for 1973 the Supplementary Benefits Commission stated: 'The adequacy of family benefits in general, and the new child benefits in particular, seems to us to be the most urgent concern of the whole field of social security' (Cmnd 6615, p. 17). This was reiterated in the next report, and in its response to the review which preceded the reorganization in 1979–80 of supplementary benefits, the Commission went on to affirm: 'Further improvements in child benefit and help for the unemployed – particularly in the form of better opportunities for work – are the most urgent of our proposals' (*Response of the SBC*, 1979, p. 40). From our different remit we endorse those priorities. *We recommend as an immediate goal the raising of the level of child benefit to 5.5 per cent of average gross male industrial earnings – in November 1979 equivalent to the rate for a dependent child of a sick or unemployed person (£5.70 including child benefit)*. [The latter sum would have to be increased to about £7.00 by April 1981 to keep pace with earnings.] In the longer term, we recommend that larger child benefits be paid for older children, perhaps with age bands corresponding to those used by the SBC. Also in the longer term we should like to see age-related child benefit rates index-linked to average gross male industrial earnings, or, because an increasing number of women are entering employment and because in many cases both husband and wife have earnings, to some other perhaps more appropriate standard (such as average net disposable personal income). Otherwise it will be difficult to maintain the 'tax equity' as well as the 'need-serving' functions of child benefit. One-parent families present special problems, and in our view their financial needs too would be better met through an increase in child benefit.

2. Infant care allowance

A re-grouping of resources on behalf of young mothers with infants is required. In principle, needs at child-birth are met through the maternity benefit and maternity grant. But the grant has not been maintained during inflation and would need to be raised to *about £100* from the present £25.00, which has not been changed since 1969, to restore its value to that equivalent to the payment when first introduced. We recommend that *the grant should be increased to £100 to acknowledge the high cost to parents of child-birth*.

The special responsibilities of caring for young children, other than through the married man's tax allowance, are, however, not yet recognized in Britain. Some countries – Hungary is one example – have introduced infant care allowances in addition to child benefit. The case for the introduction of a home responsibility payment has been made in Britain:

The benefit would be paid to all families in which there were children or other dependants needing home care, except those where the social insurance benefit included a dependant's allowance for the wife. In the case of children such a benefit could presumably be paid simply by paying an addition to the child benefit payable for the eldest dependent child in the family, and it might be better presented in this way. The payment for the care of adult dependants would then be a separate benefit, a development of the present invalid care allowance. (Meade Report, p. 287. See also pp. 498–9)

The Child Poverty Action Group has proposed a more differentiated scheme, whereby women with children under 5 would receive twice as much as those with dependent children of school age (Select Committee on Tax Credit, Vol. II, pp. 325–30). The allowance could be phased in, beginning with all births after a particular date. *We recommend the introduction of an infant care allowance of approximately the same level as of child benefit, to be paid to mothers of children under 5 years of age, to be phased in over a period of five years.* As suggested later (p. 190), the cost might be met not so much from new resources as by restricting the scope of the married man's tax allowance to wives with dependants.

Beyond these initial elements of an anti-poverty strategy, a number of other steps need to be taken.

3. Pre-school education and day care

In Chapter 8 we recommended that local authorities should be under a statutory obligation to ensure an adequate provision of day care facilities (taking this term to include not only places in day nurseries but also in nursery classes, and with trained and registered childminders). To emphasize the importance we attach to this recommendation as well as its central place in any policy devoted to meeting the developmental needs of the under-5s, we further elaborate on it at this point.

It is well known that the desire for day provision on the part of parents of under-5s greatly exceeds what is currently available. A survey in 1977 found that 'provision was wanted for twice as many children as were receiving it, so that whilst 32 per cent of children were using facilities, they were desired for 64 per cent (Bone, 1977). The survey also found that this unmet need was class related (see Table 40) and that cost was a significant factor in inhibiting usage of such facilities by the children of working-class parents.

The same survey also looked at the demand for facilities judged on the basis of the number of 'disadvantaged' children who might benefit from them. The need criteria used, which more or less correspond to those leading to priority admission to day nursery, were as follows:

Need Group A	*Need Group B*
Child had only one parent	Child already allocated to need group A
or	or
Child had two parents but father's income was less than 150 per cent of long-term SB level	Child's mother was worried he might be handicapped (no definite diagnosis)
or	or
Child's household accommodation was two or more bedrooms less than standard	Child was 3 or 4 years old and soiled himself more than twice a week
or	or
Child's household accommodation was inadequate in four ways	Child's mother classified as 'depressed' or 'anxious'
or	or
Child was definitely handicapped (definite diagnosis)	Child had behaviour difficulties (on standard scaling)

On this basis, 15 per cent of all pre-school children fell into need group A and 36 per cent into need group B (which includes A). In fact only 28

Table 40: *Desire for day provisions for under-5s by occupational class**

	Occupational Class				
	I	*II*	*IIINM and IVNM*	*IIIM*	*IVM and V*
Day provisions used	40	40	32	29	24
Not used but desired	22	26	36	33	39
Day provisions not desired	37	33	31	36	33
Total percentage†	100	100	100	100	100

*This survey used a different social class breakdown including a 'semi-skilled non-manual' (IVNM) category.

† Includes a few instances of 'not known'.

Source: Bone, 1977, Table 3.2.

per cent of all children in need group A were making use of any facilities for day provision and 30 per cent in need group B. All these figures are, perhaps, rather crude and we were unable to make a more detailed calculation of the need for day provision, but clearly the unmet need is substantial. What has to be remembered is that although the poorest children experience multiple forms of deprivation a very large proportion of children can be said to experience one or more forms of it. It is difficult to distinguish between deprived and non-deprived children and there are degrees of gradation, but by any calculation the unmet need is very substantial indeed. On the most conservative of estimates, the difference between the 36 per cent of children whose health and cognitive and psychological development (or financial circumstances, with the risks that might ultimately be entailed) make their need for day care overwhelming, and the 27 per cent of all under-5s who currently receive some provision (9 per cent of some 3¼ million under-5s in England and Wales), amounts to a minimum need of some 300,000 places. (This of course is based on the impossible assumption that all current places are taken up by children in need.) If the criterion of parental *desire* for some day provision were to be adopted, then the number of places available would have to be doubled, according to Bone's survey. This implies the creation of some 900,000 extra places in England and Wales.

The health and developmental needs of children, especially children rendered at risk by their environments, lead us to emphasize the importance of day facilities for under-5s catering for *both* these needs, and provided on an adequate scale. The precise pattern of such provision will necessarily vary with local conditions. It is clear that all available resources in the community must be used to their utmost: childminders, voluntary organizations and parents. More efficient use of existing facilities, such as nursery schools and classes, is also required. We are eager to see local authorities sponsoring collaborative arrangements between parents and others in the local community to complement the extended statutory services for the under-5s. This represents the principle of prevention at the local level. To reiterate the recommendation we have already made in Chapter 8: *We recommend that a statutory obligation should be placed on local authorities to ensure adequate day care in their area for children under 5, and that a minimum number of places (the number being raised after regular intervals) should be laid down centrally.*

Before leaving this topic it should also be made clear that different forms of provision – day care, nursery classes, playgroups, childminders etc. – cater for different needs. Local authority day nursery places are largely restricted to children regarded by social workers as 'at risk', or living in poor housing, or where a single parent is anxious to go to work. Staffed by nursery nurses they are less specifically concerned with the child's cognitive development than are nursery schools or classes. Our own view of the close relationship between health, social well-being and cognitive development in children leads us to argue for much greater integration between these forms of provision. This is of course widely acknowledged (as in the joint DES/DHSS circular *Co-ordination of Provision for the Under-Fives* of January 1978). So too is the need for more flexible provision of nursery education which caters better for the needs of working mothers (CPRS, 1978). It must be borne in mind that not only is the proportion of under-5s with mothers in paid employment rising (25 per cent in 1976) but that empty school places (due to the decline in the population of school age) represent an inefficient use of resources.

4. Nutrition: School milk and meals

In Chapter 6 we drew attention to the importance of the nutrition of children for their development. The DHSS booklet *Eating for Health* stated:

> If all were to enjoy the best possible diet, the variation in average height and weight of different socio-economic groups in the United Kingdom would probably be less marked. The attained height of adults depends to some extent on nutrition during growth as children and in particular during the most rapid period of growth as babies. Any persistent restriction of diet in a young child may impair growth to such an extent that the affected child never reaches its full hereditary endowment of height. (DHSS, 1978, pp. 12–13)

This booklet goes on to point out the remarkable gains, notably in perinatal mortality, which followed wartime food rationing, despite the overall shortages of food, and the introduction of such welfare foods as cod-liver oil and welfare orange juice: 'The unequal distribution of food, which had restricted the diet of families with low incomes, was made equitable by this system which included food subsidies on and control of the price of meat, bread, sugar, milk, potatoes, butter, margarine, cheese' (p. 16). The wartime scarcities which led to these policies fortunately no longer exist. It nevertheless remains important to *ensure* that all children are adequately nourished, if all are to achieve their potential for healthy growth.

In 1967 the Committee on Medical Aspects of Food Policy commissioned a nutritional survey of pre-school children, which was carried out in 1967–8 and eventually published in 1975. The acknowledged under-representation of large families, poor families and immigrant families in this survey must to some degree reduce the confidence which can be placed in the assessment of the adequacy of nutrition among these 'at risk' groups. The study nevertheless showed a clear decline in vitamin intake (A, C, D) with rising family size, and declining occupational class and income. Protein consumption rose with income though there was no trend with family size or occupational class. Calcium intake showed no trend. Total energy consumption actually rose with increasing family size, declining social class and falling income (except among the poorest families) – but some of this trend was certainly due to extra consumption of 'added sugar' – sweets, biscuits, soft drinks etc. – in poorer, larger working-class families. (DHSS, *Reports on Health and Social Subjects*, No. 10, 1975.)

Although the report concluded that there is 'no evidence that our pre-school children were underfed', it was hard to reconcile this with some of the statistics revealing under-nutrition and deprivation among some poor minorities. The proportions of children found to have intakes below 80 per cent of the recommended levels of specific nutrients varied from 20 to 30 per cent in some cases of energy, total protein and iron and around half were below that level for vitamin C (p. 27). The survey also showed the importance of milk in the diet of children. Although this was age-related, even at the age of $3\frac{1}{2}$ to $4\frac{1}{2}$ milk continued to provide, on average, 16 per cent of total energy intake, 26 per cent total protein and 62 per cent calcium and 42 per cent riboflavin.

A study of a sample of about 1,000 children resident in Kent aged 8–11 and 13–15, carried out between September 1968 and March 1970, throws some light on the nutritional status of older children. The sample was weighted to include larger numbers of children from occupational classes IV and V, large families, and families lacking fathers, and included a dietary assessment over a one-week period. Important conclusions were that: there was no clinical evidence of nutritional deficiency, and significant differences in average daily nutrient intake were not associated with class, number of siblings, or whether or not the mother worked. However, the *quality* of the child's diet (expressed in nutrients per 1,000 kcals) was class-related, falling with declining occupational class (Cook, et al., 1973). The study also showed that differences in nutrient intake and quality of diet were not explained by income differences when other class-related factors were held constant (Jacoby et al., 1975).

Few today would therefore dissent from the view that given the importance of adequate nutrition for a child's development, and in the absence of a comprehensive food policy, attention quite properly focuses on school milk and meals. Between 1946 and 1968, one third of a pint of milk was available free every school day to all school children. From 1968 it ceased to be provided to secondary school pupils. In 1971 it was stopped for all children after the end of the school year of their seventh birthday, except where the school doctor recommended otherwise. Late in 1978 local authorities were once more permitted, though not obliged, to provide milk for 7–11-year-olds. In 1971, when the reduced availability of school milk was accompanied also by an increase in the price of school meals, the Committee on Medical Aspects of Food Policy (COMA) was asked to monitor the effects of these changes. Its Sub-Committee on Nutritional Surveillance issued an interim report in 1973 in which it indicated the dimensions on which effects would be monitored: height, obesity and dental caries were central.

So far as provision of milk to primary school children aged 7+ is concerned, the evidence, though not clear-cut, does not indicate a significant effect on growth. The earlier study of Kent children to which we referred above, conducted in 1968–70, found that, among 8–11-year-olds, those who regularly drank school milk had significantly higher intakes of energy, calcium and animal protein, but that this was not associated with height or other measures of nutritional status (Cook et al., 1975a). The same research group, conducting a national surveillance study of a longitudinal kind under COMA auspices, found that between 1972 and 1973 the *growth* of 6–7-year-olds was not influenced by availability of school milk. The same held true of a special sample of children from occupational classes IV and V (formed by aggregation of successive age cohorts) (Cook et al., in press). A study of 7–8-year-olds in South Wales, employing a sample deliberately weighted in favour of large families and occupational classes IV and V, also found that growth over twenty-one months was unaffected by provision of school milk (Baker et al., 1978). Cook et al. summarize by stating 'the availability of school milk has no real effect on group well-being where drinking milk at home is almost universal'. It has however been suggested that linear growth may not be a wholly adequate measure of the benefits of milk consumption. Reed, for example, has referred to the need also to take account of bone status (Reed, 1978).

Moreover, current policy towards provision of school milk has to be judged, and developed, in the light of the continuing fall in household consumption of liquid milk revealed by the National Food Survey. In 1977 this average household consumption was 4.54 pints per person per week, compared with 4.71 pints in 1976 and 4.76 pints in 1975 (*National Food Survey*, 1977, p. 7). Moreover, the survey shows that in 1977 of 7–9-year-olds in lower-income families with three or more children, 12 per cent consumed less than 2 pints per week in the home, and over 25 per cent less than 3 pints.

It is clear that current policy must therefore be kept continuously under review, in the light of these trends, and also in the light of further research on growth and development.

The evidence in relation to provision of schools meals is more clear-cut. School meals are intended to provide about one third of the daily allowance of nutrients and energy for a child, and are recommended to contain, on average, 29g total protein, 880 kcals energy, and 32g fat. We have no evidence on the range in nutritional quality of the meals in practice provided. We have no doubt that this meal is the principal source of essential nutrients for many low-income children. Many may be offered a poor-quality evening meal, and many come to school without breakfast. (This sixteen hour 'fast' may well affect the child's powers of concentration, and hence his ability to profit from his schooling.) It should be regarded as a matter of importance – on education *and* health grounds – to ensure that all children receive a school meal or an adequate substitute at least during term time. To leave school children, especially young school children, to make their own free choices of what food is to be purchased would be wrong. Children will frequently prefer to consume foods high only in sugar and other sources of energy. As an inadequate substitute for a nutritious meal, this is likely to lead to increases in obesity and in dental caries.

Certainly, great importance has been attached to the nutritional variety and adequacy of school meals by a number of official committees. For example, the Working Party on the Nutritional Aspects of School Meals has commented: 'We do not think it is safe to assume that all children necessarily receive a satisfactory diet at home. We are especially concerned that all children should receive enough protein at school since any shortfall in the midday meal might easily not be made up in other meals or snacks and drinks consumed outside school' (DES, 1975, p. 8).

The survey of Kent children aged 8–11 and 13–15 offers some support to these views (Cook et al., 1975b). Consumption of school meals (about 80 per cent overall) proved to be higher among children without fathers, with working mothers, etc. Distinguishing children who had all five, or no, school meals in the test week, the study found that younger children who had school meals had higher lunchtime intakes of nearly all nutrients (and more nutrients per 1,000 kcals) than those who did not. It also found that children from classes IV and V taking school meals obtained a very much higher proportion of their total weekday nutrient intake from their lunches than did children from the same classes who did not. The same was not consistently true of class I/II children.

Taking these findings together with known biases in the information, it is possible to conclude, with the authors, that

families without a father, those in lower social classes, and with large numbers of children relied to a greater extent than others on the intake of nutrients important for growth from school meals. This reliance may or may not depend on a conscious decision. The present study took place before recent large increases in the cost of protein-rich foods and such families may now rely even more on the food intake from school meals.

Yet the percentage of pupils receiving school meals (whether free or paid for) is falling: from 70 per cent in 1975 to 62 per cent in 1977. There are a number of explanations for this, partly cost, partly poor quality and partly administrative inertia.

At present local authorities administer a government scheme making school meals free for children of parents receiving supplementary benefit or parents whose income is below certain limits laid down in national regulations. In May 1978 about 15 per cent of school children were getting it. The limits are revised regularly, normally when supplementary benefit scales are increased. In recent years the Department of Education has estimated that about three quarters or four fifths of children eligible to receive school meals free are in fact receiving them. Others consider the right figure may be no higher than 60 per cent. Part of the problem arises in fluctuating incomes and frequent assessments or reassessments, but also in the fluctuation in standards of living brought about by changing household dependencies. Experimental campaigns by the government, especially in 1967 and 1968, have shown that take-up can be increased substantially through letters addressed directly to parents and through advertisements. But because of the numbers of children passing through the schools and fluctuations in family living standards, quite apart from the effect of inflation, higher take-up rates do not endure. Twice in 1977 and again in 1978 the Secretary of State for Education was asked to renew the approach adopted in 1967 and 1968 and issue a simple letter to all parents advising them about free school meals. Although an estimated half a million children were not obtaining free dinners although entitled to them, this invitation was not accepted. Whatever the exact short-fall, there is no doubt that it is substantial and there have been a large number of research studies demonstrating that means-tested exemption from charges for school meals is not a satisfactory way of helping poor families. Field, 1975; Field and Townsend, 1975; Townsend, 1979.) A recent study has shown that there are even wide variations among areas with similar characteristics. 'This type of analysis can help to identify areas where there may be low take-up to inadequate efforts by local authorities and central Government' (Bradshaw and Weale, November 1978, p. 22).

In our view any reduction in the provision of school meals, or in eligibility for free meals, would mean putting further at risk the development of significant numbers of children. A study carried out by a team from St

Thomas's hospital showed that children receiving free school meals are significantly shorter than those who do not. Though the study was not designed to assess the value of school meals in terms of growth, the indicators are 'that free school meals are going to the right group of children and that withdrawal might well prejudice their future development' (Rona et al., 1979).

Moreover from the perspective of this report it is clear to us that expansion in such provision, elimination of inequalities in provision, and elimination of the barrier to take-up which means-testing represents, are essential aspects of a policy designed to break the continuing association between social class and health in its broad sense. We are aware that much of what we have said about school meals is very different from current government policy and much orthodox opinion in the teaching profession. Nevertheless, in our view the evidence strongly supports a change of direction.

We believe that the number of schools with facilities for providing meals for all or most of their pupils can be increased, and that more consultation with parents about the organization and administration of meals would be an important element in raising quality. Children from families living in poverty sometimes attend schools lacking facilities for meals, and although others go home at mid-day for meals because their parents believe they can provide a more nutritious meal for them, there is no doubt that some would get meals at school if they were an automatic right.

At the same time the attitude of a school does seem to influence the consumption of school meals and the eating habits of children generally. It is therefore important that teachers should understand the importance of adequate nutrition for a child's physical development and concentration in school. Moreover meals are also a social occasion when some of the intentions of an education can be consolidated. School staff are apt to underestimate the value of social relationships that can be developed.

We accordingly recommend:

i. *That the provision of nutritionally adequate meals at all schools should be required of local authorities and that the service should be extended in areas where there is under-provision;*

ii. *That there should be regular consultations between local authority representatives, community dietitians, and parents and teachers from each school in turn, over the provision and quality of school meals;*

iii. *That meals be provided in schools without charge.*

5. *Accidents to children*

In Chapter 2 we drew attention to the fact that the steepest gradients in childhood mortality are found with accidents, a fact all the more disturbing now that accidents account for one third of deaths of children. Moreover there has been little improvement in this class differential over the period 1959–63 to 1970–72. It is remarkable, given these facts and given that there is a known course of action which could be put into effect rapidly without great cost to the public, that so little has been done.

Although accidents in the home are not the largest single group of accidents to children it is probably in the home that major progress could be made most quickly. Regulations could be introduced immediately to produce a safer home environment, and these could be applied stringently to public housing. Risks of falls from roofs and staircases can be reduced without great cost by safer design, and the positioning of windows could make a substantial difference. Much could also be done to reduce the dangers from household equipment, especially the dangers from fire and burning. There is still a great deal which can be done to reduce the risks of poisoning by the clearer packaging of dangerous substances. Although important work has been done by RoSPA and the Health Education Council in educating the public, it is likely that 'safety devices built in as a constant feature of the environment are more effective than attempts to alter people's behaviour'.

The problem, as elsewhere in preventive health, is that there is no focus for government action, and although the new voluntary Joint Committee on Accident Prevention may help, a clear initiative is needed from a powerful Minister if adequate co-operation is to be forthcoming from the Department of Environment, the Department of Trade and the local authorities.

Outside the home, traffic accidents are the single most serious factor. Despite the laudable attempts of town planners to separate traffic from pedestrian ways there are still over 700 children killed on the roads each year. Although it is important to give due recognition to the accident prevention campaign in schools and elsewhere, the only reliable long-term answer is to give children safe areas in which to play. Moreover, if there is a need to step up safety education it is the motorists, especially young drivers, who should be the target. Motorists need to be made more sensitive to the presence of children in the areas they drive through, and conscious of the way in which children behave on the roads.

Apart from the specific dangers of road traffic it is likely that the working-class child lives in a more dangerous physical environment than middle-class children. Derelict slum housing about to be cleared, deserted canals, mineshafts and factories, railway lines, rubbish tips; all these present potential dangers to the child in the urban-industrial area. Given the ingenuity and sense of adventure of children it is difficult to conceive of such areas ever being made danger-free, but more could be done by environmental health authorities to monitor the risks and keep the owners of such properties up to the required standards of safety protection.

When accidents happen there is no lack of concern for the child to see he gets the best treatment possible, but unfortunately public attitudes soon return to their normal complacency. If childhood accidents are to be reduced and the gradients between social classes minimized, the issues must be kept before the public gaze. The voluntary organizations both local and national have the important role here in stimulating the political will for action.

We recommend that the Health Education Council should be provided with sufficient funds to mount child accident prevention programmes in conjunction with the Royal Society for the Prevention of Accidents. These programmes should be particularly directed at local authority planners, engineers and architects.

6. Paying for the programme

The annual cost of our proposals might be roughly as follows:

1. increase in child benefit from £4 to £5.70 for each child £970 m.

2. infant care allowance (on assumption that there are 600,000 births per annum) £180 m. in first full year (rising to £870 m. after five years)

3. expansion of day provision £150 m.

4. free school meals £200 m.

We do not regard it as our function, nor are we technically equipped, to make specific recommendations as to how the costs of our proposals might best be met. We would suggest, however, that the additional tax allowance now made to married couples without dependants be considered as a source of savings to be set against the proposals we have made for increasing the well-being of families and children.

The wider community

1. A comprehensive disability allowance

Evidence suggests that disabled people are more likely than their able-bodied contemporaries to be living below or on the poverty line (Table 41). There are also indications that among disabled people income is inversely related to severity of disability. (Townsend, 1979, Chapter 20; Harris et al., Vol. III, 1972.)

As a result of such findings, a strong case developed in the late 1960s and early 1970s for the introduction of a comprehensive allowance scheme for all disabled people. It was felt that equally disabled people were very unequally treated under different income security schemes. While there were fairly elaborate provisions for the war-disabled and those disabled in industry, those who were injured in home accidents, people who were congenitally handicapped, disabled housewives and disabled elderly people had little or no entitlement to additional income. But in 1974, while adopting different positive proposals for improvement of income benefit, both major political parties failed to commit themselves in principle to the phased introduction of a comprehensive scheme. Today major anomalies still exist and have been documented at length (Royal Commission on the Distribution of Income and Wealth, Report No. 6 (1978), Chapter 4, pp. 115–19, 152). The Snowdon Working Party stated (1976): 'The evidence clearly demonstrates the need for the fundamental methodical reforms advocated (by DIG and the Disability Alliance) to rectify the anomalous structure of disablement benefits whereby two people with equal handicaps and needs may end up with widely differing financial help to meet them' (p. 9).

After allowing for savings because of existing schemes, the introduction of a disablement allowance by stages has been costed at a little under £500 m. (Disability Alliance, 1978). Included in this estimate of costs are disabled elderly people. We believe that the establishment of such an allowance represents a major means of reducing inequalities of health and restoring equity between disabled and non-disabled people and we recommend accordingly that *a comprehensive disablement allowance for people of all ages should be introduced by stages at the earliest possible date*. There are of course other supporting measures, especially in improving the employment and wage rates of disabled people, which are important. We believe that the first step must be to establish equity for the most severely disabled people of all. At the present time there is a choice between introducing an allowance at a low rate, say £6, for all severely disabled children and adults in sup-

Table 41: *Numbers and percentage of total and disabled population living in poverty or on the margins of poverty (1977)*

Level of income	Total population		All ages (000s)	Disabled over pensionable age (000s)	Sick and disabled under pensionable age (000s)	Disabled of all ages (000s)
	Over pensionable age (000s)	Under pensionable age (000s)				
Below supplementary benefit level	760	1,270	2,020	250	70	320
Receiving supplementary benefit	2,000	2,160	4,160	790	240	1,030
At or up to 40 per cent above supplementary benefit level	3,010	4,830	7,840	860	400	1,260
More than 40 per cent above supplementary benefit level	2,750	35,960	38,720	690	1,380	2,070
Total	8,520	44,220	52,740	2,590	2,090	4,680
Below supplementary benefit level	8.9	2.9	3.8	9.7	3.3	6.8
Receiving supplementary benefit	23.5	4.9	7.9	30.5	11.5	22.0
At or up to 40 per cent above supplementary benefit level	35.3	10.9	14.9	33.2	19.1	26.9
More than 40 per cent above supplementary benefit level	32.3	81.3	73.4	26.6	66.0	44.2
Total	100	100	100	100	100	100

Note: The estimate of sick and disabled persons under pension age applies to those sick or disabled for three months or more and includes dependants in the income unit.

Source: DHSS (SR3), Analysis of FES 1977 for columns 1, 2, 3 and 5. The distribution of column 4 is based on evidence about those of pensionable age 'appreciably or severely incapacitated' in Townsend, 1979, p. 712 (and survey printout).

plementation of other income benefits and developing a scheme parallel to the main features of the war pensions and industrial injuries disablement pension schemes (into which the mobility allowance might be merged), introducing first a 100 per cent rate of payment (equivalent to the rate of £38 per week payable from November 1979 under the war and industrial injury disablement pension schemes). Even if the aggregate national sum available under either option were the same we believe the latter would be the right option. The net cost of establishing an allowance for 100 per cent disablement (the first stage) for people of all ages and causes of disablement would be approximately £24 m. at November 1979. (At November 1978 the cost was estimated by the Disability Alliance at £20 m.)

2. Improving working conditions

In our studies of inequalities in health we have been struck by the ill-developed nature of conceptions of deprivation at work. Although the hazards of working in particular industries have been carefully documented in the past, and detailed studies made of hours of work and conditions in which strikes and other conflicts between management and labour have occurred, generalizations of working conditions or work situations across industries have not been pursued very far. The point can be made by analogy. Generalization about diets, clothing, leisure-time pursuits, housing conditions and even environmental conditions are readily made, and standards of overcrowding, facilities and amenities are defined nationally for housing and are commonly understood and discussed. As a consequence, discussion about remedial measures is based upon statistics about the members who live in overcrowded or slum housing and lack particular amenities. Such standards do not exist for the world of work. There are no measures of the number in employment who have bad or deprived conditions of work, the industries or areas in which they are to be found and the degree to which they also experience bad housing conditions and low incomes.

So far as health is concerned the emphasis has been on safety and specific identifiable risks of accident or of contamination by toxic substances. For example, the Robens Committee, set up by the government in 1972 to look at health and safety at work, did not attempt to collect evidence about safety and health in relation to general working conditions. Neither did it attempt to pursue the interrelationship between fatal accidents, deaths and injuries arising from prescribed industrial diseases and occupational mortality and morbidity, for each of which independent sets of statistics exist. The importance of reports on occupational mortality to a better understanding of the work situation as well as to the circumstances outside work remains to be plumbed.

In Table 42 the wide differences between some occupations are illustrated. The marked gradient from sedentary non-manual to heavy unskilled manual work, which with some exceptions the table shows, is accompanied by wide variations between the mortality rates for specific occupations within each occupational class.

Table 42: *Mortality by occupation unit: men aged 15–64 (selected examples)*

Occupations units	Direct age-standardized death rate (per 100,000)	S M R
Relatively low death rate		
University teachers	287	49
Physiotherapists	297	55
Paper products' makers	302	50
Managers in building and contracting	319	54
Local authority senior officers	342	57
Company secretaries and registrars	362	60
Ministers of the Crown, M Ps, senior government officials	371	61
Office managers	377	64
Primary and secondary school teachers	396	66
Sales managers	421	70
Architects, town planners	443	74
Civil service executive officers	467	78
Postmen	484	81
Medical practitioners	494	81
Relatively high death rate		
Coalminers (underground)	822	141
Leather products' makers	895	147
Shoemakers and shoe repairers	898	156
Machine-tool operators	934	156
Watch repairers	946	154
Coalminers (above ground)	972	160
Steel erectors, riggers	992	164
Fishermen	1028	171
Deck, engineering officers and pilots, ship	1040	175
Labourers and unskilled workers, all industries	1247	201
Policemen	1270	109
Deck and engine-room ratings	1385	233
Bricklayers' labourers	1644	274

Specific and well-known work hazards, characteristic of many manual occupations and differing from one to another, are one factor. But in the light of the analysis of this report, we consider that in addition to these hazards, and associated risks of accidents and of certain occupational injuries and diseases, a wider variety of job characteristics may be implicated. These would include security and material rewards of employment, patterns of work (such as shift-work), conditions of work and welfare and other amenities. However, the *extent* to which work conditions, interpreted in this broad fashion, are responsible for differences in rates of occupational mortality remains uncertain and requires further research (although the work of Fox and Adelstein, 1978, suggests that other and more general elements of the 'class' factor may also be important).

Nevertheless, reduction in inequalities between occupations in their work conditions may be of importance in reducing inequalities in health. *We recommend that representatives of the DHSS, the Department of Employment, the Health and Safety Commission, together with representatives of the trade unions and CBI, should draw up minimally acceptable and desirable standards of work; security; conditions and amenities; pay; and welfare or fringe benefits.*

A national study found that in 1968, 20 per cent of the employed population, representing over 4½ million people, had poor conditions of work (Townsend, 1979, p. 453) and a list of individual examples from a random sample called attention 'both to the diverse hazards and frequent poor conditions of manual work'. They also suggested uncertainty or ignorance on the part of many about the hazards involved with dust, noise and chemicals. Doctors, for whatever motives, as well as employers, may withhold information, and the importance of the role of union safety representatives (the legal right to which workers have enjoyed since October 1978) is clear. There is still a tendency to accept poor working conditions as an inevitable accompaniment of particular jobs, and attention needs to be devoted to the question of enlightened standards which *can* be introduced, as in public housing and town planning. Among the matters which we hope will attract more attention are facilities for meals, warmth and shelter from bad weather, a dry and secure place for outer clothes and other belongings, access to a telephone, availability of first aid and first aid equipment, 'unsocial' hours, warmth, humidity, light, noise, availability of machinery to avoid or reduce the physical stress of the work, washing and toilet facilities, and facilities for changing clothes. In many of these instances regulations under current legislation are non-existent, or partial, or complex and confused (TUC, 1978).

What we are calling for is more preventive work by government departments, employers and unions and would hope to see a shift of emphasis in the work and functions (as defined by legislation) of the Health and Safety Commission and Executive, and the Employment Medical Advisory Service. It is fair to say that although there are provisions for both bodies to follow positive policies they are at present restricting their activities to specific hazards and general questions of safety. The need for legislation defining acceptable working conditions and basic employer welfare benefits is urgent.

3. Housing

Housing conditions are associated with health status in a variety of ways. Inadequate heating (or a form of heating which is too expensive for a resident) can give rise to hypothermia in old people (Wicks, 1978). Overcrowding can produce respiratory and other diseases (some of the studies are reviewed by Benjamin, 1965, who, however, pointed out that class explained more of the inter-area variance than housing). It can also produce adverse psychological responses and may give rise to mental illness.

High-rise living is known to have deleterious consequences for children. In some areas (such as Tower Hamlets) TB is common among the homeless vagrants and represents a real problem for the health authorities.

It is families with children, and especially large poor families with many children, who are most likely to be living in overcrowded conditions. Overcrowding adds to the health risk under which working-class children labour, and the extent to which such children, and especially those born into larger families, are being brought up in overcrowded conditions is unacceptable. Bone's survey of pre-school children found that 10 per cent of them inhabited dwellings inadequate on at least one of four criteria: overcrowding; no separate unshared bathroom; shared WC; no sole use of permanent fixed water supply (Bone, 1977, p. 26). But this percentage was highly class-related: 3 per cent in class I increasing to 29 per cent in classes IVM and V. For some of these children there is a risk of ill-health throughout, because chronic respiratory disorder (for example) in childhood is an all too effective predictor of adult suffering. Such considerations tend not to weigh as heavily with housing departments as they should.

We showed in Chapter 2 (on the basis of the new OPCS longitudinal study) that there is an association between tenure and SMR, independent of the occupational class of the household head. Of course, this does not demonstrate that being a tenant *causes* ill-health. But we wish to stress that the rights and privileges which are so unequally associated with housing tenures *are* associated with health both in the negative sense of freedom from ascertainable clinical disease and in the positive sense of welfare. Fear of eviction is the sort of situation which has been related to clinical depression in women (Brown and Harris, 1978). Security in housing does have health benefits and should be equally available for all. Accessible play areas for young children are vital and owner-occupation often meets this need, by virtue of garden space available. Gardening is one of the most popular outdoor leisure pursuits for people in Britain who have access to a garden, and we have already indicated the health benefits attaching to active outdoor recreation. We believe that there must be a much greater extension of the rights and privileges associated with owner-occupation to the tenants both of local authorities and private landlords. Health considerations are certainly among the factors which justify such extension.

In order to allow good housing policy to play its part in promoting health we consider the *most essential step is to co-ordinate policies in the council and owner-occupied sectors*. The changing pattern of housing tenure has been leading to problems of access to housing for the poor and mobile, which have gradually become more acute in recent years. Only in part has that been due to the decline of the privately tenanted sector. In part it has been due to rigidities in the management of council housing, together with a very uneven flow of new housing. There needs to be a more vigorous programme of rehabilitating rented housing which is obsolescent. This includes many thousands of council housing units. Comparisons need to be made between the tenures so that priorities in improvement policies and the allocation of resources, but also new standards of space, amenities and access to play areas, including gardens, can be determined. *We therefore recommend a substantial increase in local authority improvement spending under the 1974 Housing Act.*

But broad equity between the sectors must be achieved in other ways as well. The previous administration tended over-optimistically to reiterate the view that there was no longer any overall shortage of housing, while allowing local authorities to refuse housing to such groups as homeless single and childless couples. Secondly, the rights and opportunities of tenants need to be reviewed in the light of conditions enjoyed by owner-occupiers. The previous administration experimented with a 'Tenants Charter', but in some respects this was half-hearted, and among the most important measures to be introduced are freedom of movement, freedom to carry out minor improvements and repairs (and benefit from them in the terms under which the tenancy may be passed on subsequently), greater freedom in the rules of residence and more effective representation in the management of housing estates.

A number of housing charities believe that local authorities have been interpreting their obligations under the 1977 Housing Act rather too loosely. Some councils are exploiting the loop-hole of 'intentional' homelessness while others have taken advantage of the fact that the Act does not impose any standard for homeless accommodation. Moreover the Act allows local authorities to refuse accommodation to single homeless and childless couples.

We believe the legislation on homelessness deserves strengthening along the lines recommended by the housing charities. With the dwindling of the private rented sector, local authorities must provide rented accommodation for a wider range of households, including the single and childless, who are unable to enter owner-occupation. *We recommend, therefore, that local councils should increasingly be encouraged to widen their responsibilities to provide for all types of housing need which arise in their localities.*

We also believe that the sale of council houses badly needs to be placed in the changing context of the relationship between the different housing sectors. If, in the long run, a better balance could be struck in the conditions enjoyed in the two sectors, objections in principle to interchange of stock could be minimized. But indiscriminate sales may worsen housing opportunities for families needing to rent; they may reduce the quality and attractiveness of the council housing stock; and, by introducing a new basis to the relationships in many estates, they may affect the cohesion of existing communities.

Finally, a further aspect of the relationship of housing to health concerns the housing of the disabled. If the institutionalization of disabled people is to be avoided, as we have recommended, there must be sufficient provision of sheltered and adapted housing. This implies a much better working relationship than is frequently the case today between social service and health authorities and housing departments, so that necessary adaptations to dwellings can be obtained easily. We have elsewhere recommended that serious consideration should be given to the possibility that social service departments assume responsibility for the management of sheltered housing. A second aspect of such collaboration concerns policy over the re-housing of disabled people, which seems generally to be inadequate. The Working Party on Housing of the Central Council for the Disabled wrote in its (1976) report, of local authority policy:

... unless the disabled person *also* happens to be living in overcrowded accommodation with few amenities, his position on the waiting list is likely to be low indeed, even if he has the maximum medical points possible ... But the housing difficulties that are peculiarly associated with disability ... require a separate type of solution ... the priority given to disabled people should not be decided at an individual level – as tends to happen at present – but should be decided within an overall strategy of priorities within the housing policies of the authority as a whole.

... [T]he existing system means that a disabled person may not be rehoused until the situation has reached a desperate pitch. By that time the move may really be too late: his physical condition may have deteriorated too rapidly – possibly aggravated by his inadequate housing – so that he is not in a position to settle into a new environment ... Where a disabled child is concerned, to move the family to suitable housing when the child is grown and the situation has reached breaking point may work against the educational development of the child and his ability to learn to cope independently ... (Working Party on Housing of the Central Council for the Disabled, *Towards a Housing Policy for Disabled People*, 1976, pp. 58–60)

We therefore recommend that special funding on the lines of joint funding for health and local authorities should be developed by the government to encourage better planning and management of housing, including adaptations and provisions of necessary facilities and services for disabled people of all ages by social service and housing departments. This recommendation is on the same lines as that made by the Snowdon Working Party, which argued that one immediate priority was 'to develop a real choice of life-style for the severely disabled through joint planning and financing by the Department of Environment and the Department of Health and Social Security'. We also endorse that Working Party's plea for the 'urgent establishment of schemes for non-institutional accommodation for severely disabled people living in every area of the country' (Report of the Snowdon Working Party, 1976, p. 32).

Towards a co-ordinated government policy

We believe that an improvement in the nation's health should be a priority for government. The evidence of various indicators of mortality shows that in this respect Britain's record in recent years has not compared well with other countries. We should like to see drastic reduction in rates not only of perinatal and infant death, but of the extent of chronic and acute sickness and of physical and mental handicap, much of which develops in the period around birth, as well as promotion of health in its positive sense of 'well-being' and functional capacities.

The costs of sickness – the direct costs of the National Health Service, of supporting care, and of sickness benefits, as well as the indirect costs of sickness for productivity – though not easily calculated *in toto*, are very great. Acute care provided in hospitals demands an increasing share of national resources. The financial costs of bouts of ill-health, chronic sickness and handicap to individuals and families – especially poor families – are frequently immense. These private costs are not fully captured in financial terms. The alarming prevalence of depressive illness, especially among working-class women, cannot be without profound effect on family life and child-rearing, irrespective of the misery the women themselves suffer.

It is also our view that the attempt to reduce, and ultimately eliminate, the social inequalities in health which we have documented offers the greatest opportunity for achieving this overall improvement. It is surely no accident that, as we showed in Chapter 5, those countries such as Sweden and Norway which have particularly low mortality rates also seem to have greatly reduced inequalities in health. This argument is quite separate from the argument – to which we also attach great weight – that simple justice demands that this attempt be made.

Part of what is required involves attention to those regions and small areas, for example in the inner cities, where concentrations of sickness are high and levels of service provision low. Another part involves attention to improvements that can be made and new measures that can be introduced for families in all areas of the country. A third part involves attention to the vicious cycle by which, through a variety of mechanisms, poor families are locked into material, educational, environmental and social disadvantage for a lifetime and even sometimes for generations, with all that this implies for their health.

Our analysis has shown that inequalities in health have complex, multi-causal explanations. They seem to be rooted in the general nature and conditions of activity, both in work and outside work, and in the styles and standards of living of different occupational classes. Some factors have a clear causal association with ill-health: inadequate access to and use of (particularly preventive) health services; the hazards attaching to certain occupations; overcrowded and damp housing, and smoking. But there remains much that is probably not explicable in any direct fashion and meanwhile must be attributed to the pervasive effects of the class structure.

It follows, and our recommendations reflect this fact, that a reduction in health inequalities depends upon contributions from within many policy areas. Our recommendations have involved reference to community and preventive health services, to the personal social services, to health education in a very broad sense including the promotion of physical recreation, to social security measures, to uptake of school meals, to improvement in working conditions, to housing and to measures directed specifically at minority groups and notably in inner city areas. Clearly such a range of services and policies involves many departments of central government: DHSS, DOE, DES, DE (and the Health and Safety Executive), MAFF, the Department of Transport and the Home Office, as well as the Welsh

Office and the Scottish and Northern Ireland Offices. Our objectives will be achieved *only* if each department makes its appropriate contribution and this in turn, we believe, requires a better degree of co-ordination than presently exists. The fact is of course that housing, leisure, education and other relevant policies have important objectives traditionally associated with them: there is always the danger that this potential contribution to the reduction of health inequalities will receive little attention in departmental decision-making.

Machinery of government

For this reason, *we propose recourse to Cabinet Office machinery*, in order to ensure that this does not happen. A broadly based programme of work needs to be explicitly adopted, and seen to be adopted. Our analysis is very much within the spirit of the Joint Approach to Social Policy (JASP), and we envisage that a Ministerial and, secondly, an Officials Committee, corresponding to those established under JASP, would provide appropriate fora: we would certainly wish the Central Policy Review Staff to be involved. It would then be for these committees regularly to consider developments and to propose developments in relevant policies from the perspective of health inequalities. Major initiatory responsibility would be vested in the Department of Health and Social Security, and we envisage the two committees being chaired respectively by a Minister and by a senior DHSS official having major responsibilities for health and prevention. They should have before them relevant statistical material, provided by government statisticians, and relating to changes in uptake and provision of services, changes in relevant distributional aspects, and evaluation of policies. New methods of transmitting the information reviewed would have to be adopted, not least because it would need to reach a wider, public audience.

There would have to be local counterparts of national co-ordinating machinery, and a joint approach to health policies would be necessary at local level to a greater extent than at present. This might take a number of forms – inter-departmental action, for example, to reduce environmental pollution and squalor and redistribute skilled manpower to communities where the risk to health was high, acceleration of joint funding schemes, and the establishment of joint committees for planning and for the monitoring and supervision of hazards to health.

The need for a joint framework for social policies has been increasingly acknowledged in recent years. Of course, a co-ordinated approach could achieve a variety of objectives. One would be simply to warn central departments earlier than at present of forthcoming plans of individual departments.

Another would be to work out more smoothly than at present the over-lapping functions of two or more departments (a good example is nursery education and day nurseries – in the interests of child health). But others would include large-scale reallocation of priorities, for example a decision to reduce the rate of expansion in expenditure of one major social service, such as education, and greatly increase the rate of expansion of another, such as health. For this, however, support independent of central administration may be required, as we argue below. We appreciate that there are a wide range of possibilities, and that a joint approach could mean a great deal or very little. But considering that the government accepted, in the early 1960s, the need for plans for hospitals and for community care and that since then there have been a stream of plans of wider and lesser scope, developments in the actual co-ordination of social policies, as distinct from the reorganization of individual services, has been slow. (The progress since the JASP initiative has been traced by Plowden, 1977.) No doubt this is attributable to the precedence currently given not only by the government but by other bodies to economic over social objectives in policy, to a failure to appreciate the interrelatedness of policies, but above all to the stultifying effects of public expenditure control which has dominated all attempts of planning during the mid- and late-1970s. In the last fifteen years social planning has been, for the central government, predominantly one of control of public expenditure (Diamond, 1975; Glennerster, 1976; Heclo and Wildavsky, 1976). It would be wrong to suppose that this form of control could be changed overnight, because it has penetrated administrative practice at every level, or that there will not be financial and institutional constraints on more imaginative social planning. But the formulation of new social objectives by the government can only be sustained if certain changes are also made in the mechanisms of planning and administration.

A Health Development Council

Finally, and distinct from this machinery, although with the same objective in mind, we *propose the establishment of a Health Development Council*. This would be an independent body, with a small staff of seconded civil servants. Strictly its functions would be advisory, but the Council would, we recommend, play a key role in social planning. It would be invited to consider and spell out longer-term strategies to reduce inequalities of health and improve general family living standards, evaluate progress in relation to this aim, with particular reference to the roles of particular government and local authority departments and services, marshal a range of outside expertise, consult the public at every stage and play a major part in explaining the need for certain developments. Opportunities should be afforded to it of commenting on, and contributing to, plans, including expenditure programmes, which are to be published by the government on matters relevant to its concerns.

Although we are aware of the arguments against proliferation of such standing advisory bodies, we make this proposal for three particular reasons. First, the existence of the Council would provide some guarantee that, when initial enthusiasm had abated, the attempt at inter-departmental co-ordination through a Cabinet sub-committee did not 'run out of steam', as some would say happened with the original JASP initiative. Second, by virtue of its public existence such a body could serve both to keep the issue of health inequalities in the public eye, and enlist widespread support. This is essential, and the development of comparable machinery at the local level (perhaps based on existing Health and Local Authority Joint Consultative Committees) could be invaluable. Third, the Council would be in a position to assist Ministers in formulating longer-term strategies.

Conclusion and summary

In discussing actions outside the health care system which need to be taken to diminish inequalities of health we have been necessarily selective in this chapter. We have attempted to pay heed to those factors which are correlated with the *degree* of inequalities. Secondly, we have tried to confine ourselves to matters which are immediately practicable, in political, economic and administrative terms, which will none the less, properly maintained, exert a long-term structural effect. And thirdly, we have continued to feel it right to give priority to young children and mothers, disabled people and measures concerned with prevention. Above all we consider that the *abolition of child poverty should be adopted as a national goal for the 1980s*. We recognize that this requires a redistribution of financial resources far beyond anything achieved by past programmes and is likely to be very costly. Our recommendations here are presented as a modest first step which might be taken towards this objective.

i. As an immediate goal the level of child benefit should be increased to $5\frac{1}{2}$ per cent of average gross male industrial earnings, or £5.70 at November 1979 prices.

ii. Larger child benefits should be progressively introduced for older children, after further examination of the needs of children and consideration of the practice in some other countries.

iii. The maternity grant should be increased to £100.

iv. We recommend the introduction of an infant care allowance over a five-year period, beginning with all babies born in the year following a date to be chosen by the government.

Beyond these initial elements of an anti-poverty strategy, a number of other steps need to be taken.

v. Provision of meals at school should be regarded as a right. Representatives of local authorities and community dietitians should be invited to meet representatives of parents and teachers of particular schools at regular intervals during the year to seek agreement to the provision and quality of meals. Meals in schools should be provided without charge.

vi. The Health Education Council should be provided with sufficient funds to mount child accident-prevention programmes in conjunction with the Royal Society for the Prevention of Accidents. These programmes should be particularly directed at local authority planners, engineers and architects.

vii. A comprehensive disablement allowance for people of all ages should be introduced by stages at the earliest possible date, beginning with people with 100 per cent disablement.

viii. Representatives of the DHSS and DE, HSE, together with representatives of the trade unions and CBI, should draw up minimally acceptable and desirable conditions of work.

ix. Government departments, employers and unions should devote more attention to preventive health through work organization, conditions and amenities, and in other ways. There should be a similar shift of emphasis in the work and functions of the Health and Safety Commission and Executive, and the Employment Medical Advisory Service.

x. Local authority spending on housing improvements under the 1974 Housing Act should be substantially increased.

xi. Local authorities should increasingly be encouraged to widen their responsibilities to provide for all types of housing need which arise in their localities.

xii. Policies directed towards the public and private housing sectors need to be better co-ordinated.

xiii. Special funding, on the lines of joint funding, for health and local authorities should be developed by the government to encourage better planning and management of housing, including adaptations and provision of necessary facilities and services for disabled people of all ages by social service and housing departments.

Our recommendations reflect the fact that the reduction in health inequalities depends upon contributions from within many policy areas, and necessarily involving a number of government departments. Our objectives will be achieved *only* if each department makes its appropriate contribution. This in turn requires a greater degree of co-ordination than exists at present.

xiv. Greater co-ordination between government departments in the administration of health-related policies is required, by establishing interdepartmental machinery in the Cabinet Office under a Cabinet subcommittee along the lines of that established under the Joint Approach to Social Policy (JASP), with the Central Policy Review staff also involved. Local counterparts of national co-ordinating bodies also need to be established.

xv. A Health Development Council should be established with an independent membership to play a key advisory and planning role in relation to a collaborative national policy to reduce inequalities in health.

Summary and Recommendations

1. Most recent data show marked differences in mortality rates between the occupational classes, for both sexes and at all ages. At birth and in the first month of life, twice as many babies of 'unskilled manual' parents (class V) die as do babies of professional class parents (class I) and in the next eleven months four times as many girls and five times as many boys. In later childhood the ratio of deaths in class V to deaths in class I falls to 1.5–2.0, but increases again in early adult life, before falling again in middle and old age. A class gradient can be observed for most causes of death, being particularly steep in the case of diseases of the respiratory system. Available data on chronic sickness tend to parallel those on mortality. Thus self-reported rates of long-standing illness (as defined in the General Household Survey) are twice as high among unskilled manual males and 2½ times as high among their wives as among the professional classes. In the case of acute sickness (short-term ill-health, also as defined in the General Household Survey) the gradients are less clear.

2. The lack of improvement, and in some respects deterioration, of the health experience of the unskilled and semi-skilled manual classes (class V and IV), relative to class I, throughout the 1960s and early 1970s is striking. Despite the decline in the rate of infant mortality (death within the first year of life) in each class, the difference in rate between the lowest classes (IV and V combined) and the highest (I and II combined) actually increased between 1959–63 and 1970–72.

3. Inequalities exist also in the utilization of health services, particularly and most worryingly of the preventive services. Here, severe under-utilization by the working classes is a complex result of under-provision in working-class areas and of costs (financial and psychological) of attendance which are not, in this case, outweighed by disruption of normal activities by sickness. In the case of GP, and hospital in-patient and out-patient attendance, the situation is less clear. Moreover it becomes more difficult to interpret such data as exist, notably because of the (as yet unresolved) problem of relating utilization to need. Broadly speaking, the evidence suggests that working-class people make more use of GP services for themselves (though not for their children) than do middle-class people, but that they may receive less good care. Moreover, it is possible that this extra usage does not fully reflect the true differences in need for care, as shown by mortality and morbidity figures. Similar increases in the use of hospital services, both in-patient and out-patient, with declining occupational class are found, though data are scanty, and possible explanations complex.

4. Comparison of the British experience with that of other industrial countries, on the basis of overall mortality rates, shows that British perinatal and infant mortality

rates have been distinctly higher and are still somewhat higher than those of the four Nordic countries and of the Netherlands, and comparable with those of the Federal Republic of Germany. Adult mortality patterns, especially for men in the younger age groups, compare reasonably with other Western industrialized countries: the comparison for women is less satisfactory. The rate of improvement in perinatal mortality experienced by Britain over the period since 1960 has been comparable to that of most other countries. In the case of infant mortality (which is generally held to reflect social conditions more than does perinatal mortality) all comparable countries – especially France – have shown a greater improvement than has Britain. France, like Britain and most other countries considered (though apparently not Sweden), shows significant class and regional inequalities in health experience. It is noteworthy that through the 1960s the ratio of the post-neonatal death rate (between four weeks and one year) in the least favoured social group to that in the most favoured fell substantially in France. Also important probably has been a major French effort to improve both attendance rates for ante-natal care and the quality of such care. Very high rates of early attendance are also characteristic of the Nordic countries; so too are high rates of attendance at child welfare clinics, combined with extensive 'outreach' capacity. In Finland, for example, whenever an appointment at a health centre is missed, a health visitor makes a domiciliary call. We regard it as significant also that in Finland health authorities report not on the volume of services provided, but on the proportion of all pregnant women and of all children of appropriate ages who register with Health Centres.

5. We do not believe there to be any single and *simple explanation* of the complex data we have assembled. While there are a number of quite distinct theoretical approaches to explanation we wish to stress the importance of differences in material conditions of life. *In our view much of the evidence on social inequalities in health can be adequately understood in terms of specific features of the socio-economic environment:* features (such as work accidents, overcrowding, cigarette smoking) which are strongly class-related in Britain and also have clear causal significance. Other aspects of the evidence indicate the importance of the health services and particularly preventive services. Ante-natal care is probably important in preventing perinatal death, and the international evidence suggests that much can be done to improve ante-natal care and its uptake. But beyond this there is undoubtedly much which cannot be understood in terms of the impact of so specific factors, but only in terms of the more diffuse consequences of the class structure: poverty, working conditions, and deprivation in its various forms. It is this acknowledgement of the *multicausal* nature of health inequalities, within which inequalities in the material conditions of living loom large, which informs and structures our policy recommendations. These draw also upon another aspect of our interpretation of the evidence. We have concluded that early childhood is the period of life at which intervention could most hopefully weaken the continuing association between health and class. There is, for example, abundant evidence that inadequately treated bouts of childhood illness 'cast long shadows forward', as the Court Committee put it.

6. We have been able to draw upon national statistics relating to health and mortality of exceptional quality and scope, as well as upon a broad range of research studies. We have, however, been conscious of certain inadequacies in the statistics and of major lacunae in the research. For example it is extremely difficult to examine health experience and health service utilization, in relation to income and wealth.

7. Moreover, we consider that the *form* of administrative statistics may both reflect and determine (as the Finnish example quoted above suggests) the way in which the adequacy and the performance of a service is understood: hence it acquires considerable importance. We also consider systematic knowledge of the use made of the various health services by different social groups to be inadequate: though this is less the case in Scotland than in England and Wales. While conscious of the difficulties in collecting and reporting of occupational characteristics within the context of administrative returns, we feel that further thought must be given to how such difficulties might be overcome. We argue that the monitoring of *ill-health* (itself so imperfect) should evolve into a system also of monitoring *health* in relation to social and environmental conditions. One area in which progress could be made is in relation to the development of children, and we propose certain modifications to community health statistics.

(1) *We recommend that school health statistics should routinely provide, in relation to occupational class, the results of tests of hearing, vision, and measures of height and weight. As a first step we recommend that local health authorities, in consultation with educational authorities, select a representative sample of schools in which assessments on a routine basis be initiated.* (Chapter 7, p. 135)

8. *Accidents* are not only responsible for fully one-third of child deaths, but show (with respiratory disease) the steepest of class gradients.

9. We should like to see progress towards routine collection and reporting of accidents to children indicating the circumstances, the age and the occupational class of the parents. In relation to traffic accidents there should be better liaison between the NHS and the police, both centrally and locally.

(2) *We therefore recommend that representatives of appropriate government departments (Health and Social Security, Education and Science, Home Office, Environment, Trade, Transport), as well as of the NHS and of the police, should consider how progress might rapidly be made in improving the information on accidents to children.* (Chapter 7, p. 136)

10. The Child Accident Prevention Committee, if suitably constituted and supported, might provide a suitable forum for such discussions, to be followed by appropriate action by government departments. Further,

(3) *We recommend that the Health Education Council should be provided with sufficient funds to mount child accident prevention programmes in conjunction with the Royal Society for the Prevention of Accidents. These programmes should be*

particularly directed at local authority planners, engineers and architects. (Chapter 9, p. 190)

11. While drawing attention to the importance of the National Food Survey as the major source of information on the food purchase (and hence diet) of the population, we are conscious of the scope for its improvement.

(4) *We recommend that consideration be given to the development of the National Food Survey into a more effective instrument of nutritional surveillance in relation to health, through which various 'at risk' groups could also be identified and studied.* (Chapter 7, p. 136)

12. We have already referred to the difficulties in examining health experience in relation to income and wealth. In principle this can be done through the General Household Survey in which the measure of income now (since 1979) corresponds to the more satisfactory measure employed in the Family Expenditure Survey. However,

(5) *We recommend that in the General Household Survey steps should be taken (not necessarily in every year) to develop a more comprehensive measure of income, or command over resources, through either (a) a means of modifying such a measure with estimates of total wealth or at least some of the more prevalent forms of wealth, such as housing and savings, or (b) the integration of income and wealth, employing a method of, for example, annuitization.* (Chapter 1, p. 49)

13. Beyond this, we feel that a comprehensive research strategy is needed. This is best regarded as implying the need for careful studies of a wide range of variables implicated in ill-health, in their *interaction over time*, and *conducted in a small number of places*. Such variables will necessarily include social conditions (and the interactions of a variety of social policies) as well as individual and behavioural factors. Any major advance in our understanding of the nature of health inequalities, and of the reason for their perpetuation, will require complex research of a multidisciplinary kind.

(6) *The importance of the problem of social inequalities in health, and their causes, as an area for further research needs to be emphasized. We recommend that it be adopted as a research priority by the DHSS and that steps be taken to enlist the expertise of the Medical Research Council (MRC), as well as the Social Science Research Council (SSRC), in the initiation of a programme of research. Such research represents a particularly appropriate area for departmental commissioning of research from the MRC.* (Chapter 7, p. 137)

14. We turn now to our recommendations for policy, which we have divided into those relating to the health and personal social services, and those relating to a range of other social policies. Three objectives underpin our recommendations, and we recommend their adoption by the Secretary of State:

– To give children a better start in life.

– To encourage good health among a larger proportion of the population by preventive and educational action.

– For disabled people, to reduce the risks of early death, to improve the quality of life whether in the community or in institutions, and as far as possible to reduce the need for the latter.

Thirty years of the Welfare State and of the National Health Service have achieved little in reducing social inequalities in health. But we believe that if these three objectives are pursued vigorously inequalities in health can now be reduced.

15. We believe that *allocation of resources* should be based on need. We recognize that there are difficulties in assessing need, but we agree that standardized mortality ratios (SMRs) are a useful basis for broad allocation at regional level. At district level, further indicators of health care and social needs are called for. These should be developed as a matter of urgency, and used appropriately to reinforce, supplement or modify allocation according to SMRs. *However, a shift of resources is not enough: it must be combined with an imaginative (and in part necessarily experimental) approach to health care and its delivery.*

(7) *Resources within the National Health Service and the personal social services should be shifted more sharply than so far accomplished towards community care, particularly towards ante-natal, post-natal and child health services, and home-help and nursing services for disabled people. We see this as an important part of a strategy to break the links between social class or poverty and health.* (Chapter 8, p. 144)

(8) *The professional associations as well as the Secretary of State and the health authorities should accept responsibility for making improvements in the quality and geographical coverage of general practice, especially in areas of high prevalence of ill-health and poor social conditions. Where the number or scope of work of general practitioners is inadequate in such areas we recommend health authorities to deploy or redeploy an above-average number of community nurses attached where possible to family practice. The distribution of general practitioners should be related not only to population but to medical need, as indicated by SMRs, supplemented by other indicators, and the per capita basis of remuneration should be modified accordingly.* (Chapter 8, p. 153)

16. Moreover, we consider that greater integration between the planning process (and the establishment of priorities) and resources allocation is needed. In particular the establishment of revenue targets should be based not upon the current distribution of expenditure between services, but that distribution which it is sought to bring about through planning guidelines: including a greater share for community health.

(9) *We recommend that the resources to be allocated should be based upon the future planned share for different services, including a higher share for community health.* (Chapter 8, p. 150)

17. Our further health service-related recommendations, designed to implement the objectives set out above, fall into two groups.

18. We first outline the elements of what we have called a District Action Programme. By this we mean a general programme for the health and personal social services to be adopted nationwide, and involving necessary modifications to the structure of care.

19. Second, we recommend an experimental programme, involving provision of certain services on an experimental basis in ten areas of particularly high mortality and adverse social conditions, and for which special funds are sought.

District action programme

Health and Welfare of mothers and pre-school and school children

(10) *A non-means-tested scheme for free milk should now be introduced beginning with couples with their first infant child and infant children in large families.* (Chapter 8, p. 142)

(11) *Areas and districts should review the accessibility and facilities of all ante-natal and child-health clinics in their areas and take steps to increase utilization by mothers, particularly in the early months of pregnancy.* (Chapter 8, p. 151)

(12) *Savings from the current decline in the school population should be used to finance new services for children under 5. A statutory obligation should be placed on local authorities to ensure adequate day care in their area for children under 5, and that a minimum number of places (the number being raised after regular intervals) should be laid down centrally. Further steps should be taken to reorganize day nurseries and nursery schools so that both meet the needs of children for education and care.* (Chapter 8, p. 154 and Chapter 9, p. 182)

(13) *Every opportunity should be taken to link revitalized school health care with general practice, and intensify surveillance and follow-up both in areas of special need and for certain types of family.* (Chapter 8, p. 155)

20. Some necessary developments apply to other groups as well as children and mothers.

(14) *An assessment which determines severity of disablement should be adopted as a guide to health and personal social service priorities of the individual, and this should be related to the limitation of activities rather than loss of faculty or type of handicap.* (Chapter 8, p. 155)

21. Though we attach priority to the implementation of this recommendation in the care of disabled children, we believe that it must ultimately apply to all disabled people. We recognize that such assessments are now an acknowledged part of 'good practice' in providing for the disabled – we are anxious that they should become standard practice.

The care of elderly and disabled people in their own homes

22. The meaning of community care should be clarified and much greater emphasis given to tendencies favoured (but insufficiently specified) in recent government planning documents. (See Recommendation 7.)

(15) *A Working Group should be set up to consider:*

i. *the present functions and structure of hospital, residential and domiciliary care for the disabled elderly in relation to their needs, in order to determine the best and most economical balance of future services;* (Chapter 8, p. 159) and

ii. *whether sheltered housing should be a responsibility of social service or of housing departments, and to make recommendations;* (Chapter 8, p. 157)

(16) *Joint funding should be developed and further funding of a more specific kind should be introduced, if necessary within the existing NHS budget, to encourage joint care programmes. A further sum should be reserved for payment to authorities putting forward joint programmes to give continuing care to disabled people – for example, post-hospital follow-up schemes, pre-hospital support programmes for families, and support programmes for the severely incapacitated and terminally ill.* (Chapter 8, p. 160)

(17) *Criteria for admission to, and for continuing residence in, residential care should be agreed between the DHSS and the local authority associations, and steps taken to encourage rehabilitation, and in particular to prevent homeless elderly people from being offered accommodation only in residential homes. Priority should be given to expansion of domiciliary care for those who are severely disabled in their own homes.* (Chapter 8, p. 157)

(18) *The functions of home helps should be extended to permit a lot more work on behalf of disabled people; short courses of training, specialization of functions and the availability of mini-bus transport, especially to day centres, should be encouraged.* (Chapter 8, p. 160)

Prevention: the role of government

23. Effective prevention requires not only individual initiative but a real commitment by the DHSS and other government departments. Our analysis has shown the many ways in which people's behaviour is constrained by structural and environmental factors over which they have no control. Physical recreation, for example, is hardly possible in inner city areas unless steps are taken to ensure that facilities are provided. Similarly, government initiatives are required in relation to diet and to the consumption of alcohol. Legislation and fiscal and other financial measures may be required and a wide range of social and economic policies involved. We see the time as now opportune for a major step forwards in the field of health and prevention.

(19) *National health goals should be established and stated by government after wide consultation and debate. Measures that might encourage the desirable changes in people's diet, exercise and smoking and drinking behaviour should be agreed among relevant agencies.* (Chapter 8, p. 162)

(20) *An enlarged programme of health education should be sponsored by the government, and necessary arrangements made for optimal use of the mass media, especially television. Health education in schools should become the joint responsibility of LEAs and health authorities.* (Chapter 8, p. 161)

24. The following recommendation should be seen not only as a priority in itself but as illustrative of the determined action by government necessary in relation to many elements of a strategy for prevention:

(21) *Stronger measures should be adopted to reduce cigarette smoking. These would include:*

a. *Legislation should be rapidly implemented to phase out all advertising and sales promotion of tobacco products (except at place of purchase);*

b. *Sponsorship of sporting and artistic activities by tobacco companies should be banned over a period of a few years, and meanwhile there should be stricter control of advertisement through sponsorship;*

c. *Regular annual increases in duty on cigarettes in line with rises in income should be imposed, to ensure lower consumption;*

d. *Tobacco companies should be required, in consultation with trades unions, to submit plans for the diversification of their products over a period of ten years with a view to the eventual phasing out of sales of harmful tobacco products at home and abroad;*

e. *The provision of non-smoking areas in public places should steadily be extended;*

f. *A counselling service should be made available in all health districts, and experiment encouraged in methods to help people reduce cigarette smoking;*

g. *A stronger well-presented health warning should appear on all cigarette packets and such advertisements as remain, together with information on the harmful constituents of cigarettes.* (Chapter 8, p. 162)

We have already recommended that steps be taken to increase utilization of antenatal clinics, particularly in the early months of pregnancy (Recommendation 11). Given early attendance there are practical programmes for screening for Down's Syndrome and for neural tube defects in the foetus. In relation to adult disease, screening for severe hypertension is practicable, and effective treatment is available.

(22) *In the light of the present stage of knowledge we recommend that screening for neural tube defects (especially in high risk areas) and Down's Syndrome on the one hand, and for severe hypertension in adults on the other, should be made generally available.* (Chapter 8, p. 164)

Additional funding for ten special areas

(23) *We recommend that the government should finance a special health and social development programme in a small number of selected areas, costing about £30 m. in 1981–2.* (Chapter 8, p. 165)

25. At least £2 m. of this sum should be reserved for evaluation research and statistical and information units. The object would be both to provide special help to redress the undeniable disadvantages of people living in those areas but also to permit special experiments to reduce ill-health and mortality, and provide better support for disabled people. Some elements of such a programme are illustrated, particularly in connection with the development of more effective ante-natal services. (Chapter 8, pp. 165–7)

Measures to be taken outside the health services

26. In discussing actions outside the Health Care system which need to be taken to diminish inequalities of health we have been necessarily selective. We have attempted to pay heed to those factors which are correlated with the *degree* of inequalities. Secondly, we have tried to confine ourselves to matters which are practicable now, in political, economic and administrative terms, and which will none the less, properly maintained, exert a long-term structural effect. Third, we have continued to feel it right to give priority to young children and mothers, disabled people, and measures concerned with prevention.

27. Above all, we consider that the *abolition of child-poverty* should be adopted as a national goal for the 1980s. We recognize that this requires a redistribution of financial resources far beyond anything achieved by past programmes, and is likely to be very costly. Recommendations 24–27 are presented as a modest first step which might be taken towards this objective.

(24) *As an immediate goal the level of child benefit should be increased to 5½ per cent of average gross male industrial earnings, or £5.70 at November 1979 prices.* (Chapter 9, p. 179)

(25) *Larger child benefits should be progressively introduced for older children, after further examination of the needs of children and consideration of the practice in some other countries.* (Chapter 9, pp. 178–9)

(26) *The maternity grant should be increased to £100.* (Chapter 9, p. 179)

(27) *An infant care allowance should be introduced over a five-year period, beginning with all babies born in the year following a date to be chosen by the government.* (Chapter 9, p. 180)

28. Beyond these initial elements of an anti-poverty strategy, a number of other steps need to be taken. These include steps to reduce accidents to children, to which we have referred above (Recommendation 3). Further,

(28) *Provision of meals at school should be regarded as a right. Representatives of local authorities and community dietitians should be invited to meet representatives of parents and teachers of particular schools at regular intervals during the year to seek agreement to the provision and quality of meals. Meals in schools should be provided without charge.* (Chapter 9, p. 188)

(29) *A comprehensive disablement allowance for people of all ages should be introduced by stages at the earliest possible date, beginning with people with 100 per cent disablement.* (Chapter 9, p. 191)

(30) *Representatives of the DHSS and DE, HSE, together with representatives of trade unions and CBI, should draw up minimally acceptable and desirable conditions of work.* (Chapter 9, p. 195)

(31) *Government departments, employers and unions should devote more attention to preventive health through work organization, conditions and amenities, and in other ways. There should be a similar shift of emphasis in the work and function of the Health and Safety Commission and Executive, and the Employment Medical Advisory Service.* (Chapter 9, pp. 195–6)

(32) *Local authority spending on housing improvements under the 1974 Housing Act should be substantially increased.* (Chapter 9, p. 197)

(33) *Local authorities should increasingly be encouraged to widen their responsibilities to provide for all types of housing need which arise in their localities.* (Chapter 9, p. 198)

(34) *Policies directed towards the public and private housing sectors need to be better co-ordinated.* (Chapter 9, p. 197)

(35) *Special funding, on the lines of joint funding, for health and local authorities should be developed by the government to encourage better planning and management of housing, including adaptations and provision of necessary facilities and services for disabled people of all ages by social services and housing departments.* (Chapter 9, p. 199)

29. Our recommendations reflect the fact that reduction in health inequalities depends upon contributions from within many policy areas, and necessarily involves a number of government departments. Our objectives will be achieved *only* if each department makes its appropriate contribution. This in turn requires a greater degree of co-ordination than exists at present.

(36) *Greater co-ordination between government departments in the administration of health-related policies is required, by establishing inter-departmental machinery in the Cabinet Office under a Cabinet sub-committee along the lines of that established under the Joint Approach to Social Policy (JASP), with the Central Policy Review Staff also involved. Local counterparts of national co-ordinating bodies also need to be established.* (Chapter 9, p. 201)

(37) *A Health Development Council should be established with an independent membership to play a key advisory and planning role in relation to a collaborative national policy to reduce inequalities in health.* (Chapter 9, p. 202)

30. Within such co-ordinating machinery major initiatory responsibility will be vested in the Department of Health and Social Security, and we recommend that the Cabinet Committees we have proposed be chaired by a Minister, and by a senior DHSS official respectively, having major responsibility for health and prevention. Similarly it will be an important obligation upon the DHSS to ensure the effective operation of the Health Development Council.

Appendix of Tables

Table 1. *Percentage of economically active men in different occupational classes 1931, 1951, 1961, 1966, 1971 (England and Wales)*

Occupational class (Registrar General)	1931*		1951*		1961†	1966‡	1971
I	1.8	(2.2)	2.7	(3.2)	4.0	4.5	5.0
II	12.0	(12.8)	12.8	(14.3)	14.9	15.7	18.2
III	47.8	(48.9)	51.5	(53.4)	51.6	50.6	50.5
IV	25.5	(18.2)	23.3	(16.2)	20.5	20.6	18.0
V	12.9	(17.8)	9.7	(12.9)	8.9	8.8	8.4
Total	100.0	(100.0)	100.0	(100.0)	100.0	100.0	100.0
Number (thousands)	13,247		14,064		14,649	15,686	15,668

* Percentages have been weighted to allow for changes in classification between the 1931 and 1961 censuses: *The General Report, 1951* and *The General Report, 1961* allow the percentage change for each class between censuses to be calculated and the figures to be adjusted accordingly to bring both the 1931 and 1951 figures into line with the 1960 classification. Figures in brackets are based on the classification at that time. The estimates for 1931 and 1951 are necessarily crude – the latter partly for the reasons carefully listed in *The General Report 1961*, p. 193.

† Substantial numbers who were unclassified in 1961 (518,000) have been excluded. (Only 84,034 unclassified in 1971 have been excluded.)

‡ Percentages given are for economically active and retired males. Substantial numbers who were unclassified in 1966 have been excluded.

Sources: Census 1951, *General Report*, Table 66, p. 147; Census 1961, *General Report*, Table 55, p. 193; Census 1966, *Economic Activity Tables Part III*, Table 30, p. 416; Census 1971, *Economic Activity Tables Part IV*, Table 29, p. 96 (10 per cent sample).

Table 2. *Percentage of men aged 25 and over in five occupational classes in 1951, 1961 and 1971 (England and Wales), according to 1960 (and 1970) classification of occupations*

Age	Year	Professional I	Intermediate II	Skilled III	Partly skilled IV	Unskilled V
25–34	1951	2.1	7.9	54.5	26.8	8.6
	1961	5.3	12.9	55.9	18.4	7.5
	1971	7.5	18.1	53.2	15.2	6.1
35–44	1951	2.1	12.6	49.0	26.7	9.8
	1961	4.3	16.6	53.4	18.8	6.9
	1971	6.2	20.7	50.5	16.1	6.6
45–54	1951	1.9	13.1	43.5	28.5	12.9
	1961	3.3	18.8	48.5	21.1	8.2
	1971	4.8	21.3	48.8	17.9	7.3
55–9	1951	1.8	14.0	39.9	29.5	14.7
	1961	2.9	17.8	45.0	23.5	10.8
	1971	4.0	20.5	46.3	20.2	9.1
60–64	1951	1.7	13.6	38.3	30.0	16.3
	1961	2.6	17.5	42.7	24.5	12.7
	1971	3.7	18.7	45.3	21.4	10.9
65–9	1951	1.9	13.3	42.6	29.1	15.0
	1961	2.7	17.9	41.8	24.5	13.1
	1971	3.4	17.2	43.2	22.5	13.7
70+	1951	1.9	14.7	46.1	25.4	11.8
	1961	3.2	19.2	41.7	24.0	11.9
	1971	3.3	19.4	44.0	21.6	11.8
Total	1951	1.9	11.9	47.1	27.5	11.5
	1961	3.9	16.8	49.3	21.0	9.0
	1971	5.2	19.7	48.8	18.1	8.3

Note: An attempt has been made in this table to allow for changes of classification brought about after the introduction of the 1960 Classification of Occupations (there were only a few further changes in the 1970 classification and the figures from the 1961 and 1971 Censuses did not need to be adjusted before being compared). However, for 1951 we have changed the figures for each age group by the proportion suggested for all age-groups in an exercise reported in *The General Report*, General Register Office, Census 1961, Great Britain, HMSO, 1968, p. 193. The 1961 data were re-classified for a sample using the 1951 classification and compared with the 1961 data classified according to the 1960 Classification of Occupations. We have worked back to the 1951 data for social classes and changed the figures for each class by the proportion suggested by the results of the exercise carried out by the GRO. The 1951 figures given above must be treated as approximate only. But they are more nearly comparable with the 1961 and 1971 Census results than the figures published in the 1951 Census reports.

The table gives estimates by age as well as class of the distribution in 1951, 1961 and 1971. For men aged 25 and over the percentage in class V declined from 11 to 8 and in class IV from 27 to 18 in the twenty years 1951 to 1971 (most of the corresponding increase taking place in class II, but also class I). However, the rate of change slowed down in 1961–71 and it can be seen that between a fifth and a quarter of those in the youngest age groups continued to be found in classes IV and V. Overall, substantially more than a quarter of economically active men remained in class IV and V in 1971.

Sources: General Register Office, Census 1951, England and Wales, Occupation Tables, HMSO, 1956; General Register Office, Census 1961, England and Wales, Occupation Tables, HMSO, 1966, Table 20; Office of Population Censuses and Surveys, Census 1971, Great Britain, *Economic Activity Tables, Part IV*, HMSO, 1975, Table 29.

Table 3. *Two versions of trends in the distribution of wealth (Britain)*

Year	Inland Revenue data series B*				Atkinson and Harrison (assumption B3)†			
	Top 1%	Top 5%	Top 10%	Top 20%	Top 1%	Top 5%	Top 10%	Top 20%
1960	38.2	64.3	76.7	89.8	34.4	60.0	72.1	83.6
1964	34.4	59.3	73.5	88.4	34.7	59.2	72.0	85.2
1966	31.8	56.7	71.8	87.8	31.0	56.1	69.9	84.2
1968	32.7	59.0	73.8	89.4	33.6	58.6	72.0	85.4
1970	29.0	56.3	70.1	89.0	30.1	54.3	69.4	84.9
1972	29.9	56.3	71.9	89.2	32.0	57.2	71.7	85.3

* Assuming that persons not covered by the Inland Revenue estimates have no wealth.
† Assuming that the value of certain property not accounted for by estate data but estimated by means of the balance-sheet method is distributed between the population included in the estate data and the population excluded. This is their 'central estimate'.

Sources: Royal Commission on the Distribution of Income and Wealth, *Report No. 5, Third Report on the Standing Reference*, Cmnd 6999, HMSO, 1977, p. 76; A. B. Atkinson and A. J. Harrison, *Distribution of Personal Wealth in Britain*, Cambridge University Press, 1978, p. 159.

Table 4. *Distribution of personal income – study of the incidence of taxes and benefits (1961 to 1975, U K). Percentage shares of final income received by given quantile groups, and supplementary statistics (1961 to 1975). Income unit: households.*

Quantile group	Final income			
	1961	1965	1971	1975
Top 10 per cent	23.7	23.3	23.7	22.4
11–20 per cent	15.1	15.2	15.6	15.4
21–30 per cent	12.8	12.8	12.8	13.0
31–40 per cent	11.1	11.1	11.0	11.2
41–50 per cent	9.8	9.8	9.6	9.7
51–60 per cent	8.6	8.5	8.3	8.4
61–70 per cent	7.2	7.1	6.9	7.0
71–80 per cent	5.8	5.7	5.4	5.7
81–90 per cent	4.3	4.3	4.1	4.3
91–100 per cent	1.7	2.3	2.5	2.9
Difference as a percentage of the median between highest and lowest deciles	149	149	158	149
Upper and lower quartiles	75	77	83	81
Median £ pw	15	18	26	52
GINI coefficient %	32.9	32.2	33.0	31.1

Note: While this table shows no pronounced trend in the distribution of final income, it is also true that fringe benefits (employer welfare and public sector subsidies) have grown in importance, and probably this has been to the relative advantage of higher income groups. (See for example Royal Commission on Distribution of Income and Wealth Report, No. 13, Chapter 4 and Appendix H, 1975.)

Source: Royal Commission on the Distribution of Income and Wealth.

Table 5. *Recent trends in death rates by occupational class men aged 15–64 (England and Wales)*

Occupational class	Age-standardized death rate per 100,000 living at ages 15–64		
	1951	1961	1971
I	103	82	79
II	108	87	83
III	116	106	103
IV	119	108	113
V	137	134	123

Note: Adjustments have been made by the OPCS to improve comparability between censuses.

Source: OPCS, *Occupational Mortality, Decennial Supplement, 1970–72, England and Wales*, HMSO, 1978, p. 174 (supplemented by the OPCS).

References

Introduction

Abel-Smith, B., *An International Study of Health Expenditure*, Public Health Papers, No. 32, WHO, 1967. *Value for Money in Health Services*, Heinemann, 1976. 'The Cost of Health Services', *New Society*, 12 July 1979. 'Towards a Healthier Population', *New Society*, 15 October 1981.

Banks, M. H., et al., *Young People Starting Work*, Interim Report to MSC, MRC Social and Applied Psychology Unit, University of Sheffield, 1980.

Best, G., *Health Care Resources in Redbridge and Waltham Forest: A Comparative Study of Resource Provision Levels in the Seventeen North East Thames RMA Health Districts*, Redbridge and Waltham Forest Area Health Authority, September 1981.

Bevin, G., Copeman, H., Perris, J., and Rosser, R., *Health Care Priorities and Management*, Croom Helm, 1980.

Black, D. (1981a), 'Inequalities in Health', *British Medical Journal*, 2 May.
(1981b), 'Inequalities in Health', Lecture in memory of Dr Christie Gordon, mimeo, University of Birmingham.

Blume, S., 'Explanation and Social Policy: The "Problem" of Social Inequalities in Health', *Journal of Social Policy*, 1982.

Bradshaw, J., Edwards, H., Staden, F., and Weale, J., 'Area Variations in Infant Mortality, 1975–1977', *Journal of Epidemiology and Community Health*, 1981.

Brennan, M., and Lancashire, R., 'Association of Childhood Mortality with Housing Status and Unemployment', *Journal of Epidemiology and Community Health*, 1978.

Brenner, M. H., 'Mortality and the National Economy: A Review and the Experience of England and Wales 1936–1976', *Lancet*, 15 September 1979.

Burchell, A., 'Inequalities in Health: Analysis of the 1976 General Household Survey', Government Economic Service Working Paper No. 48, DHSS, 1981, Economic Adviser's Office, Blackfriars Road, London SE1 8EU, October 1981.

Centre for Health Studies, *A Proposal for Co-operative Multidisciplinary Studies of the Complex Social Causation and Prevention of Ill-Health*, Yale University, November 1977.

Chandra, R. K., *Immunology of Nutritional Disorders*, Arnold, 1980.

COHSE, Research Bulletin, occasional series, London, Confederation of Health Service Employees, December 1980.

Colledge, M., *Unemployment and Health*, North Tyneside Community Health Council, Stephenson House, Stephenson Street, North Shields NE30 1ET, 1981.

Collins, E., and Klein, R., 'Equity and the NHS: Self-Reported Morbidity, Access and Primary Care', *British Medical Journal*, 25 October 1980.

Cooper, P., 'Thames Barrier', *Times Health Supplement*, 20 November 1981.

Deitch, R., 'The Debate on the Black Report', *Lancet*, 18 July 1981.

DHSS, *Care in the Community: A Consultative Document on Moving Resources for Care in England. Reply to the Second Report from the Social Services Committee on Perinatal and Neonatal Mortality*, Cmnd 8084, HMSO, December 1980.

Djukanovic, V., and Mach, E. P., *Alternative Approaches to Meeting Basic Health Needs in Developing Countries* (a joint UNICEF and WHO study), Geneva, WHO, 1975.

Dowding, V. M., 'New Assessment of the Effects of Birth Order and Socioeconomic Status on Birthweight', *British Medical Journal*, 28 February 1981.

Doyal, L., *The Political Economy of Health*, Pluto Press, 1980.

Fagin, L., *Unemployment and Health in Families*, DHSS mimeo, 1981.

Forster, D. P., 'The Relationship Between Health Needs, Socio-Environmental Indices, General Practitioners' Resources and Utilisation', *Journal of Chronic Disease*, Vol. 32, 1979.

Godber, Sir G., 'Health Care During a Recession', *Update*, 15 May 1981.

'GP's Report from the Frontline on Jobless Countries' (A summary of cases reported in the *British Medical Journal*), *Guardian*, 24 August 1981.

Gravelle, H. S. E., Hutchinson, G., and Stern, J., 'Mortality and Unemployment: A Cautionary Note', Centre for Labour Economics, London School of Economics, Discussion Paper No. 95, September 1981.

Gray, A., *On the Black Report: Inequalities in Health, a Summary and Comment*, Aberdeen, Health Economics Research Unit, University of Aberdeen, November 1981.

Hollingsworth, J., and Rogers, 'Inequality in Levels of Health in England and Wales, 1891–1971', *Journal of Health and Social Behaviour*, Vol. 22, September 1981.

House of Commons, Second Report from the Social Services Committee, Session 1979–80, *Perinatal and Neonatal Mortality*, London, HMSO, July 1980. Third Report from the Social Services Committee, Session 1979–80, *The Government's White Papers on Public Expenditure: The Social Services*, London, HMSO, 9 July 1980.

IDS Health Group, *Health Needs and Health Services in Rural Ghana*, Institute of Development Studies, University of Sussex, June 1978.

Lalonde, M., *A New Perspective on the Health of Canadians*, Ottawa, Information Canada, 1975.

LeGrand, J., 'The Distribution of Public Expenditure: The Case of Health Care', *Economica*, Vol. 45, May 1978. 'Inequality in Health', *British Medical Journal*, 11 July 1981.

Morris, J. N. (1980a), 'Social Inequalities Undiminished', *Lancet*, 13 January 1979; *Health Visitor*, Vol. 53, September 1980.
  (1980b), 'Equalities and Inequalities in Health', *British Medical Journal*, 11 October.
  (1980c), 'Medicine's Order of Priorities', *The Times*, 19 September.

OHE Briefing, 'Doctors, Nurses and Midwives in the NHS', Office of Health Economics, No. 18, November 1981.

OPCS, *General Household Survey, 1979*, HMSO, 1981.

OPCS Monitor, 'Adult Heights and Weights Survey', 27 October 1981.

Popay, J., 'Unemployment: A Threat to Public Health', in Burghes, L., and Lister, R., *Unemployment: Who Pays the Price?*, CPAG, November 1981.

Radical Community Medicine, No. 4, Autumn 1980.

Ramsden, S., and Smee, C., 'The Health of Unemployed Men', *Employment Gazette*, London, September 1981.

Simanis, J. G., 'Medical Care Expenditure in Seven Countries', *Social Security Bulletin*, March 1973.

Stern, J., 'Unemployment and its Impact on Morbidity and Mortality', Centre for Labour Economics, London School of Economics, Discussion Paper No. 93, September 1981.

Townsend, P., 'The Policy Implications of a Positive Approach to Health', *Health Visitor*, February 1982.

TUC, *The Unequal Health of the Nation*, a TUC Summary of the Black Report, TUC, 1981.

Vetter, N. J., Jones, D. A., and Victor, C. R., 'Variations in Care for the Elderly in Wales', *Journal of Epidemiology and Community Health*, Vol. 35, 1981.

Watkins, S., and Elton, P., 'Inequalities in Health: A Response', a paper prepared for a working party of the North West Regional Health Authority (unpublished) 1981.

World Bank, *World Development Report 1981*, OUP, 1981.

Wynn, M. and A., 'Nutrition Counselling in the Prevention of Low Birth-weight: Some Conclusions About Ante-Natal Care Following a Visit to Canada', Foundation for Education and Research in Childbearing, 27 Walpole Street, London SW1, 1975. *Prevention of Handicap and the Health of Women*, London, Routledge, 1979. 'The Importance of Nutrition Around Conception in the Prevention of Handicap', Annual Conference of British Dietetic Association, 1981 (to be published by John Libby).

1: Concepts of Health and Inequality

Abel-Smith, B., *The Hospitals 1800–1948*, Heinemann, 1964.

Birch, H. G., and Gussow, J. D., *Disadvantaged Children: Health, Nutrition and School Failure*, New York, Harcourt, Brace and World, 1970.

Black, D., 'The Paradox of Medical Care', *Journal of the Royal College of Physicians*, 13, 57, 1979.

Brown, G. W., and Harris, T., *Social Origins of Depression: A Study of Psychiatric Disorder in Women*, Tavistock, 1978.

Culyer, A. J., Lavers, R. J., and Williams, A., in Shonfield, A., and Shaw, S. (eds.), *Social Indicators and Social Policy*, Heinemann, 1972.

Disability Rights Handbook for 1980, Disability Alliance, 1979.

Dollery, C., *The End of an Age of Optimism*, Nuffield Provincial Hospitals Trust, 1978.

Dubos, R., *Mirage and Health*, Allen & Unwin, 1960.

Help for the Disabled, Louis Harris International, 1974.

McKeown, T., *The Role of Medicine: Dream, Mirage or Nemesis?*, Nuffield Provincial Hospitals Trust, 1976.

Marshall, W. A., *Human Growth and Its Disorders*, Academic Press, 1977.

Mechanic, D., *Medical Sociology: A Selective View*, New York, Free Press, 1968.

Morris, J. N., *Uses of Epidemiology*, 3rd edn, Churchill Livingstone, 1975.

Royal Commission on the Distribution of Income and Wealth, Reports Nos. 1, 4, 5 and 7, Cmnds 6171, 6626, 6999 and 7595, London, HMSO, 1975–9.

Sackett, D. L., Chambers, L. W., MacPherson, A. S., Goldsmith, C. H., and Macauley, R. G., 'The Development and Application of Indices of Health: General Methods and a Summary of Results', *American Journal of Public Health*, Vol. 67, No. 5, 1977.

Sigerist, H. E., *Civilisation and Disease*, University of Chicago Press, Phoenix Edition, 1962 (first published Cornell University Press, 1943).

Stevenson, T. H. C., 'The Vital Statistics of Wealth and Poverty', *Journal of the Royal Statistical Society*, Vol. 91, 1928.

Susser, M. W., and Watson, W., *Sociology in Medicine*, Oxford University Press, 1971.

Tuckett, D. A. (ed.), *An Introduction to Medical Sociology*, Tavistock, 1976.

2: The Pattern of Present Health Inequalities

Gans, B., 'Health Problems and the Immigrant Child', in CIBA Foundation, *Immigration: Medical and Social Aspects*, 1966.

Hood, C., Oppé, T. E., Pless, I. B., and Apte, E., *West Indian Immigrants: A Study of One-Year-Olds in Paddington*, Institute of Race Relations, 1970.

Logan, W. P. D., and Cushion, A. A., *Morbidity Statistics from General Practice*, HMSO, 1960.

Ministry of Pensions and National Insurance, *Report of an Inquiry into the Incidence of Incapacity for Work*, HMSO, 1964.

OPCS, *Occupational Mortality 1970–72, Decennial Supplement*, HMSO, 1978.

Oppé, T. E., 'The Health of West Indian Children', *Proceedings of the Royal Society of Medicine*, 57, 1967, pp. 321–3.

Smith, D., *The Facts of Racial Disadvantage: A National Survey*, PEP, 1976.

Thomas, H. E., 'Tuberculosis in Immigrants', *Proceedings of the Royal Society of Medicine*, 61, 1968.

3: Trends in Inequality of Health

Fit for the Future: The Report of the Committee on Child Health Services (Court Report), Cmnd 6684, HMSO, 1977.

McKeown, T., *The Role of Medicine*, Nuffield Provincial Hospitals Trust, 1976.

Morris, J. N., 'Health and Social Class', *Lancet*, 7 February 1959.

OPCS, *Occupational Mortality, Decennial Supplement, 1970–72, England and Wales*, HMSO, 1978.

Registrar General's Decennial Supplement, England and Wales, 1961: Occupational Mortality Tables, HMSO, 1971.

4: Inequality in the Availability and Use of the Health Service

Bone, M., *Family Planning Services in England and Wales*, HMSO, 1973.

Brotherston, J., 'Inequality: Is It Inevitable?', in Carter and Peel (eds.), *Equalities and Inequalities in Health*, Academic Press, 1976.

Bulman, J. S., Richards, N. D., Slack, G. L., and Willcocks, A. J., *Demand and Need for Dental Care*, OUP, 1968.

Buxton, M. J., and Klein, R. E., 'Distribution of Hospital Provision: Policy Themes and Resource Variations', *British Medical Journal*, 1, 1976, p. 299.

Cartwright, A., *Human Relations and Hospital Care*, Routledge, 1964. *Parents and Family Planning Services*, Routledge, 1970.

Cartwright, A., and O'Brien, M., 'Social Class Variations in Health Care', in Stacey, M. (ed.), *The Sociology of the NHS*, Sociological Review Monograph 22, 1976.

Clarke, M., *Trouble with Feet*, Occasional Papers on Social Administration, Bell, 1969.

Coombe, V., 'Health and Social Services and Minority Ethnic Groups', *Journal of the Royal Society of Health*, 96, 1976.

Douglas, J. W. B., and Rowntree, G., 'Supplementary Maternal and Child Health Services', *Population Studies*, 2, 1949.

Forster, D. P., 'Social Class Differences in Sickness and General Practitioner Consultations', *Health Trends*, 8, 1976, p. 29.

General Household Survey Reports, 1971–7.

Gordon, I., 'Social Status and Active Prevention of Disease', *Monthly Bulletin of the Ministry of Health*, 10, 1951.

Gray, P. G., et al., *Adult Dental Health in England and Wales in 1968*, HMSO, 1970.

Jones, D. R., and Masterman, S., 'NHS Resources: Scales of Variation', *British Journal of Preventive and Social Medicine*, 30, 1976, p. 244.

Martin, D., *Social Aspects of Prescribing*, Heinemann, 1957.

Martin, J. and Morgan, M., *Prolonged Sickness and the Return to Work*, HMSO, 1975.

Martini, C. J. M., et al., 'Health Indexes Sensitive to Medical Care Variation', *International Journal of Health Services*, 7, 1977, p. 293.

Morris, J. N., *The Uses of Epidemiology*, 3rd edn, Churchill Livingstone, 1975.

Noyce, J., Snaith, A. H., and Trickey, A. J., 'Regional Variations in the Allocation of Financial Resources to the Community Health Services', *Lancet*, 1974.

Rickard, J. H., 'Per Capita Expenditure of the English Area Health Authorities', *British Medical Journal*, 1, 1976, p. 299.

Sheiham, A., and Hobdell, M. H., 'Decayed, Missing and Filled Teeth in British Adult Populations', *British Dental Journal*, 126, 1969, p. 401.

Skrimshire, A., *Area Disadvantage, Social Class and the Health Service*, Department of Social and Administrative Studies, University of Oxford, 1978.

Titmuss, R. M., *Commitment to Welfare*, Allen & Unwin, 1968.

Townsend, P., *The Last Refuge*, Routledge, 1962.

Townsend, P., and Wedderburn, D., *The Aged in the Welfare State*, Bell Occasional Papers on Social Administration, 1965.

Tudor Hart, J., 'The Inverse Care Law', *Lancet*, 1, 1971.

West, R. R., and Lowe, C. R., 'Regional Variations in Need for and Provision and Use of Child Health Services in England and Wales', *British Medical Journal*, October 1976, p. 843.

5: International Comparisons

Anderson, O. W., *Health Care – Can There Be Equity?*, New York, Wiley, 1972.

Chase, H. C., 'Infant Mortality and Its Concomitants 1960–1972', *Medical Care*, 15, 8, August 1977, p. 662.

Denmark, *Medicinsk Fødselsstatistik*, Copenhagen, 1974.

Derrienic, F., Ducimetière, P., et Kritsikis, S., 'La mortalité cardiaque des Français actif d'âge moyen selon leur catégorie socio-professionelle et leur région de domicile', *Revue d'Épidémiologie, Médecine Sociale, et Santé Publique*, 25, 1977, p. 131.

Dinh Quang Chi, and Hemery, S., 'Disparités régionales de la mortalité infantile', *Économie et Statistiques*, 1977, 85, pp. 3–12.

Doguet, M. L., 'Les prestations familiales en France: Bilan et perspectives', *Revue Française des Affaires Sociales*, 32, 1, January–March 1978, pp. 3–48.

Geijerstam, G., 'Low Birth Weight and Perinatal Mortality', *Public Health Report*, 84, November 1969, pp. 939–48.

Germany, *Bevölkerung und Kultur*, Reiche 7: *Gesundheitswesen 1974*, Wiesbaden, Statistisches Bundesamt, 1974.

Kaminski, M., Blondel, B., Bréart, G., Franc, M., Du Mazaubrun, C., 'Issue de la grossesse et surveillance prénatale chez les femmes migrantes. Enquête sur un échantillon représentatif des naissances en France en 1972', *Revue d'Épidémiologie, Médecine Sociale, et Santé Publique*, 26, 1, 1978, pp. 29–46.

Lerner, M., and Stutz, R. N., 'Have We Narrowed the Gap between the Poor and the Non-Poor? Narrowing the Gaps 1959–61 and 1969–71 – Mortality', *Medical Care*, 15, 8, August 1977, p. 620.

Lindgren, Gunilla, 'Height, Weight and Menarche in Swedish Urban School Children in Relation to Socio-Economic and Regional Factors', *Annals of Human Biology*, 3, 1976, 6, pp. 501–28.

Maynard, A., 'The Medical Profession and the Efficiency and Equity of Health Services', *Social and Economic Administration*, 12, 1, 1978, p. 3.

Morris, J. N., 'Scottish Hearts', *Lancet*, 3 November 1979.

Naytia, S., 'Social Group and Mortality in Finland', *British Journal of Preventive and Social Medicine*, 31, 4, 1977, p. 231.

Netherlands, *Compendium Gezondheidsstatistiek Nederland*, Centraal Bureau voor de Statistiek, 1974.

Norway, *Sosialt Utsyn 1977*, Oslo, Statistisk Sentralbyra, 1977.

Pharaoh, P. O., and Morris, J. N., 'Postneonatal Mortality', in Sartwell, P. E. (ed.), *Epidemiological Reviews* I, 1979, pp. 170–83.

Purola, T., Kalimo, E., Nyman, K., and Sievers, K., *The Utilization of the Medical Services and its Relationship to Morbidity, Health Resources and Social Factors*, Helsinki, Research Institute for Social Security, 1968.

Rona, R. J., Swan, A. V., and Altman, D. G., 'Social Factors and Height of Primary School Children in England and Scotland', *Journal of Epidemiology and Community Health*, 32, 1978, pp. 147–54.

Rumeau-Rouquette, C., et al., 'Evaluation épidémiologique du programme de santé en périnatologie. I Région Rhône-Alpes 1972–1975', *Revue d'Épidémiologie, Médecine Sociale, et Santé Publique*, 25, 1977, p. 107.

Salkever, D. S., 'Economic Class and Differential Access to Care: Comparisons among Health Care Systems', *International Journal of Services*, 5, 1975, 3, p. 373.

Sjolin, S., 'Infant Mortality in Sweden', in Wallace, Helen M. (ed.), *Health Care of Mothers and Children in National Health Services*, Cambridge, Mass., Ballinger, 1975.

Wilson, R. W., and White, E. L., 'Changes in Morbidity, Disability and Utilization Differentials between the Poor and the Non-Poor. Data from the Health Interview Survey 1964 and 1973', *Medical Care*, 15, 8, 1977, p. 636.

Wynn, M., and A., *The Protection of Maternity and Infancy* (A Study of the Services for Pregnant Women and Young Children in Finland with Some Comparisons with Britain), Council for Children's Welfare, 1974. *Prevention of Handicap of Perinatal Origin* (An Introduction to French Policy and Legislation), Foundation for Education and Research in Childbearing, 1976.

6: Towards an Explanation of Health Inequalities

Abel-Smith, B., and Townsend, P., *The Poor and the Poorest*, Bell, 1965.

Banks, J. and O., *Feminism and Family Planning*, Routledge, 1964.

Baird, D., 'Epidemiology of Congenital Malformations of the Central Nervous System in (a) Aberdeen and (b) Scotland', *Journal of Biosocial Science*, 6, 1974, p. 113. 'The Epidemiology of Low Birth Weight: Changes in Incidence in Aberdeen, 1948–1972', *Journal of Biosocial Science*, 6, 1974, p. 323.

Bernstein, B., *Class, Codes and Control*, Routledge, 1971.

Birch, H. G., and Gussow, J. D., *Disadvantaged Children: Health, Nutrition and School Failure*, New York, Harcourt, Brace and World, 1970.

Brennan, M. E., 'Medical Characteristics of Children Supervised by the Local Authority Social Services Department', *Policy and Politics*, 1, 1973, 3, p. 255.

Brenner, M. H., 'Fetal, Infant, and Maternal Mortality during Periods of Economic Instability', *International Journal of Health Services*, 3, 1973, 2, p. 145. 'Estimating the Social Costs of National Economic Policy: Implications for Mental and Physical Health and Criminal Aggression', Joint Economic Committee, US Congress, US Government Printing Office, Washington DC, 1976. 'Health Costs and Benefits of Economic Policy', *International Journal of Health Services*, 7, 1977, 4.

Brown, G., and Harris, T., *Social Origins of Depression*, Tavistock, 1978.

Colley, J. R. T., and Reid, D. D., 'Urban and Social Class Origins of Childhood Bronchitis in England and Wales', *British Medical Journal*, 2, 1970, p. 213.

DHSS, *Eating for Health*, 1978.

DHSS, *Nutrition among the Elderly*, 1980.

Doll, R., Hill, A. B., and Sakula, J., *British Journal of Preventive and Social Medicine*, 1960.

Douglas, J. W. B., and Waller, R. E., 'Air Pollution and Respiratory Infection in Children', *British Journal of Preventive and Social Medicine*, 20, 1966, 1.

Eichenwald, H. F., and Fry, P. C., 'Nutrition and Learning', *Science* 163, 1969, p. 644.

Eyer, J., 'Hypertension as a Disease of Modern Society', *International Journal of. Health Services*, 5, 1975, 4, p. 539. 'Prosperity as a Cause of Death', *International Journal of Health Services*, 7, 1977(a), 1, p. 125. 'Does Employment Cause the Death Rate Peak in Each Business Cycle?', *International Journal of Health Services*, 7, 1977(b), 4, p. 625.

Fuchs, V., *Who Shall Live? Health, Economics, and Social Choice*, New York, Basic Books, 1974.

Goldberg, E. M., and Morrison, S. L., 'Schizophrenia and Social Class', *British Journal of Psychiatry*, 109, 1963, p. 785.

Hellier, J., 'Perinatal Mortality 1950 and 1973', *Population Trends*, 10, Winter 1977.

Holman, R. T., *Poverty: Explanations of Social Deprivation*, Robertson, 1978.

Illsley, R., 'Social Class Selection and Class Differences in Relation to Stillbirths', *British Medical Journal*, 2, 1955, p. 1520.

Janerich, D. T., 'Maternal Age and Spina Bifida: Longitudinal Versus Cross-Sectional Analysis', *American Journal of Epidemiology*, 96, 1972, p. 389.

Lawrence, K. M., Carter, C. O., and David, P. A., 'Major CNS Malformations in South Wales II', *British Journal of Preventive and Social Medicine*, 22, 1968, p. 212.

Leeder, S. R., Corkhill, R., Irwig, L. M., Holland, W. W., and Colley, J. R. T., 'Influence of Family Factors on the Incidence of Lower Respiratory Tract Illness during the First Year of Life', *British Journal of Preventive and Social Medicine*, 30, 1976, p. 203.

Lewis, O., *The Children of Sanchez*, New York, Random House, 1967.

McKeown, T., *The Modern Use of Population*, Arnold, 1976.

Miller, F. J. W., Court, S. D. M., Knox, E. G., and Brandon, S., *The School Years in Newcastle-upon-Tyne, 1952–1962*, Oxford University Press, 1974.

Morris, J. N., *Uses of Epidemiology*, 3rd edn, Churchill Livingstone, 1975. 'Social Inequalities Undiminished', *Lancet*, 13 January 1979, 87.

Morris, J. N., and Heady, J. A., 'Social and Biological Factors in Infant Mortality: I. Objects and Methods', *Lancet*, 1955, i, p. 343.

Morris, J. N., and Titmuss, R. M., (a) 'Health and Social Change: I The Recent History of Rheumatic Heart Disease', *Medical Officer*, 26 August, 9 September 1944. (b) 'Epidemiology of Peptic Ulcer', *Lancet*, 30 December 1944, p. 841.

OPCS, *Occupational Mortality 1970–72*, HMSO, 1978. *Trends In Mortality*, HMSO, 1978.

Powles, J., 'Health and Industrialization in Britain', Proceedings First World Congress on Environmental Medicine and Biology, Paris, 1974.

Rutter, M., and Madge, N., *Cycles of Disadvantage*, Heinemann, 1976.

Stedman-Jones, G., *Outcast London*, Oxford, Clarendon Press, 1971.

Thompson, P., *The Edwardians*, Paladin, 1976.

Townsend, P., *Poverty in Britain*, Penguin Books, 1979.

Wilson, H., and Herbert, G. W., *Parents and Children in the Inner City*, Routledge, 1978.

8: Planning the Health and Personal Social Services

Acheson Report, *Primary Health Care in Inner London: A Report of a Study Group Commissioned by the London Health Planning Consortium*, 1981

Action on Smoking and Health, *European Survey of Smoking in Public Places*, 1976.

Alberman, E. D., Morris, J. N., and Pharaoh, P. O., 'After Court', *Lancet*, 20 August 1977.

Brennan, M. E., and Lancashire, R., 'Association of Childhood Mortality with Housing Status and Unemployment', *Journal of Epidemiology and Community Health*, 32, 1978, 1.

Butler, J. R., Bevan, J. M., and Taylor, R. C., *Family Doctors and Public Policy*, Routledge, 1973.

Carstairs, V., and Morrison, M., *The Elderly in Residential Care*, Scottish Health Studies No. 19, Edinburgh, SHHD, 1972.

Department of Health and Social Security (and the Welsh Office), *The Census of Residential Accommodation 1970*, HMSO, 1975. *Priorities for Health and Personal Social Services in England: A Consultative Document*, HMSO, 1976. *Prevention and Health*, Cmnd 7047, HMSO, 1977. *The Way Forward*, HMSO, 1977. 'The DHSS Perspective', in Barnes, J. and Connelly, N., *Social Care Research*, Bedford Square Press, 1978. *A Happy Old Age*, 1978. Circular HC(78)5, *Health Services Development: Court Report on Child Health Services*, January 1978. *Local Authority Social Service Summary of Planning Returns 1976–77 to 1979–80*, HMSO, 1978. *Report of the Committee of Inquiry into Mental Handicap Nursing and Care* (Jay Report), Cmnd 7468, HMSO, 1979.

Expenditure Committee, First Report, Session 1976–7, *Preventive Medicine*, HC 169–i, HMSO, 1977. Ninth Report, Session 1976–7, Chapter V, 'Spending on the Health and Personal Social Services', HC, HMSO, 1977.

Fitzherbert, K., *Child Care Services and the Teacher*, Temple Smith, 1977.

Forster, H. D. P., Frost, B., Francis, B., and Heath, P., 'Need and Demand for Health Care', University of Sheffield.

Gardner, M. J., Crawford, M. D., and Morris, J. N., 'Patterns of Mortality in Middle and Early Old Age in the County Boroughs of England and Wales', *British Journal of Preventive and Social Medicine*, 23, 1969, 3.

Graham, H., 'Problems in Antenatal Care', unpublished paper, DHSS/CPAG conference, 'Reaching the Consumer in the Antenatal and Child Health Services', April 1978.

Kimbell, A., and Townsend, J., *Residents in Elderly Persons' Homes*, Cheshire CC Social Services Department, April 1974.

Lind, G., and Wiseman, C., 'Setting Health Priorities: A review of Concepts and Approaches', *Journal of Social Policy*, 7, 4, 1978.

Morris, J. N., 'Social Inequality Undiminished', *Health Visitor*, September 1980.

Plank, D., *Caring for the Elderly: Report of a Study of Various Means of Caring for Elderly People in Eight London Boroughs*, GLC, 1977.

Report of the Royal Commission on the National Health Service (Merrison Report), Cmnd 7615, HMSO, 1979.

Rutter, M., Tizard, J., and Whitmore, K., *Educational Health and Behaviour*, Longman, 1970.

Rutter, M., et al., 'Attainment and Adjustment in Two Geographical Areas: Some Factors Accounting for Area Differences', *British Journal of Psychology*, 126, 1975.

Scottish Home and Health Department, *Towards an Integrated Child Health Service*, Edinburgh, HMSO, 1973.

Smith, D., *The Facts of Inequality*, Penguin Books, 1980.

Townsend, P., *The Last Refuge*, Routledge, 1962. 'The Needs of the Elderly and the Planning of Hospitals', in Canvin, R. W., and Pearson, N. G. (eds.), *Needs of the Elderly for Health and Welfare Services*, University of Exeter, 1973.

Tuckett, D., 'Choices for Health Education: A Framework for Decision Making', Health Education Studies Unit, 1979.

9: The Wider Strategy

Baker, J. A., et al., 'School Milk and Growth in Primary School Children', *Lancet*, 11, 1978, p. 575.

Benjamin, B., *Social and Economic Factors Affecting Mortality*, Mouton, The Hague and Paris, 1965.

Bone, M. *Pre-School Children and the Need for Day Care*, OPCS Social Survey Division, HMSO, 1977.

Bradshaw, J., Edwards, H., Staden, F., and Weale, J., 'Area Variations in Infant Mortality 1975/77', *Journal of Epidemiology and Community Medicine*, November 1978.

Brown, G. W., and Harris, T., *The Social Origins of Depression*, Tavistock, 1978.

Cook, J., Altman, D. G., Moore, D. M. C., Topp, S. G., Holland, W. W., and Elliott, A., 'A Study of the Nutritional Status of School Children', *British Journal of Preventive and Social Medicine*, 27, 2, 1973.

Cook, J., Altman, D. G., Jacoby, A., Holland, W. W., and Elliott, A., 'School Meals and Nutrition of School Children', *British Journal of Preventive and Social Medicine*, 29, 3 September 1975.

Cook, J., Altman, D. G., Jacoby, A., and Holland, W. W., 'The Contribution Made by School Milk to the Nutrition of Primary School Children', *British Journal of Nutrition*, 1975, 34, 91.

Cook, J., Irwig, L. M., Chinn, S., Altman, D. G., Florey, C. du V., 'The Influence of Availability of Free School Milk on the Height of Children in England and Scotland', *Journal of Epidemiology and Community Health* (in press).

Department of Education and Science, *Nutrition in Schools*, Report of the Working Party on the Nutritional Aspects of School Meals, HMSO, 1975.

DHSS, *A Nutrition Survey of Pre-School Children 1967–68*, Reports on Health and Social Subjects, No. 10, HMSO, 1975.

DHSS, *Eating for Health*, HMSO, 1978.

DHSS and DES, *Joint Circular on Co-ordination of Provision for Under-5s*, January 1978.

Disability Alliance, *Disability Rights Handbook for 1979*, November 1978.

DHSS and Supplementary Benefits Commission, *Response of the Supplementary Benefits Commission to 'Social Assistance: A Review of the Supplementary Benefits Scheme in Great Britain'*, HMSO, 1979.

Diamond, J., *Public Expenditure in Practice*, Allen & Unwin, 1975.

Field, F., and Townsend, P., *A Social Contract for Families*, Poverty Pamphlet, 19, Child Poverty Action Group, 1975.

Field, F., *Children Worse Off under Labour?*, Poverty Pamphlet 32, London, Child Poverty Action Group, February 1978.

Fox, A. J., and Adelstein, A. M., *Journal of Epidemiology and Community Health*, 23, 1978, p. 73.

Glennerster, H. (ed.), *Labour's Social Priorities*, London's Fabian Research Series 327, 1976.

The Great Child Benefit Robbery, Child Benefit Now Campaign, London Child Poverty Action Group, April 1977.

Harris, I. A., et al., *Income and Entitlement to Benefit of Impaired People in Great Britain*, Vol. 3 of *Handicap and Impairment in Great Britain*, HMSO, 1972.

Heclo, H., and Wildavsky, A., *The Private Government of Public Money*, Macmillan, 1976.

Howe, J. R., *Two-parent Families: A Study of their Resources and Needs in 1968, 1969 and 1970*, Statistical Report Series No. 14, HMSO, 1971.

Jacoby, A., Altman, D. G., Cook, J., Holland, W. W., and Elliott, A., 'Influence of Some Social and Environmental Factors on the Nutrient Intake and Nutritional Status of School Children', *British Journal of Preventive and Social Medicine*, 29, 2, June 1975.

Land, H., 'The Introduction of Family Allowances: An Act of Historic Justice?', in Hall, P., Land, H., Parker, R., and Webb, A., *Change, Choice and Conflict in Social Policy*, Heinemann, 1975.

Land, H., 'The Child Benefit Fiasco', in Brown, M., and Jones, K. (eds.), *The Yearbook of Social Policy in Britain 1977*, Routledge, 1978.

Institute for Fiscal Studies, *The Structure and Reform of Direct Taxation*, Report of a Committee chaired by Professor J. E. Meade, Allen & Unwin, 1978.

Ministry of Pensions and National Insurance, *Financial Circumstances of Retirement Pensioners*, HMSO, 1966.

Ministry of Social Security, *Circumstances of Families*, Report of an Inquiry by the Ministry of Pensions and National Insurance with the co-operation of the National Assistance Board, HMSO, 1967.

National Food Survey, *Household Food Consumption and Expenditure*, Ministry of Agriculture, Food and Fisheries Annual Report, 1977.

Plowden, W. J. L., 'Developing a Joint Approach to Social Policy', *The Yearbook of Social Policy in Britain 1976*, Routledge, 1976.

Reed, F. B., *Lancet*, 2, 1978, pp. 675–6.

Report of the Snowdon Working Party, *Integrating the Disabled*, National Fund for Research into Crippling Diseases, 1976.

Rona, R. J., Chinn, S. and Smith, A. M., 'Height of Children Receiving Free School Meals', *Lancet*, 8 September 1979, p. 534.

Royal Commission on the Distribution of Income and Wealth, *Report No. 6, Lower Incomes*, Cmnd 7175, HMSO, May 1978.

Safety and Health at Work (Robens Report), Cmnd 5034, HMSO, July 1972.

Select Committee on Tax Credit, Session 1972–3, Vol. I, *Report and Proceedings of the Committee*, Vol. II, Evidence, HMSO, 1973.

Social Trends, Cmnd 7439, HMSO, 1979.

Supplementary Benefit Report 1973, Annual Report of the SBC 1973, Cmnd 6615, HMSO, 1974.

Townsend, P., *Poverty in Britain*, Penguin Books, 1979.

Trades Union Congress, *Handbook of Safety and Health at Work*, TUC, 1978.

Wicks, M., *Old and Cold*, Heinemann, 1978.

Wilson, H., and Herbert, G. W., with Wilson, J. V., *Parents and Children in the Inner City*, Routledge, 1978.

Working Party on Housing of the Central Council for the Disabled, *Towards a Housing Policy for Disabled People*, 1976.

Index

Abel-Smith, B., 13, 41, 116
accidents: causes of child death, 125–6; class differential, 126, 127, 189–90; importance of child-accident reporting, 136, 137, 138; strategy for child-accident prevention, 189–90; at work, 130, 132, 133, 193
Alberman, E. D., 152
American Medical (Europe), 32
Anderson, O. W., 95
ante-natal care, 81, 82, 87, 106–7, 108, 118, 134, 151, 163–4, 171, 172
Asclepius, 41

Baird, D., 124
Banks, J. and O., 122
Banks, M. H., 19
behavioural/cultural explanation of health inequality, 118–23
Bernstein, B., 121
Best, G., 31
Bevan, J. M., 154
Birch, H. G., 42, 129
birth: class incidence of mortality and low birth-weight, 123; groups at risk, 123; mortality rates, 123; *see also* ante-natal care; infant mortality; perinatal mortality
Black, D., 17, 19, 29, 39, 40, 42
Black Report: appointment of working group, 14–15; and availability and distribution of resources, 24–6; broad findings, 15–16; and causes of inequalities in health, 19–23; government reaction to, 16–18; purpose, 14; support for basic principles of NHS, 31; and unequal access to NHS, 23–4
Blume, S., 40
Bone, M., 177, 180, 181, 182, 196
Boxall, M., 155
Bradshaw, J., 19, 143, 187
Brandon, S., 129
Brennan, M., 128, 148
Brenner, M. H., 19, 117, 118
British Medical Journal, 16, 24
British United Providential Association (BUPA), 32
Brotherston, J., 14–15, 82
Brown, G. W., 44, 46, 128, 197
Bulman, J. S., 82
Butler, J. R., 154
Buxton, M. J., 87

Canada, 13, 111
Carter, C. O., 123
Cartwright, A., 76, 79, 81
Central Council for the Disabled, 198–9

cervical screening, 81, 82
Chandra, R. K., 19
Chase, H. C., 104
Child Benefit Act 1975, 178
Child Poverty Action Group, 180
children: causes of death and illness class-related, 126–30; child benefit, 178–9, 203; child guidance system, 155; death from accidents, 125, 126, 127–8, 135–6; handicapped children, 154, 155; importance of child-accident reporting, 136, 137, 138; infant care allowance, 179–80, 204; need for health education in schools, 161, 167, 171; need for more research into child health, 137, 138; need for provision of school health statistics in relation to class, 135–6; nutrition: school milk and meals, 183–8; physical development affected by material deprivation, 129; policy for elimination of child poverty, 177–80; pre-school education and day care, 180–83; priority for children at start of life, 141; respiratory disease, 125, 126–7, 128, 129; school health work, 154–5; strategy for accident prevention, 189–90
chiropody, 82, 83
cigarette-smoking, 118, 119, 132, 133, 139; need for anti-smoking policy, 162–3, 167, 171
class gradient in health standards: care of infirm and disabled, 84–5; and concepts of 'social class', 47; and female mortality, 69–70; and GP consultations, 61–3, 77–80; illness and, 61–4; and infant mortality, 70–71; and male mortality, 66–9; and mortality of elderly, 71; mortality rates, 15–16; occupation as basis of, 48–9; recent studies, 19–22; trends in morbidity, 72–3; use of hospital services, 80–81; use of preventive and promotive services, 81–3; *see also* inequalities in living standards; middle class; occupational class; working class
Colledge, M., 19
Colley, J. R. T., 126
Collins, E., 24
Committee on Medical Aspects of Food Policy (COMA), 135, 183, 185
community care: and elderly, 157–60; and mentally handicapped, 156–7; shift of resources towards, 144–6, 150; vagueness of DHSS definition, 143
Community Health Councils, 164
Confederation of British Industry (CBI), 195

236 Index